THE KURDISH POLITICAL STRUGGLES IN IRAN, IRAQ, AND TURKEY

A Critical Analysis

A. Manafy

UNIVERSiTY PRESS OF AMERICA,® INC.
Lanham • Boulder • New York • Toronto • Oxford

Library of Congress Control Number: 2005924237
ISBN 0-7618-3003-0 (paperback : alk. ppr.)

Contents

Chapter One

Who are the Kurds?

The Kurds live in Kurdistan, which literally means "land of the Kurds." It is a mountainous region with some of the most beautiful scenery in the world. The area's natural beauty is reflected in their cultural folklore. The poems and songs resonate with the Kurds' cultural traditions and sufferings.

Kurdish people live mainly in Iran, Iraq, and Turkey. They can also be found in Syria, the former Soviet Union, and Lebanon, as well as Germany, where they are employed as wage laborers. Prominent Kurdish intellectuals live in exile in France, Sweden, and other European countries, where in spite of their exile they continue to be effective in internationally promoting the Kurdish cause. The focus of this study centers on the Kurdish liberation struggles in Iran, Iraq, and Turkey.

There are no officially recognized borders in Kurdistan because the Kurds have never had a state. However, Kurdistan is strategically located in the Middle East:

"... at the heart of the high and rugged mountains of the Zagros Range, spanning the ridges northwest to southeast. In the west, these mountain folds give way to rolling hills falling to the Mesopotamian plain. To the north, the mountains slowly turn to the steppe-like plateau and highlands of what used to be known as Armenian Anatolia.[1]

Although the Kurds have lived in Kurdistan for centuries, they have never had a state of their own. A concept of the state cannot be found in Kurdish history. The Kurds are characterized as brave, proud, quarrelsome, stubborn, and tough-minded, their character perhaps conditioned by the harsh mountainous areas they inhabit. Centuries of struggle have proven that no invader or conqueror has been able to convert or assimilate them. In a sense, they are born into struggle. They claim that the mountains are their only loyal friends because it is true that this rugged terrain has provided protection for the Kurds, hindering hostile invaders and preventing cultural assimilation. The Kurds possess a uniquely autonomous and independent culture that remains pure and unabsorbed by other cultures.

However, it is also true that the Kurd's isolated mountainous existence has prevented the development of independently minded, politically cohesive, and class-conscious organizations in Kurdistan. The mountains, due to impassable peaks, inadequate communication networks, roughed transportation systems, and remoteness to urban areas have created an island of tribally oriented organization with conservative feudal and semi-feudal norms and values.

Nonetheless, the Kurds have been socialized to depend on, accept, and internalize the tribal values of the village head, who is either called a *Shaikh* or *Momusta*. *Momustas* are religious leaders with some degree of religious education, and rely on the landed-class for financial support. In return, these religious leaders support and reinforce the possessive values of the landlords and landed peasantry. The rural Kurds are kept away from the modern urban centers where they would be exposed to a pluralistic culture and have the opportunity to associate with other political forces. Due to individual isolationism and attachment to one's own tribe or clan, the Kurds are unaware that other minorities or classes are as oppressed as they are. This is basically true in Iraq and Iran, and to some degree in Turkey. In Turkey, there is evidence of Kurdish affiliation with progressive political parties in an effort to promote class alliance, which, in turn, advances the Kurdish cause. The Kurd's isolated existence has impeded the development of fierce nationalism that has dominated other parts of the Middle East. However, the mountains have functioned as strategic shields preventing hostile intrusion, and in this capacity they have benefited the Kurds.

Kurds are stereotypically conceived as being a courageous people. For instance, Rostam-e zal, the historic and heroic figure of ancient Persia, is linked to a Kurdish tribe. It is also claimed that Pishdadi and Kayani kings of ancient Persia might have been Kurds. Bahram Chubin, too, was of Kurdish descent. Farhad, a Kurd from the Kalhur tribe who lived at the time of the Persian king, Khesrov-Parviz (who was also in love with Shereen), expressed his love for Shereen through sweet melodies and Persian poems. According to Sharafnameh, Nezami-i Ganjavi, the leading Persian poet, was also of Kurdish ancestry.[2]

Shaikh Muhammad Mardukh-i Kurdistani (Kurdish) contends that the Kurds are of Aryan origin, Indo-Europeans with the oldest cultural tradition.[3] Tavahoudi's argument also supports the claim that the Kurds are of Aryan origin.[4] However, many Kurds believe that they descended from the Medes.[5] Gazi Mohammad, a great spiritual leader of Mahabad and himself a Kurd, claimed that

Kurds were descendants of Medes, and did not hesitate to call Mahabad, the Land of Medes. In spite of this remarkable statement, Gazi Mohammad and his followers held Pan Kurdish aspiration hoping to have Mahabad replace Syria and Sulaymaniya, centers of culture and the Kurdish Nationalist movement. To this end, two political papers entitled "Kurdistan," and two literary magazines, *Hawar* and *Hilal,* were published in the Kurdish language. Kurds look to Mahabad as a source of hope and inspiration as it remains the center of political struggle and nationalistic activities geared toward liberation.[6]

Minorskii attributes the Kurdish language, in spite of variation in dialects, to Persian languages of the northwest. The differences that exist between the Kurdish and Farsi languages can be found in all other dialects in the Kurdish region. According to Minorskii, the Kurdish language was originally the language of a group of people who lived in the same geographic area. Consequently, Kurdish seems to have been the language of Kurds before they chose to live in the mountains. Minorskii does not exclude the possibility that Medes might not have influenced the various Persian dialects. Based on geographic and historical realities, Kurdish language development may have taken place in the Median territory called "Atropatene," which is now called Azerbaijan.[7]

Minorskii claims that the concepts of *kortchekh, kordukh,* and *kordikh* can be found in the geography of Armenia. He claims that the evolution and development of the Kurds took place in the Lake Urmia area. The concept of *Mâhkert,* meaning the Kurdish territory, was established in 4th century BC. An analysis of the word *Kurmanj* illustrates that Kurdish origin is attributable to Medes. If the suffix "j" is omitted from the end of the word *kurmanj,* there remains Kur(d), and in the second part we have the word "man," which Minorskii relates to Medes. Based on this historical reality, it is likely that the Kurds are of Medes origin.[8]

Whatever their origin may be, the Kurds remain divided. Tavahoudi cited Molana Salahaddin, the tutor of Sultan Muradkhan and the emperor of the Ottoman Empire, who claimed that the Kurds are united only in one realm: religion. The tribal and feudal influence on Kurdish thinking has led to contradictory behavior. On the one hand, the Kurds are fiercely independently minded, yet on the other hand, they are deeply attached to the dictates of their tribal leaders. They have lost their autonomy and have become totally dependent on their leaders, the tribal chieftains. For Stephan C. Pelletiere, this type of tribal control is the leading feature of the nomadic tribe. Since nomadic tribes are constantly on the move and "vulnerable to predators," they have to follow the decisions and organization set forth by their leaders.[9]

Pelletiere further asserts that today in Kurdistan, tribalism and nomadism are largely replaced by feudalism and semi-capitalistic development has taken

Country	Percentage	Total Population	Kurds
Turkey	19%	40,200,000	7,500,000
Iraq	23%	10,500,000	2,000,000 - 2,500,000
Iran	34%	34,000,000	3,500,000
Syria	8.5%	7,300,000	500,000
USSR	N/A	N/A	0.1
		TOTAL	13,500,000 to 15,000,000

Figure 1. Population Estimates for 1975
Source: Adopted from Martin Van Bruinessen, *Agha, Shaikh and State: The Social and Political Structures of Kurdistan* (London: Zed Press, 1992), 15.

place in Kurdistan. However, the Aghas, who were encouraged by the British to secure and privatize tribal lands, still command Kurdish loyalty in some parts of Kurdistan, and in the remote and primitive regions of Kurdistan, tribalism still persist.[10] In terms of numbers, the estimates of Kurdish populations vary (see Figures 1 and 2 population estimates).

Country	Percentage	Total Population	Kurds
Turkey	19%	57,000,000	10,800,000
Iraq	23%	18,000,000	4,100,000
Iran	10%	55,000,000	5,500,000
Syria	8%	12,500,000	1,000,000
USSR	NA		500,000
Elsewhere	NA		700,000
		TOTAL	22,600,000

** * Estimates in round numbers.**

Figure 2. Population Estimates for 1991*
Source: Adopted from David McDowall, "The Kurds, A Nation Denied," London: *Minority Rights Publications,* 1992, p. 12.

Discrepancies in the statistics on the Kurdish population make the estimates unreliable. Population numbers are either exaggerated or minimized. Turkey, for instance, maintains that Kurds do not exist at all. However, the Turkish government states the existence of "mountain Turks." While states downplay the number of Kurds for security reasons, the opposition forces maximize population estimates. The authors of *People Without a Country* claim that there are over five million Kurds in Iran (1975 estimates), over 6 million in Turkey (1970 estimates), about 3 million in Iraq (1975 estimates), almost one million in Syria (1976 estimates), and approximately 200,000 in the USSR (1970 General Census). These figures total 15 million Kurds.[11]

Pelletiere approximates the Kurdish population in Turkey, Iran, Iraq, Syria, and the USSR between 7 and 7.5 million. A breakdown of this figure illustrates the following: 3 million in Turkey, approximately 2 million in Iran and 2 million in Iraq, and a very small number of Kurds in Syria and the former Soviet Union. Pelletiere claims that the Kurds are only politically important in Turkey, Iran, and Iraq.[12]

The accuracy of Kurdish population estimates are difficult to determine. In order to obtain a reasonable estimation, a median figure is calculated, which reveals a population between 14 and 15 million. Van Bruinessen's population estimates appear to be the most accurate, but irrespective of their numbers, the Kurds do exist and the Kurdish political question constitutes the most important compelling and overriding political factor in the Middle East. These 15 million Kurds have a legitimate possessive claim to a vast homeland that consists of roughly 200,000 square miles, an area equal to France,[13] or slightly smaller than the state of Texas. In terms of numbers, the Kurdish population is approximately equal to the population of the state of Texas, and almost more than three times the population of all oil producing states in the Persian Gulf (using 1990 estimates for the United Arab emirates: 1.6 million, Qatar; 422,000, Bahrain; 489,000, Kuwait; and 2 million in the Persian Gulf).

Language presents another problem. Some scholars see language as a bond of integration, which when lacking prevents a group's unity and solidarity. Unfortunately, the Kurds have yet to develop a single systematized written or spoken language.[14] I found this substantiated by my own observation. In the summer of 1993 and 1995, I noticed that the Kurds of Ushnavieh (west of Lake Urmia) and Nagadeh (west of Mahabad) could not understand the dialect I introduced to them in a video from the southeastern Kurds in the area of Turkey. Nonetheless, it is said that Kurdish is an Iranian language of Indo-European origin.

Due to the existence of different dialects, and although some speak more than one dialect, most Kurds have communication problems with other Kurds when using their mother tongue. The Kurdish dialects are Kurmanji, Sorani,

Zaza, Gurani, and Sine,i (Sanandaji). Kurmanji is spoken by the Syrian Kurds, and the Kurds of the former Soviet Union speak North Kurmanji. The Kurmanji dialect is also spoken by the Kurds of Northern Khorasan, an eastern Iranian state. South Kurmanji, or Sorani, is spoken by the majority of Kurds in Iran and Iraq. In Iraq, Sorani is the predominant dialect of the Sulaymaniya, Erbil, Mosul, Rawanduz, and Kirkuk Kurds. In Iran, Sorani is spoken by a plurality of Kurds inhabiting the southern part of Lake Urmia to the west of Kermanshahan. Other subdialects include Kermanshahi, Laki, and Gurani. These subdialects are spoken in Iranian Kurdistan, running from Kermanshah to Sanandaj, though the dialect spoken by the Kurds of Kermashah is different from the northern dialects. The dialect spoken by Kermanshah Kurds is what was called the dialect of the Kalhur and Zangana tribes. Hence, the Kermanshahi dialect, based on Sanandaji's claim, is the dialect of Shi,i Kurds. Today, the Gurani, Sanjabi, and Kalhur tribes, along with those living between Kangavar and Gasr-i Shirin, and from Ravansar to Iylam, speak the Kermanshi dialect. It is also spoken by the Ahl-e Haqq (people of the truth). Zaza is spoken by the Kurds of Dersim (now called Tunceli), Siverek, and Modki, near Bitlis. It is believed that Zaza and Gurani are closely related.[15]

The plurality of Kurdish dialects creates the problem of intelligibility, which undermines the creation of national solidarity based on a politicized identity. But why are there conflicting dialects? Sanandaji mentions two valid explanations. First of all, the Kurdish dialects are not protected or enriched by scientific and literary efforts. Since the Kurds are often deprived of reading and writing in their own mother tongue, a unified or unitary dialect has not been established. Secondly, the high, impassable mountains, remoteness of the Kurdish rural areas from one another, lack of transportation and communication systems among different tribes, and constant isolation of one group from another have led to the development of different dialects. More importantly, attempts at Arabization, Turkification, or deKurdification by the states in the region have further exacerbated the problem.[16]

With respect to religion, the Kurds are predominantly the followers of Sunni Islam. They, on majority, are followers of the Shafi-ite school of Islamic law. The Kurds of Turkey, however, are Sunni Muslims following the Hanafite school. Both schools feel that the Quran (the Islamic Holy Book) is the final word, and every Islamic idea or issue must be in conformity with the Holy Book or encounter rejection. Both schools believe in cultural tradition and (Ijma) consultation. The major difference between the two is that Hanafite rite is more flexible than Shafi-ite rite. The Hanafi school values Islamic and pre-Islamic norms and values, and the Shafi-ite school only accepts the Islamic cultural tradition. Hanafism is more inclusive than Shafiism.[17] It must be emphasized that not all Kurds adhere to Sunni Islam. In the provinces of Khanagin and Kermanshah, a majority of Kurds are the followers of Shi,i Islam. Seven to 10 percent of the Kurds are followers of Shi,i Islam, although Izady estimates these followers between 5 and 7 percent of the total Kurds living in Kurdistan.[18]

Politically, the Shi-i Kurds of Iran have not involved themselves in nationalistic political action, but an Iraqi faction of Shi-ism has become deeply involved in political praxis against the former dictator's, Saddam Hussein, regime. Although they were militant during Saddam's rule, they now generally side with the United States

According to Van Bruinessen, some Kurds (especially in northwestern Kurdistan) are adherents of Alavis, and it is common that some from this group speak Zaza. There are also Alavis who speak Kurmanji. The majority of the Alavis living in Turkey are Turks, not Kurds. In Turkey, by contrast, the Zaza-speaking Alavis are a small minority.[19]

In south and southeastern Kurdistan, there is a small sect called Ahl-e Haqq (people of the truth). The followers of Ahl-e Haqq, based on Sanandaji's opinion, are those who, as a result of excessive admiration, strive to promote Ali, the prophet's son-in-law, to the level of God. Hence they are called Aliullahi, which means those who worship Ali, the manifestation of God. Sanandaji believes that this approach is not conducive to Islamic values since it has been influenced by Zoroastrian, Christian, and Manchurian ideas and, as such, represents an Agnostic belief system. The followers of this school are seen as Shafi-ite Kurds and are located in Kermanshah, especially in Shahabad and around Kerend-e-Gharb (west Kerend).

Yazidism is another sect followed by the Kurds, especially by the rural and pastoral Kurds living in Iraq, Turkey, and in the Mosul, Diyarbakier, Sanjar, and Shaikhan regions. It must be noted that Yazid murdered Imam Hossein, the third Shi,i Imam (the second son of Ali, the son-in-law of Prophet Mohammad). Some interpreters link the followers of the Yazidi school to Yazid implying that the followers of this school adhere to the devil. However, Yazidis do not believe that they are worshippers of the devil, since Yazid was not the founder of their religion. Based on Yazidis' conviction, the founder of Yazidism was Adam's son, who married a God-ordained angel. The result of this miraculous marriage was a son called Yazdan, therefore Yazidis have descended from Adam's son, Yazdan.[20] According to McDowall, the notion that stereotypes Yazidis as devil worshippers is abusive and incorrect. Rather, Yazidism is what he calls a synthetic religion, which contains the elements of Zoroastrian, Manchurian, Jewish, Nestorian Christian, Muslim, and Sufi belief systems.[21]

Yazidis are located in southwest Mosul and their sanctuary is located in Shaikhan. During the 1830s and 1840s, many of them left Shaikhan and relocated in the Caucaus because of religious persecution by the Turks, Kurds and Arabs. Today, approximately 100,000 Yazidis remain, and their persecution continues based on the false allegations of devil worshipping.

Since 1950, Yazidis have been involved in the Kurdish nationalist movement, and in 1974 they were participants in Barzani's rebellion. Still, the Yazidis are forced to abandon their Kurdish identity. According to Izadi, "There is now also a movement to strip the Yazidis of their Kurdish identity by either declaring them an independent ethnic group apart from the Kurds, or by attaching them to the Arabs."[22] They are referred to as "Umayyad Arabs" by the Iraqi and Syrian governments, implying they are the followers of Yazid ibn Mu'awiyya, as explained earlier. The majority of Yazidis are now in the Caucaus, Syria, Jazira, Sanjar Heights, and Iran.[23]

There are also Kurds who follow Sufism, which is the "right path to truth." The adherents of the Sunni Sufi order are called Naqshbandi and Qadiri, and the Shafi-ite Sufi followers constitute Nimat Ullahi and Khaksari.[24] The oldest Sunni Sufi order is the Qadiri named after its founder, Abdul-Gadir Gilani (AD 1077–1166), also referred to as Gaylani. In Iraq, the present leader of the Patriotic Union of Kurdistan (PUK) organization, Mom Jalal Talabani, belongs to the Gadiris line of Sufism. The Kurds of southern Iraq and eastern Kurdistan in Iran are Gadiris. Gadiris can also be found in the western and southern areas of western Azerbaijan in Iran between Naghadeh and Piranshahr, in a village called Gurveh. The headquarters of this Sufi order are located in the ancient town of Barzanji, around Sulaymania. According to Izadi, Shaykh Mahmud, who led the Kurdish upheaval against "the British mandate of Iraq," was the leader of "Gadiri Sufi house of Barzanji."[25]

Baha al-din Nagshband of Bukhara (AD 1317–1389) established the Nagshbandi order. Turkish tribes permeated the Middle East in the twelfth century and brought with them the Nagshbandi order. Today, the followers of this order are those Kurds who live in northern and "to some extent western Kurdistan," while the Kurds from central and eastern Kurdistan are adherents of the Gadiri order. The Kurdish democratic party of Iraq and its leadership under Barzani are affiliated with Nagshbandi Sufism.[26]

The Nematollahi Sufi order can be traced to the fifth Shafi-ite Imam. His *khanaga* (a Sufi lodge) is located at the popular pilgrimage site in Mahan of Kerman (Iran). Many of his followers called him the King of Arifan, which means Gnostic or learned.[27] However, Bruinessen contends that this Sufi group is an aristocratic Dervish order.[28] Nematollahis also have a *khanaga* in Sanandaj, Tehran, and at Kermanshah in Iran. Khaksari Sufis are related to a Dervish called Seyyed Jalal Al-din-e Haidar, and can be found in most Iranian cities. They also have *khanagas* in Kurdistan, especially in Kermanshah.[29]

The Gadiri Dervishes feel that the happiness of spirit is caused by the pleasure of an action, which is called *zikr* (verbal praying). The repetition of *zikr* promotes spiritual unconsciousness, which is considered the highest level of spiritual attainment. This state of spiritual unconsciousness enables the Dervishes to swallow swords, eat broken glass, walk barefoot on fire, stab themselves with a sword or dagger, or drive a stick through their tongue or flesh, seemingly, without harm. Dervishes believe that *Mashaikh's* (plural of Shaikh) spirits are the source of inspiration and protect them from injury.[30] This belief system embraces superstition and mystification. But based on my personal observation, the Dervishes consciously believe in what they do. It is considered a level of perfection to be in proximity with the spirit of Gouse, Shaikh Gilani, who is closer to God.

Bruinessen characterizes this spiritually unconscious state of the Dervish as an attack of epilepsy, a sudden loss of consciousness, a result of biological malfunctioning.[31] Bruinessen's generalizations may not hold concerning hundreds of other Dervishes whom I have personally observed practicing this apparently self-inflicted behavior. Although this behavior is not practically understood, it is inaccurate to conclude, as Bruinessen does, that Dervishes who indulge in this behavior are simply epileptics.

However, I do agree with Bruinessen's assessment that some of the Sufi orders, such as the Naqshbandi and Qadiri, are people-based. Their followers are poor and from the lower classes and they do not play a political role in Kurdish nationalism. The development of these organizations into class-based political consciousness and social liberation movements remains to be seen. Presently, the governments in the regions view these orders as expressions of religiosity, passivity and mystification, and as conservative and politically neutral modes of thought that are not subject to censorship, repression, and control. However, in the summer of 1995, I witnessed a political raid on a Sufi meeting at Urmia, Iran by the police. Before the raid I had an opportunity to talk to the senior member of the order, who was apolitical and very spiritual.

Dervishism resembles the Cynic and Stoic schools of thought. The Cynics believed that self-control, especially control of one's passion, was the highest virtue, and virtue was the only good. The leading student of this philosophy was Antisthenes (445–365 BC), who felt that virtue was capable of creating happiness. It is liberation from want, the abolition of egoism, and the practice of self-control. It was a protest against social distinction.[32] Similarly, Dervishism is a protest against social distinction. All Dervishes are equal to one another and each constitutes Kant's "kingdom of ends," meaning that each person is an end in himself. No one has a right to use another as a means of accomplishing one's selfish ends or ideals, and these values animate

Dervish discourse. They sympathize with the sufferings of humanity and dispossessed. Dervishism offers an invitation to those who are suffering, an opportunity to join the Dervish's kingdom for spiritual perfection inspired by divinity. In reality, everybody has a place around the Dervish's meal cloth. In Dervish homes in Kurdistan, the meal is served upon a tablecloth that is placed on the floor. Attending guests and family sit around the tablecloth and after praying they begin their meal. Male and female are served separately in different rooms since it is against Islamic Sharia and ethical values to have one's wife, daughters, or even maids sit around the same table cloth with men.

Like some Cynics, notably Crates, who lived in the latter part of the 4th century BC, Dervishes believe in fatalism. It is the will of God should you suffer from illness, poverty, and enslavement. By accepting your misfortune you obey the will of God, and perfect your moral virtues. The Dervish acceptance of the status quo and their passivity are facilitated by their fatalistic beliefs.

Dervish practice is also similar to Stoic philosophy, which preaches the doctrine of self-control and the adoption of an attitude of indifference to worldly affairs. Thus, the exercise of control over one's passion is a virtue; self-discipline leads to the control of passions by reason. Like Stoicism, Dervishism is a doctrine of withdrawal and protests earthly social conventions. The devotee seeks to enter a spiritual realm where societal problems and defects are of no consequence. In the spiritual realm one can attain moral self-sufficiency through the exercise of self-control. When individuals turn inward, they can achieve freedom from the earthly world. Dervishes emphatically argue that what matters is the brotherhood of man, which belongs to the kingdom of God, not an earthly world that is morally corrupt. Dervishes do not seek salvation in this earthly world and, therefore, they are apolitical. Passivity prevails and conservatism dominates the thinking of the Kurdish Dervishes. Dervish philosophy, along with the Cynic and Stoic schools, does not pose a threat to the prevailing political orders in the Middle East.

Bruinessen's view of the epileptic Kurdish Dervishes does not hold empirically. The philosophy of Dervishism is the philosophy of moral perfection as a means of attaining the greatest spiritual good, which is a proximity to God. In order to achieve this goal, Dervishes will employ all means available to them. This is the highest stage in the recognition of God, and at this stage, as in at the peak of radicalized political consciousness, one may behave in a strange manner, like the Chinese student in the Tiananmen Square democracy movement. This student threw himself in front of an army tank in protest against his government's repressive policies. In reality, the practices of the "epileptic" Dervish and the Chinese student protester reflect a higher spiritual or social consciousness, but are not organized and Dervishes constitute a small minority within the Islamic religion.

In essence, the defining Kurdish value is pluralism, a birthright as well as a human right. It is a human right because human beings possess the natural right to be different. On the positive side, plurality is the strength of any political culture. But as this chapter demonstrated, the pluralism that characterizes the Kurdish groups obstructs mobilization and solidarity, which are the necessary components of the national liberation struggles.

NOTES

1. David McDowall, "The Kurds, A Nation Denied," (London: *Minority Rights Publication,* 1992), 7. See also, Mehrdad R. Izady, *The Kurds: A Concise Handbook* (Washington, D.C.: Crane Russak, Taylor, and Francis International Publishers, 1992), 1–8.

2. Kalim Tavahoudi, *Harakat-i-Tarikhi-i Kurd beh Khurasan,* 2 vols. (Tehran, Iran: Publisher Unknown, 1985), vol. 2: 88. Shahnam-i Ferdousi is cited as proof of the claims made in the aforementioned source. See also, Ali Asghar Shamim, *Kurdistan* (Tehran, Iran: Modabber Publication, 1370), 44–62.

3. Shaikh Mardukh Mohammad, *Tarikh-i Mardukh, Tarikh-i Kurd va Kurdistan* (Due to the sensitive nature of these writings, place of publication and publisher information is not included in the book, 1979), 21; Mirza Shukr Allah Sanandaji, *Tuhfah-i Nasiri Dar Tarikh va Joghrafiay-i Kurdistan* (Tehran, Iran: Amirkabeer Publications, 1987), 8–14. Augen Pittard, cited by Sanandaji, claims that the Kurds, among the other tribes of Iran, have remained more unassimilated than other tribes. The formidable mountains have prevented invasions by conquering tribes. This source, too, links the Kurds to the Aryan origin.

4. Tavahoudi, *The Hisotrical Move of the Kurds to Khorasan,* 4.

5. McDowell, *The Kurds,* 11. See also, Omar Faroughi, *Negah-i Beh Tarikh va Farhang-e Kurdistan* (Tehran, Iran: Sharg Publishers, 1363), 6–15.

6. Derk Kinnane, *Kurds and Kurdistan,* trans., Abraham Yunis (Tehran, Iran: Negah Publishers, 1372), 196–97. See also, Gerard Chaliand, ed., *People Without a Country* (Zed Press: London, 1980), 145–46.

7. V. Nikitine, *Kurds va Kurdistan,* trans., M. Gazi (Tehran, Iran: Nilofar Publication, 1366), 45–47. See also, Minorskii Vladimir Fedorovich, *Kurd,* trans., Habiballah Tabani (Tehran, Iran: Gustardeh Publishers, 1379), 27–35.

8. Nikitine, *Kurds va Kurdistan,* 52–54. See also, Vladimr Fedorovich Minorskii, *Kurd,* trans. Habiballah Tabani Nashr-e Gostardeh (Tehran, Iran, 1379), 19–25.

9. Stephen C. Pelletiere, *The Kurds: An Unstable Element in the Gulf* (London:Westview Press, 1984), 18.

10. Ibid., 15.

11. Gerard Chaliand, ed., *People Without a Country: The Kurds and Kurdistan* (London: Zed Press, 1980), 47, 108,156, 211.

12. Ibid.; Pelletiere, *The Kurds,* 16.

13. Mehrdad R. Izady, *The Kurds*, 1–12.

14. Philip G. Kreyenbroek,"On the Kurdish Language," in Philip G. Kreyenbroek and Stefan Sperl, eds., *The Kurds: A Contemporary Overview* (New York: Routledge, 1992), 68–83; Sanandaji, *Tuhfah-i Nasiri Dar Tarikh* 18–28; Izady, *The Kurds*, 167–175; Martin Van Bruinessen, *Agha, Shaikh and State* (London and New York: Zed Books, 1992), 21–22.

15. Sanandaji, *The Kurds*, 22–23; Faroughi, *Nigahi, beh Tarikh va Farhang-i Kurdistan*, 16–20. See also David McDowall, *A Modern History of the Kurds* (London: I. B. Tauris, 1996), 9–10; Kreyenbroek, "On the Kurdish Language," in Philip Kreyenbroek and Stefan Sperl, eds. *The Kurds: A Contemporary Overview*, 68.

16. Sanandaji, *Tuhfah-i Nasiri Dar Tarikh*, 22–23.

17. Ibid., 31–34. See also Bruinessen, *Agha, Shaikh*, 23–25; Izady, *The Kurds*, 133–137.

18. Izady, *The Kurds*, 133.

19. Bruinessen, *Agha, Shaikh*,.23.

20. Sanandaji, *Tuhfah-i Nasiri Dar Tarikh*, 46–52; Bruinessen, *Agha, Shaikh*, 23–25; McDowall, *Modern History*, 10–13.

21. McDowall, *Modern History*, 11.

22. Izady, *The Kurds*, 157; McDowall, *The Kurds*, 14.

23. Izady, *The Kurds*, 157–158.

24. Sanandaji, *Tuhfah-i Nasiri Dar Tarikh*, 56.

25. Izady, *The Kurds*, 160.

26. *Ibid.*, 160–161.

27. Sanandaji, *Tuhfah-i Nasiri Dar Tarikh*, 56.

28. Bruinessen, *Agha, Shaikh*, 212, 240.

29. Sanandaji, *Tuhfah-i Nasiri Dar Tarikh*, 56.

30. Sanandaji, *Tuhfah-i Nasiri Dar Tarikh*, 59–60; Izady, *The Kurds*, 161.

31. Bruinessen, *Agha, Shaikh*, 240.

32. Brian R. Nelson, *Western Political Thought From Socrates to the Age of Ideology*, 2nd ed. (New Jersey: Prentice Hall, Inc., 1996), 72–77; George Sabine, *A History of Political Theory*, 4th ed. (London: Holt, Rinehart and Winston, 1973), 136–138, 141–147.

Chapter Two

The Kurdish Liberation Struggles:
An Alternative Explanation

This chapter begins by exploring the conceptual and definitional problems associated with political or liberation struggle theory. Hence, it is crucial to define what the Kurdish struggle really is. Is it a revolutionary movement? Is it a political or social revolution? Is it a struggle for liberation from domination? Or is it a class-based political struggle, as left-leaning Kurdish political organizations claim? What is it?

In order to define the problem under investigation, we need to make analytical distinctions among the various movements and analyze their scope of social transformations. For Theda Skocpol, "Social revolutions are rapid basic transformations of a society's state and class structures; and they are accompanied and, in part, carried through by class based revolts from below."[1] The defining feature of a social revolution, based on this definition, is class conflict, which plays a dominant role in socio-political transformation. In contrast, a political revolution does not change social structures, only state structures. Yet, this type of change may not necessarily be carried through a class struggle. Although rebellions, revolts, and insurrections involve the revolt of subordinate classes,[2] they do not culminate in structural transformation.

As Figure I indicates, social revolutions lead to the transformation of A (regime) + B (state structures) and + C (class structures).

Coups may or may not change a regime. Industrialization, involving massive social change, has often been defined as a genuine revolution. But, in reality, it only changes social structure and has nothing to do with political structural transformations, nor is it accompanied by political upheaval. Without this kind of analytical differentiation, conceptual chaos and theoretical confusion will obscure the formulation of a scientific theory.

13

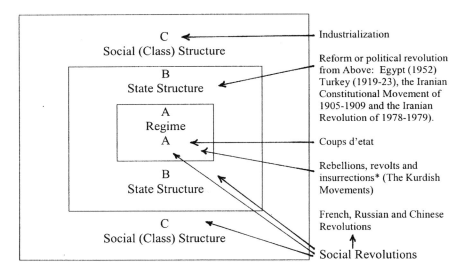

These three types of social movement have the potential for change.

Figure 1.   Demonstration of the Scope of Social Transformations
Source: Adapted from Theda Skocpol, *States and Social Revolutions,* 3–7.

According to Figure 1, the Kurdish movement is characteristically a revolt or rebellion. The Kurdish struggle has failed to materialize changes desired by their practitioners. In Iran, Iraq, and Turkey, the Kurdish movement has not been able to alter *A*, let alone *C* or *B*. Based on the history of political movements, reform from above has achieved more rights and affected more changes than the Kurdish armed rebellion. The Kurdish struggle remains peripheral to the regime, even though its major target has been A (regime).

Skocpol's theory indicates that it is impossible for a revolution to occur as long as the pre-revolutionary repressive forces of the state are in firm control. The most basic pre-condition for the outbreak of a revolution is the development of a rupture in the state and a breakup of the internal forces of domination. Once the state monopoly on coercion is weakened due to the external military pressure from the international environment, defeat in war, or political and economic crises, the situation is ripe for a revolutionary upheaval.[3] Such a structural breakdown occurred in Iran in 1978–79, in Iraq in 1991, and again in Iraq recently in 2003. There was no Kurdish upheaval although they revolted in Iran. The reason for this is that according to Skocpol, a class-based revolt from the bottom was missing. The Kurdish rebellion failed to organize class solidarity. Although the existing literature on Kurdish political issues is illuminating and substantively enlightening, it is descriptive. Conceptual and definitional problems are abundant. Due to the lack of a solid theoretical framework, the literature does not reveal the direction of the Kurdish political struggle. Some scholars equate the Kurdish struggle to a national liberation movement, a model that does not adequately explain the Kurdish struggle. National liberation theory explains the socio-political movements of dominated classes who attempt, through revolutionary struggles, to liberate themselves from the colonial and imperial structures imposed on them.

However, Kurdish leadership is quick to point out that they are fighting for liberation from internal colonialism. This explanation has merit to some degree, but it is reductionistic. Internally colonized countries are dominated by and dependent upon external dominant powers. The politics of exclusion are not accidental; they are in accord with neo-colonial expectations and interests, structurally linked to the wishes and requirements of international capital. The beneficiaries of political exclusionism are both the local and metropolitan ruling classes. The Kurdish leadership fails to realize that politics of the peripheral states are determined by the central model of the world system: dominated forces remain divided and the liberation struggle is thwarted.

The Kurdish movement lacks cohesive ideology, direction, and a well-defined strategy. The movement has failed to develop class alliances and class coalitions. In all social revolutions and national liberation movements, political class mobilization and alliances have played a critical role. Any movement cut off from mass support and political variables, such as national class solidarity, inclusionism, political consciousness, and a well-defined political ideology cannot succeed. Guerrilla warfare derives its strength from the people. In Mao Tse-Tung's opinion, "The populace is for the revolutionaries what water is for the fish."[4] To win the battle an "insurgent"[5] fish, (in our case, the Kurdish movement) needs the ocean of countryside (the peasantry). Unfortunately, the water in the Kurdish countryside is either polluted or drained by the key variables of informalism of group interaction, religio-patrimonial relations, and tribal and feudal communal differences. The Kurdish appeal to win the "hearts and minds"[6] of the people of rural Kurdistan and the allegiance of the aggrieved population of Iran, Iraq and Turkey has not been effective. In these countries, other minorities are as oppressed as the Kurds. It is this outreach failure of the Kurdish leadership, which has led non-Kurdish forces to believe that the Kurds are separatist or secessionist.

According to Eqbal Ahmad, 800,000 French army and militia troops were constrained by 35,000 Algerian guerrilla forces. By 1961, this number was reduced to five thousand Algerian fighters. The French Army had won the war militarily, but had lost politically. The land the French had dominated by force, they could not rule; the French government had failed to win the "hearts and minds" of the masses. In Ahmad's words, the French government had been out-administered and illegitimized by the FLN.[7]

It is important to consider why the peasants fought in Algeria for seven years, and why these same forces did not join the armed struggle earlier. Apparently, the time was not "ripe."[8] Similarly, in rural Kurdistan, the time is not "ripe." Without the development of an objective internal condition, a subjective determination can not be imposed on the political struggle. The idea of political consciousness in a political struggle is extremely important, otherwise, the victories will be quickly lost. According to Eric Wolf's theory, the political movements that shook the world in the twentieth century—the Mexican Revolution of 1910, the Russian Revolutions of 1905 and 1917, the Chinese Revolution from 1921 to 1945, the Vietnamese Revolution, the Algerian Revolution of 1954, and the Cuban Revolution of 1958—succeeded because the countryside was "ripe." As a result of the breakdown of traditional economic order, culminating in institutional crisis, revolutions took place with the peasantry. The triggering variable was organizational capacity guided by a well-defined ideology capable of transforming mass discontent into political action.[9]

These movements were anti-imperialist and desired liberation from domination. It is a theoretical fallacy to equate these movements with Kurdish movements, as Martin Van Bruinessen does.[10] The Kurdish movements lack mobilization propelled by class-consciousness which strive for social justice. Bruinessen agrees with the last thesis. His statement that Kurdish peasants who only verbally expressed their support for the movement in 1966, and then suddenly adopted conservatism and became "even reactionary" is contradictory.[11] Such a regressive change did not characterize the political domains of the aforementioned movements. In Iraq, the movement was consistently and hopelessly reactionary from the beginning to the very end of Mulla Mostafa-Barzani's era and continues under his son, Mom Masud Barzani. Whereas the Mexican, Russian, Chinese, Cuban, Vietnamese, and Algerian movements were anti-imperialist and led to the development of political and class-consciousness, the Kurdish movements were not. Bruinessen writes:

> The Kurdish leadership seemed to wish for more imperialist interference in the region rather than less. Mulla Mostafa Barzani repeatedly expressed his warm feelings for the United States, which he wanted Kurdistan to join as the fifty-first state, and to which he was willing to grant control of the oil in Kurdistan in exchange for support.[12]

Barzani's statement validates the reactionary and regressive nature of his movement. It also deviates from the explanatory theoretical scheme of liberation struggles. Reliance on the oppressors to liberate the oppressed has simply no empirical or theoretical basis in the history of political movements.

In the six progressive movements mentioned above, the army and the state, backed by the imperial centers, stood on the status quo, and Guerrillas supported by the masses fought to transform the prevailing order. Armed with political consciousness and theoretical knowledge, these movements were able to translate theory into political realization of its ends, which was liberation from domination and exploitation. Although the Kurdish demand is a just one, its movement is reactionary. It fails to form class alliances and embrace political coalitions with other social classes and aggrieved forces. In class societies, everyone belongs to a class, clan, or tribe and is expected to reflect the ideological values within the dominant social formation that is bound by contradictions. Conflict is the result of contradictions between the old vs. new, haves vs. have nots, and the dominant vs. dominated. These contradictions result in suppression of one class by another, and the resulting discontent is evident. Effective leadership would mitigate this problem through an inclusive organizational effort that incorporated the affected social forces into its political praxis. In all national liberation movements, political mobilization has been organized against the imperial structures in domination. In contrast, the missing link in the Kurdish struggle is the political connection between leadership and the masses. Thus, the Kurdish movement is largely defined by conservatism, and change containing ideology imposed from without, controlled and manipulated by external political powers. This circumvents the development of a national and class-based solidarity.

Barzani's statement supports this analysis. The Kurdish revolution "would accept arms from Israel if the West advised," and he (Barzani) "would be willing to let foreign oil firms into Kurdistan to exploit fields."[13] This apolitical position blocks the objective development of political consciousness from within. It also hinders the creation of an autonomous military force. The Kurdish struggle has failed to develop an organic link between the people and the army, and has failed to formulate revolutionary ideology. Tribal mentality, old fashion leadership, and corruption exercised by the notables dominating military and political structures contribute to the perpetuation of traditional realities. The Kurdish movement under Barzani's leadership failed to effectively extend its ideological and political base to the urban areas. The Kurdish revolution could not create democratic alliances with other oppositional forces due to the lack of a political base. The movement suffers from parochial and tribal values in rural areas, and in the cities it lacks any mass mobilizing bases. During the Arab and Israeli conflict, Henry Kissinger advised Barzani not to attack Iraq, and by abandoning this opportunity to secure rights for the Kurds, Barzani again proved his questionable allegiance to the Kurdish cause.[14]

Instead of linking the Kurdish movement to the progressive forces of Iran, Barzani allied himself with the Shah of Iran. Barzani's vision of the history of liberation struggles was blind, and he failed to learn from the bloody fields of political experimentalism. It was Gazi Mohammad, the President of the short-lived Republic of Mahabad, 1945–1946, who promoted him to the status of General to lead the armed forces of Kurdistan. Barzani soon forgot the Shah's attack on the newborn Kurdish Republic of Mahabad. He also failed to remember that Gazi Mohammad, his brother, Sadr Gazi, and Safe Gazi were condemned to death by the Shah's military court and at dawn on 31 March 1947, were hung in Mahabad Chwar Chera Square (a square that has four lights).[15] Today this square still has only four lights; there has been no change. In 1979, the square again became the organizing center of the Kurdish Democratic Party that had been underground for almost thirty-three years. This reflects the reactionary and traditional nature of the leadership that failed to learn from its past and relied on those whose political intention has been and is the perpetuation of the prevailing status quo, not the liberation of the oppressed.

The concept of a liberation struggle is problematic. How can it be defined and by whom? What are the limitations for liberation struggle, if any? Can we apply the concept to the cause of the oppressed forces such as the Kurds? What about the nation-states such as Iran, Iraq, and Turkey against whom the Kurds struggle for liberation? Do these states have rights to defend their internationally recognized sovereignty and be concerned about dismemberment? Each of these three countries is composed of several ethnic groups. The separation or secession of one may trigger a liberation movement by others. Yet, the dominating political structures in these countries is unable to accommodate the Kurdish cause. In a sense, the argument that an old order is dying and a new one is not allowed to be born holds perfectly. In these countries, social relations are polarized and politicized. The dominating class coercively perpetuates the prevailing order, while the ethnically dominated Kurdish forces struggle to redefine the existing geographic, historic, and ethnic boundaries.

The concept of a liberation movement is vague. There is no agreement as to what constitutes a liberation struggle. According to Baxter there is a relationship between self-determination and liberation struggles.

> The right of self-determination can, however, mean different things in different contexts. It is all very well to speak of anticolonialist struggles in Africa but does a similar right of self-determination exist in the metropolitan territory of other countries? . . . . States that have had experience with secessionist movements, such as Nigeria, Pakistan and Indonesia . . . . react with surprise and resentment to the suggestion that they have been guilty of a violation of the charter . . . . It is quite clear that one man's war of national liberation can be another man's war of national secession.[16]

Generally, states are selective in their reactions to liberation struggles. They support the struggles launched against their external foes, but they tend to suppress the movements taking place within their own boundaries. The United Nations only acknowledges liberation movements when they are classified as anti colonial struggles. In fact, Resolution 1514 of the United Nations' Charter, paragraph 6, "excludes secessionist movements from the definition of self-determination."[17] This claim can be substantiated by the United Nations' Charter, Article 1, paragraphs 2 and 55, and Resolution 2625:

> . . . all peoples have the right freely to determine without external interference, their political status and to pursue their economic, social, and cultural development, and every state has the duty to respect this right in accordance with the provisions of the Charter . . . . Nothing in the foregoing shall be construed as authorizing or encouraging any action which would dismember or impair . . . . The territorial integrity or political unity of . . . states conducting themselves in compliance with the principle of equal rights and self-determination of peoples . . . possessed of a government representing the whole people belonging to the territory without distinction as to race, creed, or color.[18]

Consequently, the United Nations' Charter does not support secessionism, or the disintegration of a state's political unity. However, Resolution 2625 clearly recognizes the people's rights of self-determination against their own governments, if such political systems discriminate against them. If this tenet of the United Nations' charter is applied to the political behavior of Iraq and Turkey concerning Kurdish rights, the violation of Resolution 2625 becomes vividly clear. The Kurds have had their political rights severely violated and have never been treated equally with respect to race or creed. Article 3 of the Universal Declaration of Human Rights maintains that "every one has the right to life, liberty and security of person." In Iraq and Turkey, Kurds do not have the right to their own lives, let alone the right to liberty, and personal security. Obviously, the Universal Declaration of Human Rights does not apply to the Kurdish people; human rights and authoritarianism do not mix. Human rights without democracy cannot be realized. Why has the international community failed to address the legal and political issues of the Kurdish people? Why doesn't the Kurdish legal and political question dominate the agenda of the world organization? Why didn't the United Nations or the United States take action against Saddam Huessin when he gassed the Kurds? The revealing answers to these important questions must be sought in the context of the prevailing world system.

According to Maxime Rodinson, "International conservatism does not believe in the rights of people, and the opportunist will support the Kurds when it suits his own ends, only to abandon them when it does not."[19] The world system is conservative and the rights of minorities, like Kurds, are subordinated to the self-defined national interests and security ideals of the world capitalist system. The Kurds' land, between the oil-rich countries and the former Soviet Union, is located in one of the world's most sensitive and strategic areas. This is the heart of the problem. The Kurds' rights conflict with the prevailing Middle Eastern status quo and the interests of the conservative world system, which require access to the oil rich areas. Although the Soviet Union has disintegrated and the Cold War has ended, the dynamics of capital accumulation remain unchanged. When Kurdish rights clash with the self-interest of local elites who support the status quo that reflects the interests of international capital, the former is subordinated to the latter.

For Samir Amin, the world capitalist system is irrational. It fails to meet the needs and rights of the people who are subject to it. "Unemployment, polarization in world development, and ecological waste are manifestations of the irrationality of the system which I call existing capitalism."[20] If the Kurds and other have-nots are systematically oppressed according to the demands of capital accumulation, it is due to the prevailing world system.

As the world system theorists argue, the prevailing world system is capitalistic, a divisive mode of production. Based on Rosa Luxemburg's research, capitalism has to either expand itself to overseas or die at home.[21] Expansion is necessary because the international arena provides access to cheaper raw materials necessary for commodity production and an exploitable labor market. This expansion creates international polarization that breeds manifold social and political problems: growing income inequalities, unemployment, alienation, marginalization, radicalization, and political violence. These variables, in turn, result in the loss of political legitimization that cater to the interests of international capital.

To guarantee the continuity of peripheral governments, the masses are excluded from the body politic, since their concerns are antithetical to the interests of international captital. In contrast to the core formations where elite hegemony is perpetuated by both cultural and political apparatuses, in the peripheries, the continuity of the ruling class hegemony depends on the state political apparatus. For Gramsci, hegemony involves the domination of bourgeois values and norms.[22] Capitalist relations of production create ideological practices that legitimize the political culture of domination and subordination. It is devised to "wrap in mystery the most basic fact of capitalist economy: that one social group exploits another."[23]

In the peripheries, however, this mystery has been unmasked and the state, as a class institution, has no choice but to use political force to defend its interests which result in alienation and subordination of the dominated groups. At the core and in the periphery of the world system, the state becomes the terrorizing arm of the ruling classes. Professor Clive Thomas identifies the state's purpose as:

> ... [the state exists to] destroy the organizations of the masses in order to assure its own security. This has meant concentrated attacks on the trade unions, on opposition political parties, and on any means of public communication. . . . not directly under control of the state.[24]

In Iran, Iraq, and Turkey, the state has attacked universities, students, critiques, and dissenting groups. The state also suppressed and/or violently eliminated Kurdish opposition, terrorized Kurds who spoke their mother tongue or wore their traditional Kurdish dress or called themselves Kurds, and punished those who did not identify themselves with the so-called totality of the whole (Turkey). Individual freedoms and rights are meaningless since unity is the highest virtue; individuals must be subordinated to the whole. Wills and desires that go against the whole are "inconsequential" and, therefore, suppressed.[25]

The state as a class institution exercises excessive force to achieve its stated end, which is the preservation of the status quo. Egbal Ahmad's argument lends support to this analysis. The ruling classes:

> . . . are even experimenting with new methods of terrorizing the people and eliminating their opposition while reducing the "visibility" of their excesses. Increasingly, people are tortured in "safe houses," in civilian quarters rather than identifiable prisons or concentration camps. Actual and potential dissenters disappear more often than they are imprisoned.[26]

In reality, this is inconsistent with the idea of unity; it alienates rather than unites. State sponsored terrorism creates disunity and barbarism. For example, the Shah's government tortured over 350,000 dissidents in Iran; the Indonesian government killed between 500,000 to one million so called Communists after the coup of 1965; and between 1968 and 1978 alone, over 30,000 people disappeared in Latin American countries.[27] State sponsored terrorism reflects conflict not unity. As this research has documented, unity created by force is precarious. Ahmad argues that torture is not entirely designed to extract information or to punish dissenting opposition groups, but to create a repressive and intimidating environment that prevents the political and social coalition of opposition groups.[28] The political state apparatus promotes this arrangement. Privately organized death squads and shock troops reinforce these ends and operate with "unofficial sanction."[29] The vitality of state sponsored terrorism is obvious. The state in many peripheral formations does not have its legitimacy derived from the consent of the ruled, and must exercise control over the means of political violence. In these social formations, the state is in conflict with the masses, and the masses are in conflict with the elites at the core of the world system. International capital uses the peripheral state as a tool to secure its own end of capital accumulation. The state in the periphery is not a local or national phenomenon, but is a product of the structural crisis of accumulation in the core of the system. Local state structures are reinforced by the international structures of domination.[30] According to Professor Thomas, the state in the periphery is not only supported by the core systems, but cannot exist without external support.[31] He argues that:

> . . . the center's ability to appropriate output from the periphery (with which to satisfy its own exploited classes) is contingent on the under development of the bourgeoisie in the periphery and on the prevention of a revolutionary transformation of political relations and state power in favor of the workers and peasants in those countries.[32]

The core plays a crucial role in arming and training the armed forces, as well as the peripheral state's secret police. The peripheral state is armed by sophisticated technologies of social control and internal surveillance, provided by the West. The goal in the peripheries is to establish a safe and stable environment for capitalization, surplus appropriation, and capital accumulation. This order, created by force in the periphery, is violent and precarious. It promotes the interests of local, national, and international classes, the state conflicting with the human rights of the masses, especially the minority groups.[33] Since the vital objective of the world system is profit maximization, it concentrates wealth and political power in the hands of the few. This promotes exclusion rather than inclusion. Morality, humanity, political, and democratic rights are defined in economic terms. The world system in its attempt to create an environment safe for global capital accumulation imposes its cultural and structural needs on the peripheries in the name of democracy and freedom. In reality, the concept of democracy occupying the universal agenda of the core is only freedom for capital accumulation and maintenance of the capitalistic relations of production. For this to be realized, "the political and economic principles of capitalism should prevail."[34] The world system has become the center of elite decision-making for the peripheries where millions of people must subordinate to, and accept without consent, decisions made against their wills.

The dominant class at the core equates democracy with capitalism, and believes that without capitalism democracy cannot be realized.[35] However, this equation fails to analytically define the two concepts. This debate is impoverished by narrow definitions and is confined to limited political rights, negating other societal and economic rights. Without state interventionism to regulate this relationship, democracy and capitalism tend to be incompatible. Capitalism, as a class system, creates economic inequalities that pose a serious threat to the realization of democratic ideals. Democracy is doomed when the prevailing world economic system "for its survival, keeps billions of people starving or undernourished, landless, poor, and overworked in the South, and makes waste and saturation consumption a necessity in the North?"[36] This does not necessarily indicate that third world countries are poor. Most countries are rich, only the people are poor. The elitist core adopted modernization theory as the theoretical framework to depict capitalistic development in the third word as a means to narrow the gap between the rich and the poor, the North and the South. In practice, the gap between the North and South has widened and the decade of efforts to narrow social, economic, and political disparities led to rising unemployment, poverty, lower consumption, and a decrease in buying power.[37] Modernization theory as a political paradigm was to promote western-style democracies. Contrary to this theoretical expectation, countries that did achieve successful socioeconomic development and modernity turned out to be authoritarian dictatorships.[38]

Martin Khor, the managing editor of the *Third World Resurgence*, states that "much of the world's output and income is channeled to a small elite (mostly in the North, but also in the South), while a large part of humanity (mostly in the South, but also a growing minority in the North) has insufficient means to satisfy its needs."[39] While the North has 20 percent of the world population, it uses up to 80 percent of the resources of the world, and its per capita income is almost fifteen times higher than that of the South.[40] According to Professor Joshua Goldstein of American University, about half of the world's population does not have access to safe drinking water. About the same percentage is homeless or living in low quality homes. Nearly half of these people are illiterate and 98 percent lack a college education. Overall, one billion people live in abject poverty. Every five seconds a child dies due to malnutrition, seven hundred every hour, sixteen thousand every day, and six million every year. Yet, in the same five seconds, the world spends over $125,000 on military matters. A thousandth of this sum can save a child's life.[41] This data support the thesis that the world capitalist system is largely responsible for human sufferings, and stifles a meaningful debate regarding North/South relations. Without a fundamental and structural transformation of the prevailing world system through mobilization from the bottom up, human rights and democratic ideals can not be realized. The Kurdish leadership ignores this reality, especially those in Iraq who rely on the prevailing system for their self-realization and self-determination. Kurdish movements, though not in Turkey, deviate completely from other national liberation struggles.

In the next chapter, the world system theory will be applied to the Kurdish political struggle. Empirical evidence will validate the impeding nature of the world system and how it blocks the realization of Kurdish rights.

NOTES

1. Theda Skocpol, *States and Social Revolutions: A Comparative Analysis of French, Russia and China* (London: Cambridge University Press, 1979), 4.

2. *Ibid.*, 4–5. I devised this typology because the Kurdish leadership calls the Kurdish struggle a revolution. As such, we must know what kind of revolution it is. Without such a distinction, the meaning and analysis of the Kurdish movement will remain vague. The concept of the Kurdish revolution was coined by Dr. Mahmud A. Osman. It is also used very commonly by the Kurds. Mahmud A. Osman, *The Kurdish Journal* 4:1 (March 1967), 3–7.

3. Skocpol, *States and Social Revolutions,* 19–24.

4. Cited by Eqbal Ahmad, "Revolutionary Warfare and Counter-Insurgency," *National Liberation Revolution in the Third World*, eds., Norman Miller and Roderick Aya (*New York: The Free Press*, 1971), 146.

5. Ibid., xvi.

6. Ibid., xix.

7. Ibid., 149–149.

8. Ibid., 149.

9. Eric R. Wolf, "On Peasant Rebellions," in Teodor Shanin, ed., *Peasants and Peasant Societies: Selected Readings* (London, Oxford: Basil Blackwell, 1987), 367–374.

10. . Martin Van Bruinessen, *Agha, Shaikh and State The Social and Political Structure of Kurdistan* (London: Zed Bookds, 1992), 2.

11. *Ibid.*; see also Derk Kinnane, *Kurdha va Kurdistan: A Short History of the Kurds and of Kurdistan* (Tehran, Iran: Negah Publishers, 1372), 14–16.

12. Bruinessen, *Agha, Shaikh*, 2.

13. Stephen C. Pettetiere, *The Kurds: An Unstable Element in the Gulf* (Boulder, Colorado: Westview Press, 1984), 174.

14. Ismet Sheriff Vanly, "Kurdistan in Iraq," in Gerard Chaliand, ed., *People Without a Country: The Kurds and Kurdistan*, (London: Zed Press, 1980), 182–192.

15. Archie Roosevelt, Jr., "The Kurdish Republic of Mahabad," in Gerard Chaliand, ed., *People Without a Country: The Kurds and Kurdistan* (London: Zed Press, 1980), 149.

16. Baxter, *The Geneva Convention of 1949 and Wars of National Liberation*, 56 Revista Di Dirito Internazionale 193–195 (1974) cited by Christopher O. Quaye, *Liberation Struggles* (Philadelphia: Temple University Press, 1991), 7. See also, Quaye, *Liberation Struggles in International Law*, 7–8; Chaliand, ed. *People Without a Country*, 149.

17. Ibid., 8.

18. See the UN Charter, Article 1, Paragraph 2 and Res. 2625.

19. Maxime Rodison, preface to Gerard Chaliand, ed., *People Without a Country the Kurds and Kurdistan* (London: Zed Press, 1980), 1–7.

20. Samir Amin, "The Future of Socialism," in *The Future of Socialism Perspectives from the Left*, William K. Tabb (New York: Monthly Review Press, 1990), 106–123.

21. Rosa Luxemburg, *The Accumulation of Capital* (New York: Monthly Review Press, 1964), 246–249.

22. Martin Carnoy, *The State and Political Theory* (New Jersey: Princeton University Press, 1984), 66.

23. Ronate Holub, *Antonio Gramsci: Beyond Marxism and Postmodernism* (New York: Routledge, 1992), 41.

24. Thomas Clive, *The Rise of the Authoritarian State In Peripheral Societies* (New York and London: Monthly Review Press, 1984), 92.

25. This view basically is a fascist view of the state and its continuity means more alienation, marginalization, and suppression. For further details see Bernard Susser, *Political Ideology in the Modern World* (Boston: Allyn and Bacon, 1995), 189–190.

26. Egbal Ahmad, "The Neo-Fascist State: Notes on the Pathology of Power in the Third World," *International Foundation for Development Alternatives*, 2:16 (September–October 1980), cited by Clive, *The Rise of the Authoritarian State*, 90.

27. Ahmad, "The Neo-Fascist State," 3 (17); Clive, *The Rise of the Authoritarian State*, 90.

28. Ahmad, "Neo Fascist State," 16; Clive, *The Rise of the Authoritarian State*, 90.

29. Clive, *The Rise of the Authoritarian State*, 91.

30. Ibid., 93.

31. Ibid., 94.

32. Ibid., 94.

33. In this respect Noam Chomsky and Edward Herman maintain that even aid from the capitalist centers to the peripheries "has been positively related to the investment climate and inversely related to the maintenance of a democratic order and human rights." For further discussion, see Noam Chomsky and Edward Herman, *The Washington Connection and Third World Fascism* (Boston, Massachusetts: South End Press, 1979), 44.

34. Thomas E. Weisskopf, "Capitalism, Socialism and the Sources of Imperialism," in G. John Ikenberry, ed., *American Foreign Policy Theoretical Essays* (Boston: Scott, Foresman and Company, 1989), 162–185. Weisskopf's analysis supports our thesis that the world capitalist system is largely responsible for conflict generating inequalities at the global level. For an excellent criticism of this article see, Robert W. Tucker, "The Radical Critique Assessed," in G. John Ikenberry, ed., *American Foreign Policy* (Boston: Scott, Foresman and Company, 1989), 185–220 and 197 for quotation cited.

35. Amin, *The Future of Socialism*, 107–108.

36. Muto Ichiyo, "For An Alliance of Hope," in Jeremy Brecher, John Brown Childs and Jill Cutler, eds., *Global Visions Beyond the New World Order* (Boston: South Ends Press, 1993), 154.

37. Richard J. Barnet and Ronald E. Miller, *Global Reach, The Power of the Multinational Corporations* (New York: Simon and Shuster, 1974), 149. In a video titled "U.S. Foreign Policy" presented at Boulder University in Boulder, Colorado, Michael Parenti stated that it is adapted from Michael Harrington's notion.

38. Alvin Y. So, *Social Change and Development, Modernization, Dependency, and World System Theories* (London: Sage Publications, 1990), Chapters 1 and 2.

39. Martin Khor Kok Peng, "Reforming North Economy, South Development, and World Economic Order," in Jeremy Brecher et al, *eds., Global Visions Beyond the New World Order* (Boston, Massachusetts: South End Press, 1993), 164.

40. Ibid., 165.

41. Joshua S. Goldstein, *International Relations*, 5th ed. (New York: Longman, 2003), 455–457.

Chapter Three

The World System Affecting the Kurdish Political Aspirations

The world system approach provides a theoretical framework that allows us to understand the Kurdish problem. Kurds are the victims of a conservative world system that suffers from its own contradictions and the anachronous structural limitations. The world system is an important unit of analysis in an investigation of the dynamics of political and social movements and struggles in the periphery.[1] The world system is divisive. The owners of the means of production, the oppressors, utilize every means to maintain the status quo, insuring their privileged position, and the oppressed struggle to change it. In terms of human suffering, the conflict has been tragic. The history of the colonial and neo-colonial era provides evidence of the atrocities inflicted on humanity, and the process of domination and exploitation continues. The Kurdish people are an example of a group that has struggled to liberate themselves from this process; a realization which has been impeded by the world system of domination and exploitation.

According to Nezan Kendal and Martin Van Bruinessen, the incapacitation of the Ottoman Empire intensified the Kurdish desire for independence. The Empire disintegrated during the nineteenth century by virtue of its own internal contradictions. Once the centralized absolutist political structures dissolved, the Kurds sought to capitalize on this event to achieve their independence. The French/British rivalry played a key role in dominating the Empire. Colonial policy, coupled with discontent, and the arbitrary absolutism and corruption of the Sultan's government, provoked nationalism and gave birth to the movement of the "Young Turks." In 1908, this movement forced Sultan Abdulhamid II, who was a symbol of "oriental despotism," to restore the constitution of 1876 and adopt a parliamentary democracy which would secure legal equality for all citizens.[2] Unable to contain the Young Turks, the sultan agreed to restore the constitution; elections were conducted and a representative system was upheld.

In April 1909, a counter-revolution, led by Sultan's supporters, including the "Milli" Kurds leaders, took place.[3] This counter-rebellion was defeated by the army. The Committee of Union and Progress, which brought about the 1908 young Turkish movement, declared itself the Party of Union and Progress (PUP) in April 1909 and captured political power in the April 1912 elections. By the end of the nineteenth century, Turkish intellectuals armed with European progressive and nationalistic ideas dominated the party leadership. Ideologically, this emerging class became allies with artisans and merchants, and constitutional optimism prevailed for a short period of time. However, the party failed to defend Turkey against imperialist onslaught during the First World War and lost massive territories following the two Balkan Wars of 1912–13.[4]

During World War I, Turkey allied itself with Germany and Austria, hoping to win back its lost territories and bring an end to Russian domination. During these four years of conflict, 1914–1918, the Kurds played a critical role. The war was labeled a "holy war," and the Kurds, being Muslems, considered participation in the war an important religious duty. A faction of the Kurds sided with the Russian army and fought against the Ottomans, failing to see that Tsarist Russia's major objective was the annexation of Kurdistan. In reality, the Russians, like other imperial and colonial powers, notably Britain and France, wanted to colonize the Kurds, Arminians, Arabs, and Turks.[5] While Russia's occupation forces were active in the East, the British forces were promoting their colonial cause in the South. In early 1916, Russia invaded Eastern Anatolia and advanced beyond Erzincan, and the British coveted Kirkuk and Mosul oil wells.[6]

The Bolshevik Revolution of 1917 revealed the unholy alliance between France and Britain. The revolution exposed the content of the Sykes-Picot agreement, a secret arrangement, which led to the "Balkanization" of the Middle East by creating artificially drawn boundaries, spheres of influences, and a new map of the region in accordance with colonial wishes and desires. The goal was to divide the Middle East between Britain and France. France obtained Syria, including Lebanon and the Cilicia region of Turkey, and took Damascus by force; the British procured Palestine and Iraq. The Tsarist Russia's share from such a plundering harvest included Istanbul and the strategically important straits.[7] However, after the social revolution of 1917 in Russia, the newly emerging Soviet government renounced its claim to the imperialized territories. The British government took advantage of the Soviet withdrawal from the occupied territories and took possession. In order to defend its colonial interests, the British created dissension between the ethnic groups. Britain, congruent with Van Bruinessen's argument, took up the Armenian cause and attempted to create an independent Armenia, which would include Van, Erzurum, Sivas, Mamuret al-Aziz, Bitlis, and Diyarbakir. An independent Armenia would also be created from the provinces of Kars, Ardaham, and Batum.[8] These were the territories occupied by Tsarist Russia, but given back to Turkey by the Soviet revolutionary government.

When the Paris Peace Conference convened early in 1919, the colonial forces, with the notion of peace, wanted to legalize illegally captured lands. Brought to fruition on 10 August 1920, the Treaty of Sevres[9] provided for the establishment of an Armenian state and an independent Kurdistan. In reality, the British were playing politics for Mosul (now Iraqi Kurdistan), an area which proved to possess extensive oil reserves. However, the possession of this oil resource presented many problems. British involvement in the extraction of this commodity would require support from the local and predominantly Kurdish, population. With this in mind, the British promised the Kurds an independent Kurdish state reflected in Section III, Articles 62 and 64 of the Sevres Treaty, albeit a promise realized only in theory. The British did not want to link this oil rich territory to the other Kurdish areas. The capture of the Kurds' land by force and subsequent attempts to obtain their consent reflects the world capitalist system's hypocrisy, not a commitment to democracy.

The British government consulted the Kurdish people of Mosul to determine the desirability of an independent Kurdistan, a deception to pacify the Kurds. Although the Kurds' answer to an independent Kurdistan was an affirmative yes, it would have to be further studied by the British government to verify that the Kurdish people "were capable of such independence."[10] This benevolent British policy, claiming to give democracy to its sphere of influence and domination, delivered hypocrisy and barbarism. It excluded the territories of Adiyaman, Malatya, Elbistan, Darende, and Divrik where an overwhelming majority of the Kurds lived, from the promised independent Kurdistan. Additionaly, Article 27 (Section II, Clauses 2 and 3) of the Sevres Treaty gave the "Kurd Dagh" area (the Kurds' Mountain), part of the Djasireh, the cities of Kilis, Aintab, Biredjik, Urfa, Mardin, Nusaybin, and Djaziret ibn Omar to the French mandate of Syria. According to Gerard Chaliand, these areas, "which were to be directly or indirectly annexed by France, accounted for about a third of the territories of Ottoman Kurdistan." The allocation to the Armenians of the Kurdish dominated territories of Van, Bitlis, Bingol, Erzincan, Mus, Karakilisa, Igdir and Erzurum proved equally as vexing. For Chaliand this accounted for about "third of Ottoman Kurdistan."[11]

The Sevres Treaty eliminated two-thirds of Kurdish lands and excluded a Persian Kurdistan from consideration, a clear violation of the Kurds' rights to property. Ironically, even under this arbitrary arrangement, the British were to control the oil rich areas. From Turkey's nationalistic point of view, the 1920 Treaty of Sevres was humiliating and led to the dismemberment of their country and the imperialist domination of the region. The treaty confirmed French occupation of Cilicia. Areas that are today considered Turkish, were placed under Greek and Italian occupation, and much of Eastern Turkey was assigned to the Armenian Republic. A small Kurdish state was also proposed, subject to a plebiscite that was never held, and the Turkish strait's zone was to be demilitarized and internationalized.[12]

Domination, colonization, "balkanization,"[13] and partition of Turkish land provoked an intensified Turkish nationalism led by Mostafa Kamal Pasha, who assumed leadership of the liberation struggle (1919–1923).[14] Kamal Pasha felt that imperialism was the main enemy and needed to be defeated through armed struggle on three fronts: the imperial forces of aggression, the sultan's corrupt palace forces (like the White Army in Russia after the Bolshevik Revolution of 1917), and the comprador bourgeoisie class. By mid 1919, the occupation forces were concentrated in Istanbul and Izmir, thus prompting Kamal Pasha to organize a national liberation guerrilla movement in the countryside. Landlord, clergy, and comprador bourgeoisie sympathizers supported the palace and forces of occupation. The Anatolian peasantry, including some factions of the Kurds, remained to be allied along similar lines.[15]

Kamal Pasha managed, through his leadership quality and appealing nationalism, to present himself as the liberator of Kurdistan and the defender of the Muslim territories dominated by infidel forces. His leadership and ideals appealed to all Muslems, Kurds and Turks, as he appealed for unity to liberate the "Muslem Father Land" from occupation. This Kamalist tactic resulted in the convening of the Erzurum Congress of 1919, which met from 23 July to 6 August 1919. This congress agreed to prevent Armenia from annexing Muslim lands and to expel the invading infidels from the Islamic territories. In fact, front-line Kurdish forces supported Turkey's war for independence. Once the eastern front was liberated, the Kurds played a dominant role in liberating Anatolia.[16] In 1919, an Armenian state was created in the southern Caucasus. Eastern Anatolia was invaded in 1920 by Armenian forces, who also planned for the forceful acquisition of the provinces promised at Sevres. On 20 October, the Armenians, armed and financed by the British government, were defeated by Kazim Karabekir, the commander of Kurdish forces on the eastern front. On the western front, the Greek armies in Anatolia were defeated.[17]

A month after the Erzurum Congress, a second congress was held at Sevres in September of 1919. There was broad-based Turkish representation at the Sevres Congress, and resolutions were passed calling upon popular resistance in the defense of Anatolian rights.[18] A representative committee elected Mostafa Kamal as president, and declared that the remaining Ottoman Empire should be placed under the leadership of the committee.[19] Later that year, elections were held for the parliament, and Kamalist candidates were chosen in each region, including Kurdistan. On 28 January 1920, this parliament adopted a document, referred to as the National Pact, calling for the national integrity and sovereignty of the newly created Turkey. Self-determination (by plebiscite) for occupied regions of the Ottoman Empire with an Arab population majority was required, and all other areas inhabited by a Muslim majority were to remain an undivided whole.[20] The response of occupation forces to nationalist demands of the parliament was to occupy Istanbul by force, arrest Parliamentarians, and dissolve this popularly elected assembly.

A meeting in Ankara on 28 April 1920 was arranged due to the farsighted political vision of nationalist members of the assembly. A result of this meeting was the institution of the Grand National Assembly of Turkey, designed to assume legislative and executive responsibilities. The assembly declared that the Turkish authorities would not honor any treaties or agreements signed by the colonially chosen administration in occupied Istanbul. This declaration led to the nullification of the Sevres Treaty.[21] If the imperial powers' plans had been placed into effect, little of the Ottoman Empire would have been left for the creation of a Turkish state. It was this threat of destruction that culminated in the Turkish national revival.[22]

By 1923, the Turks had defeated their potential enemies. This military victory, along with the victory of the Soviet social revolution, created major concern for the imperialist powers. The concern was that Mostafa Kamal Pasha also called Ataturk, meaning "Father of the Turks," an honorary title given to him by Turkey's Grand Assembly, might enter an alliance with the newly emerging revolutionary government of the Soviet Union. Hence, they favored the creation of a Turkish independent state on 24 July 1923. This calculated strategy had a twofold objective. It was to prevent Kamal from aligning with Soviet forces, and to use Turkey as a buffer zone between the Soviet Union and the western colonies in the Middle East. It was this consideration that led to the 1923 Treaty of Lausanne. This treaty revised and redefined Turkey's territorial arrangements and fixed its borders very much as they stand today.[23] However, oil was an important issue in the Lausanne agreement. The fight hinged on the vilayet of Mosul, which was originally located in the French zone. In 1925, the Supreme Council of the League of Nations gave Mosul to Iraq, a British mandate. In 1926, Turkey and Britain agreed to accept the new boundary. In addition, France agreed to give Mosul to Britain in exchange for a 25 percent share in crude oil production and a "free hand" in Syria; the United States received a 20 percent share in Turkish petroleum; Turkey gave up its rights to Mosul and in return, 10 percent of the oil produced in the area would be Turkey's; and the British agreed not to agitate the Kurds and Armenians against Turkey.[24]

The colonial forces freely imposed their own arbitrarily defined boundaries on the people of the region, which created more political and cultural problems. Although the Jewish and Turkish states were created, their political problems are far from resolved. The Arab/Israeli conflict remains unresolved, and the Turkish state is at war against its own people, Kurds and Armenians, who continue without states.[25] Before World War I, Kurdish territories were divided between the Persia and Ottoman empires. In the aftermath of colonial domination, these territories were split between Turkey, Iran, Iraq, and Syria.[26] However, colonial powers were not welcomed in the Middle East. In order to maintain their exploitation in the colonized areas, the colonizing powers, especially the British, resorted to the divide and rule strategy, pitting one ethnic group against the other. This policy heightened ethnic conflict and fragmentation. As competition for possession of resources, new markets, cheap raw materials, spheres of influence, child labor, and cheap labor in the third world intensified, it was difficult to sustain prevailing political structures in the region through divide and rule policy alone. These structures required reinforcement by centralized autocracies. Consequently, colonial powers used state fascism to defend capitalism and maintain their captured, but not earned, interests.

The world system, as an externally activating variable, has played a critical role in politicizing ethnic differences and the resulting political conflicts. British imperialism provoked Kurdish nationalist aspirations for an independent Kurdistan, but pitted Armenians and Kurds against one another to block its actualization. Since, the goal of imperialism was to appropriate the oil fields of Kurds in the south, the creation of a centralized, neo-fascist, and imperial state was the critical solution. It was not an accident that the British set up the puppet state of Iraq designed to control the vilayets of Basra, Baghdad, and Mosul. While the first two vilayets were seized from the Ottoman Empire during World War II, the latter was occupied by the British after the Armistice was signed between the Allied forces and the Sultan's Turkey in 1918. Iraq was created by the British. Oil rich provinces like Basra, Mosul, Kurkuk, and Khanagin were conveniently situated inside Iraqi boundaries, instigating hostile feelings of intense nationalism between the Kurds and Arabs.[27]

To date, the only change taken place in this state of affairs has been the replacement of colonial domination by neocolonialism. The abuse of Kurdish rights has been systematic. Whenever the internationally dominant powers wanted alteration, equation, or restoration of regional balance of power, they have used the Kurds. Once this goal was achieved, the Kurds were abandoned. For instance, Iran started supporting the Kurdish political movement in Iraq in the mid-1960s. The political objective of the Shah of Iran was to weaken Iraq's position on border disputes and navigation rights. In return, General Barzani, the leader of KDP Iraq, committed his forces to create stability in Iranian Kurdistan by executing the Kurdish rebels who had supported the rebellion against the government of Iran under the Shah. Even General Barzani extradited the fellow Kurdish rebels of Iran to the Shah's government.[28]

In April 1972, Iraq entered into a friendship treaty with the Soviet Union. This left no choice for General Barzani, the Iraqi KDP leader, but to advance the Shah's foreign policy and support the aggression against the Kurdish progressive forces operating inside Iran. The Iraqi alliance with the Soviets so concerned the U.S. government, that it provided secret funds for General Barzani through the CIA as a bribe to discourage any coalition with the Soviets and to signify American support for the Kurdish movement. The United States gave sixteen million dollars to Kurdish leadership between 1972–1975.[29] The main objective was to weaken the possibility that Iraq would become a supportive base for the Soviet Union. A coalition between Iraq and the Soviet Union would threaten American interests in the Middle East. In 1973, Kissinger, then the United States Secretary of State, flew to Tehran where he met with General Barzani. Having secured support from the United States, Barzani did not want to accept the Saddam Hussein formulated autonomy that excluded Kirkuk and Khanagin from Kurdistan. Kissinger's visit coincided with the Arab-Israeli war of 1973. Also during this time, General Barzani wished to advance his cause politically by attacking the Iraqi government, but was prevented by Kissinger. In March 1974, Saddam Hussein unilaterally proposed an autonomy law, which was rejected by General Barzani for its exclusion of crucial parts of Kurdistan.[30] This was the excuse for the 1974 war. In reality, Washington and the Shah of Iran supported the Kurdish/Iraqi conflict. The Kurds' participation in this war was extremely tense and unprecedented. In September 1974, the Iranian artillery was placed in Iraqi Kurdistan to strengthen the Kurdish front, while the Iraqi air force, using the Soviet piloted Tupolev 225, bombed Kurdish villages. Iraq also employed T62 Tanks to attack Riwanduz and Qala Diza. The Kurdish forces suffered heavy casualties in these areas. However, the Iraqi army, after fierce fighting in the area of Mountain Zozek, was boldly resisted by the Kurdish *peshmerga* (vanguard of death), and by October 1974 had retreated.[31]

While the Kurdish *peshmergas* courageously stood up to Saddam's forces, secret negotiations between Iran and Iraq took place during 1974. At an OPEC meeting in Algiers on 6 March 1975, secret arrangements between the Shah and Saddam were negotiated, mediated by Anwar Sadat of Egypt, King Hussein of Jordan, and President Boume Dienne of Algiers. The Shah of Iran was a big winner. He gained control of the Shatt-al-Arab and won major land concessions in border disputes. Once the Shah achieved these ends, the Kurds were abandoned once again, and the Kurdish movement thus collapsed. Although they were undefeated militarily, they were defeated politically.

General Barzani, nonetheless, hoped for special compensation in the Algiers agreement on 6 March 1975. However, this failed to materialize. Out of desperation, General Barzani wrote a letter to Henry Kissinger on the day of the conclusion of the Algiers' accord which reads: "The United States of America has both moral and political responsibility for our people who have fought to advance the political cause of your country." He asked Kissinger to have Iranians "support the Kurds, at those saddest and darkest moments of the Kurdish life, so that they start a guerrilla war until a political settlement is reached."[32] Kissinger never answered this letter; the United States had temporarily finished with the Kurds as the political pawns to achieve a balance of power in the area. Mostafa Barzani, the leader of the movement was exiled in Tehran, later dying of cancer in 1978. The extended struggle failed to materialize the Kurdish dream of an independent Kurdistan owing to a lack of political vision and reliance on the perpetuators of the political status quo.

During the Iran-Iraq war (1980–1988), triggered by Saddam Hussein's aggression, Iran recruited PDK-Iraq led by Masud Barzani, the late General Barzani's son, to fight on behalf of Iran against Saddam's invading forces. Iraq used KDP-Iran and Komala against Iran. The two countries made use of the other's Kurds to contribute to a weakening of their rival.[33] As soon as this devastating war was over, Saddam sought to retaliate against the Kurds who supported Iran. In August 1988, he murdered thousands of Kurds, mostly women and children, in the small town of Halabja.[34] This was during the Reagan era, and Reagan's goal was to contain the Iranian revolution, a revolution that resulted from U. S. policy contradictions associated with capital accumulation. Hence, it was not considered a major international event. Ironically, during the war, Senator Dole, along with other key senators, flew to Iraq to participate in Saddam Hussein's birthday party.[35] At that time, the goal of America's foreign policy was to use Saddam Hussein's state sponsored terrorism against Iran in defense of corporate interest. The United States was not concerned with Kurdish rights or human rights. Human rights as a concept, not its practical application, has been a tool of American foreign policy adapted to secure world domination, capital accumulation, and value extraction, a reality that Kurdish leaders never understood. Personal gain and the quest for political power have always blinded the Kurds to the reality of their defeat by colonial and imperial powers. Kurdish leaders are as guilty as the world system for the plight of the Kurdish people.

In the aftermath of the 1991 Gulf War, the United States created a neutral no-fly-zone in both northern and southern Iraq. The objective was the defense of the status quo oil producing countries. In the south, the policy aimed to control Saddam Hussein's initiatives to create the so-called imaginary "weapons of mass destruction," disabling a potential invasion of Kuwait or Saudi Arabia. In the north, "operation restore hope" initiatives were adopted to protect the Kurds from Saddam Hussein's brutality. The policy helped the Kurds and was welcomed, especially by their leader, Masud Barzani, but the policy contained other objectives. The Kurds were the agents of capital accumulation and used to balance the region's power configuration. The goal was to weaken and contain Saddam Hussein until a figurehead favoring United States policy was found. It is not so much that the United States favored the Kurds, but that Saddam Hussein was no longer acceptable to American foreign policy strategists who were obsessed with the imperial domination of the region.

The Kurds of Turkey provide the empirical evidence supporting this thesis. American foreign policy does not support Turkish Kurds, and advocates Turkey's Saddam-style assault on the Kurds in southeast Turkey. According to the *Herald International Tribune*, the Turkish government pursues state terror in Kurdistan. It uses "the scorched earth policy" in Turkish Kurdistan. Based on the *Herald Tribune's* findings, "The Kurdish villages are mostly wiped off the map, forests are burned, several oradous (this analogy between oradous and burned Kurdish villages refers to the village of Oradous in France destroyed by the German Secret Service in 1944) are perpetuated under cover in the fight against terrorism . . ."[36] As the paper reports, during a two year period, 1,638 Kurdish political activists, intellectuals, trade unionists, and teachers were assassinated and thousands of others are in prison because of their opinions.[37] Human rights activists are murdered by the Turkish "Gulag." Intellectuals are subjected to the acceptance of the state-defined ideology. Any deviation from the state-imposed ideology brings destruction for the violator(s). Ismail Besikci, a well-known sociologist and university professor, wrote thirty books, twenty-seven of which were banned. The professor became a criminal. This represents censorship and control of knowledge intended to inform and educate the public. According to the *Turkish Daily News* of 17 November 1995, Ismail Besikci was sentenced to imprisonment for two hundred years.[38] Exercising critical intellectual capacity and defending one's cultural rights is considered a crime.

The center of the world system, the United States of America, along with the Turkish government, considers the Turkish Kurds terrorists. Such a contradictory stand is based on self-interested selective perception. Turkey is an American ally, Iraq is not. Iraq allied with the United States against the Iranians with the objective of containing the Iranian revolution. When the goal was accomplished, the allied relationship was abandoned. When policy shifted in favor of the Kurds, the Kurds were utilized to undermine the internationally recognized sovereign state of Iraq, in spite of its erratic leader. At the peak of the Cold War, Turkey aided the West's Cold War policy. Now Turkey assists the United States in spreading a reactionary version of the Islamic religion to central Asian countries and allows the United States to use its military bases.[39]

The world system has betrayed the Kurdish cause. President Wilson promised the Kurds some form of statehood at the end of World War I, but when the British and French governments, the leading colonial powers of the time, learned that the proposed area for the Kurdish state contained oil, they moved to block it. In order to participate in colonial competitions and gains, the Soviet Union supported the Iranian Kurds in their struggle to create their own state at Mahabad, the capital and headquarters of the Kurdish movements. This was short lived, and the state collapsed in 1947. According to the *New York Times*, "Leaders of countries where Kurds live have often sponsored Kurdish rebellions in neighboring lands while massacring Kurds on their own territory. Syria, for example, tolerates no expression of Kurdish identity within its borders, but shelters and equips a large force of Kurds fighting against Turkey."[40] This strategy also applies to other countries where Kurds are living and fighting. This is illustrated vividly in recent developments in Northern Iraq. Masud Barzani, the leader of KDP (the Kurdistan Democratic Party), claims the reason for his alliance with Saddam was that his rival Jalal Talabani, the leader of PUK (the Patriotic Union of Kurdistan), sought support from Iran. Talabani argues the reason for his involvement with Iran was due to Barzani's Turkish support.[41] Ironically, Turkey denies its own Kurds cultural and identity rights.

Kurds have been used by both regional and international powers and are abandoned after the goals of these political powers are achieved. Neither the world system nor the regional powers is genuinely concerned for the Kurdish people. The Kurds are critical factors when they can be used as the agents of capital accumulation and the instruments in a regional balance of power. The concept of capital is divisive, and the resulting conflict is indicative of the structural crisis of the system of accumulation. As Rosa Luxemburg argues, the West takes into account only one aspect of economic development, the realm of peaceful competition, but fails to acknowledge the realm of violence that arises from the capital accumulation process. Violence and destruction are seen as independent of the realm of the accumulation process, hence, incidental to foreign policy. For Rosa Luxemburg, these two realms are structurally linked.[42] Accumulation at the global level means conflict and divisiveness. It creates polarization. In Samir Amin's words, capital accumulation has polarized the world for five centuries.[43] The Kurds, along with other forces, are victim of this prevailing reality. The realization of Kurdish political and human rights cannot be attained under the arrangements of the existing world system, which chooses capital's rights over human rights. However, the Kurdish hope for autonomy or statehood has been dashed repeatedly because of changes in international and regional power's policies, the external variables[44] In the following chapter, the internal variables that are largely responsible for and the impediments to the realization of Kurdish ideals are discussed.

NOTES

1. Samir Amin, "The Future of Socialism," in *Perspectives from the Left*, ed. William K. Tabb (New York: Monthly Review Press, 1980), 109.

2. Nezan Kendal, "The Kurds Under the Ottoman Empire," trans. Michael Pallis, in *People Without A Country: The Kurds and Kurdistan*, ed. Gerard Chaliand (London: Zed Press, 1980), 19–46; Martin Van Bruinessen, *Agha, Shaikh and State The Political Structures of Kurdistan* (London: Zed Books Ltd., 1992), 270–271. For a detailed study see Derk Kinnane, *Kurdaha va Kurdistan,* trans. Abraham Unisi (Tehran, Iran: Negah Publishers, 1372), 72–75.

3. Chris Kutschera, *The Kurdish National Movement*, trans. from French to Farsi, Abraham Unisi (Tehran, Iran: Negah Publishers, 1373), 31.

4. Berch Berberoglu, *Turkey in Crisis* (London: Zed Press, 1982), 4–5.

5. Kendal, *The Kurds Under The Ottoman Empire*, 37–38.

6. Bruinessen, *Agha, Shaikh and State*, 270–271.

7. Alasdair Drysdale and Gerald H. Blake, *The Middle East and North Africa: A Political Geography* (New York: Oxford University Press, 1985), 63–66.

8. Bruinessen, *Agha Shaikh and State*, 271–272.

9. *Ibid.*, 272; Chaliand also notes from the Treaty of Sevres:

Article 62: A Commission, having its seat in Constantinople and made up of three members appointed by the governments of Britain, France, and Italy, will, during the six months following the implementation of the present treaty, prepare for local autonomy in those regions where the Kurdish element is preponderant lying east of the Euphrates, to the south of a still-to-be established Armenian frontier and to the north of the frontier between Turkey, Syria, and Mesopotamia, as established in Article 27 II (2 and 3). Should agreement on any question not be unanimous, the members of the commission will refer it back to their respective governments. he plan must provide complete guarantees as to the protection of the Assyro-Chaldeans and other ethnic or religious minorities in the area. To this end, a commission made up of British, French, Italian, Persian, and Kurdish representatives will visit the area so as to determine what adjustments, if any, should be made to the Turkish frontier wherever it coincides with the Persian frontier as laid down in this treaty.

Article 63: The Ottoman Government agrees as of now to accept and execute the decisions of the two commissions envisaged in Article 62 within three months of being notified of those decisions.

Article 64: If, after one year has elapsed since the implementation of the present treaty, the Kurdish population of the areas designated in Article 62 calls on the Council of the League of Nations and demonstrates that a majority of the population in these areas wishes to become independent of Turkey, and if the Council then estimates that the population in question is capable of such independence and recommends that it be granted, then Turkey agrees, as of now, to comply with this recommendation and to renounce all rights and titles to the area. The details of this renunciation will be the subject of a special convention between Turkey and the main Allied powers.

If and when the said renunciation is made, no objection shall be raised by the main Allied powers should the Kurds living in that part of Kurdistan at present included in the Vilayet of Mosul seek to become citizens of the newly independent Kurdish state. Chailand, *People Without a Country,* 43.

10. Chaliand, *People Without a Country,* 43.

11. Ibid., 43–44.

12. *Ibid.*

13. Ibid., 64. This term is used by Al Sadair.

14. Chaliand, *People Without A Country,* 55; Drysdale and Blake, *The Middle East,* 63.

15. Berch Berberoqlu, *The Internalization of Capital Imperialism and Capitalist Development on a World Scale* (New York: Praeger, 1987), 124–25; Berch Berberoqlu, *Turkey in Crisis* (London: Zed Press, 1982), 9–10.

16. Chaliand, *People Without A Country,* 55–56.

17. Bruinessen, *Agha, Shaikh and State,* 272–273.

18. Chaliand, *People Without A Country,* 56; Bruinessen, *Agha, Shaikh and State,* 272.

19. Chaliand, *People Without A Country,* 56.

20. Ibid., 56–57. See also Bruinessen, *Agha, Shaikh and State,* 273.

21. Ibid., 57.

22. Drysdale and Blake, *The Middle East,* 186–189; see also Chaliand, *People Without a Country,* 57.

23. Drysdale and Blake, *The Middle East,* 55, 187; Chaliand, *People Without a Country,* 58.

24. Drysdale and Blake, *The Middle East,* 66; Chaliand, *People Without a Country,* 58–59; Bruinessen, *Agha, Shaikh and State,* 273–274.

25. Drysdale and Blake, *The Middle East,* 66.

26. Chaliand, *People Without A Country,* 60.

27. Ibid.; Drysdale and Blake, *The Middle East,* 158–159; Bruinessen, *Agha, Shaikh and State,* 13–14.

28. Chaliand, *People Without A Country,* 14–15; Bruinessen, *Agha, Shaikh and State,* 29–32.

29. Chaliand, *People Without A Country,* 14.

30. Bruinessen, *Agha, Shaikh and State,* 30.

31. Geradrd Chaliand, *The Kurdish Tragedy,* trans. Philip Black (London: Zed Books, 1994), 62–65.

32. Kutschera, *The Kurdish National Movement,* 406–07.

33. Chaliand, *The Kurdish Tragedy*, 11.

34. Halabja is a small Kuridsh town located in the Southeast of Sulaymaniya. Saddam used poison gas in killing Kurds. Bruinessen, *Agha, Shaik and State*, 42–45.

35. This is a matter of public record. It was reported live by TV networks around the world.

36. "State Terror in Turkish Kurdistan," *Herald International Tribune*, 9 June 1994, 44.

37. Ibid., 44.

38. This report has been used by *Human Rights Watch* under the title, "The Turkish Gulag Through Ten Pictures," 13–14. It documents how political activists have been either tortured, imprisoned, or assassinated. These figures are illustrated by their names, profession, and activities through their pictures. The report bases its information of Besikci's imprisonment on *Turkish Daily News*, 17 November 1995.

39. "America Arms Turkey's Repression," *Human Rights Watch* (Washington, D.C., 1995), 53.

40. Stephen Kinzer, "History's Losers Fight Neighbors and Each Other, Often Assisted by Foes," *New York Times*, 4 September 1996, A-11.

41. Thomas L. Friedman, "A View from Tehran," *New York Times*, 4 September 1996: 21.

42. Rosa Luxemburg, *The Accumulation of Capital* (New York: Monthly Review Press, 1964), 452; Immanuel Wallerstein, *The Modern World System: Capitalist Agriculture and the Origins of the European World Economy in the 16th Century* (New York, London: Academic Press, 1974), 69–70, 348; Immanuel Wallerstein, *The Capitalist World Economy* (New York: Cambridge University Press, 1979), 162. For a critical perspective, see Harry Magdoff, "Militarism and Imperialism," in *Readings in U.S. Imperialism*, ed. K. T. Fann and Donald C. Hodges (Boston, Massachusetts: Porter Sargent Publishers, 1971), 127–138; Thomas E. Weisskopf, "Capitalism, Socialism and the Sources of Imperialism," in *American Foreign Policy*, ed. John Ikenberry (Boston, Massachusetts: Scott Foresman and Company, 1989), 162–185.

43. Samir Amin, "The Real Stakes in the Gulf War," *Monthly Review* (July–Aug. 1991): 14–24; see also Amin, "The Future of Socialism," in *The Future of Socialism Perspective From the Left, ed.* William K. Tabb (New York: Monthly Review Press, 1990), 106–123. For Amin, capitalism is a world system resulting in polarization on a world scale. The expansion of capital to overseas culminates in polarization. It creates income inequality, unemployment, and marginalization that lead to politicization, radicalization, and political conflict.

44. Arno J. Mayer, "Beyond the Drumbeat: Iraq, Preventive War, Old Europe," *Monthly Review* 54:10 (March 2003): 17–21. The U.S. preemptive attack and occupation of Iraq recently vividly supports this view. Professor Mayer of Princeton University argues, "If Iraq's economic base were the cultivation of tulips for export, rather than the world's second largest oil reserve, the United States would turn a blind eye to Baghdad's arsenal of weapons. . . ."

Chapter Four

The Kurdish
Divisive Internal Problems

The Kurdish forces and the existing literature on the Kurds and Kurdistan commonly blame the Kurdish political problems on external factors, which are critical variables, indeed. However, an exclusive concentration on external intervening factors may result in reductionism. This not only reduces the value of analytical and critical thinking, but also hinders the realization of Kurdish political rights. In order to avoid reductionism, this chapter will analyze the internally divisive, self-created, and self-perpetuated Kurdish political problems. These problems are as formidable as those externally imposed on Kurds. It can be safely argued that the Kurdish liberation struggle has been defeated due to the traditional and parochial values of the Kurdish political culture injected into the movement. These values have not yet been abandoned by the Kurdish leadership.

The Kurdish movement lacks a cohesive and well-defined ideology. Ideology is defined as a belief system that identifies the central core of the political debate, teaching lessons in political consciousness and action-driven political knowledge. It is this belief system that explains and justifies a preferred political order for society either existing or proposed, providing a strategic means for its achievement.[1] Political ideology, according to Reo Christensen, is to unite the dominated forces into a political organization for effective political action.[2] For DeTracy, ideology " . . . is the definitive exposition of what was true and what was false. Its aim is two-fold: To present systematically what could be counted as authentic knowledge, and to trash all the vague metaphysics, theology, and sentimental morality that raped European thinking prior to the Enlightenment and the Revolution."[3] As such, true human needs could be distinguished from false impersonated ones. DeTracy felt that once reason was based on authentic knowledge, social problems and human sufferings would cease. Social ills are rooted in false consciousness and in a lack of understanding one's own structurally caused problems. They are deeply rooted illusions, which are associated with the status quo. If authentic knowledge dominated human society, a blue print for the realization of human ideals would be within grasp.[4] For this reason, ideology is an important mystifying feature of the class in domination, since ideology is used to conceal the image of domination. Nicos Poulantzas argues that one of the particular characteristics of the dominant bourgeois ideology is that it conceals class exploitation in a specific manner, to the extent that all traces of class domination are systematically absent from its language.[5] If ideology were not crucial, the class in power would not use it. Ideology teaches social solidarity, unity, and social mobilization. Hence, it is critical to inculcate in the Kurdish forces the values of enlightenment and the subsequent development of action-oriented liberation struggle.

Kurdish political action is divorced from theoretical and ideological guidance. It is not driven by programmatic political knowledge, but by emotionalism and sentimental cultural traditionalism. It lacks a strategic plan to achieve its politically preferred ends. Ironically, even the ends are vaguely defined. At times the leadership emphasizes cultural autonomy, other times political autonomy (or both), and sometimes an independent Kurdish country. Hence, the missing link in the Kurdish movement is what DeTracy calls authentic knowledge. A realistic analysis of the Kurdish situation would eliminate the politically inhibiting ideals based on mystification, superstition, and parochialism that dominate Kurdish political action.

Using Poulantzas' definition of ideology, Kurdish leadership needs to develop a counter-ideology and focus on raising political consciousness. Unfortunately, Kurdish political action does not transcend the existing reality, but consolidates non-Kurdish nationalism in all three countries, and promotes solidarity and support for the elites in domination. The importance of this missing link is well illustrated by the leading Russian author, Belinsky, in an open letter to Gogol in 1847:

> One cannot be silent when, under cover of religion, backed by the whip, falsehood and immorality are preached as truth and virtue . . . Russia sees her salvation not in mysticism, or aestheticism, or piety, but in the achievement of education, civilization and humane culture. Russia is in need of the awakening in the people of a feeling of human dignity, lost for so many ages in mud and filth. It needs laws and rights in accordance . . . with those of common sense and justice. It does not need sycophants who have always favored despotism and the elite perpetuated ignorance.[6]

This situation in eighteenth century Russia described by Belinsky aptly characterizes Kurdistan. The impeded realization of the political ends of the victimized and at-risk Kurdish minority requires an in-depth analysis.

According to David McDowall, approximately 75 percent of the Kurdish people are Sunni Muslems, though the Kurds of Kermanshah in Iran are mostly Shi,i Muslems. Some Kurds follow the Alavi religion, a religious sect that originated during the fifteenth century.[7] Followers of this sect are located in Anatolia, especially in the Dersim area. McDowall sees Alavism on the extreme edge of Shi,ism, a mixture of pre-Islamic, Zoroastrian, Turkoman Shaman, and Shaf-ite ideas.[8] Ahl-e Hagg is another religious sect located around Zahab and Gasr-i shirin in Iran, as well as in the areas of Sulaymaniya, Kirkuk, and Mosul. However, neither the Alavis, nor the Ahl-e Hagg are exclusively Kurds; some Alavis are Turkish and a portion of Ahl-e Hagg followers are Turkoman. Nonetheless, both religious sects follow the Iranian religious ideas of the Safavid dynasty that came to power on the basis of such heterodox beliefs.[9] Another sect called the Yazidis can be found in the Mosul regions. These people speak Kurmanji and are the most persecuted. Their religion is a synthesis of old pagan elements; Zoroastrian dualistic elements, with a manichean gnosis overlaid with Jewish, Christian, and Muslem elements.[10] Additionally, there are two schools of Sunni religious ideas, the Hanafi and Shafi-ite schools. The Sunni Turks and Arabs follow the Hanafi school, while the Sunni Kurds follow the Shafi,t school.

Other religious variations can be found in Kurdistan, such as the Sufi brotherhood. Based on McDowall's observation, this brotherhood creates both divisiveness and unity. Certainly, it strengthens the bond of unity when the Ahl-e Tarigat (the people with the same religious conviction) exercise the same Tariqat (the same spiritual values). Hence, unity is narrowly based. It does not promote political unity or national solidarity in the way McDowall theorizes. It is bound by tension when opposed by another rival, the Ahl-e Tarigat. In this regard, McDowall argues with acuity. The Shaikhs of different orders, or Shaikhs within the same order with their own followers, compete to create a network of clientalism to support their power structure. This can be demonstrated by the conflict between two Nagshbandi dynasties, the Sayyids of Nihri and the Shaikhs of neighboring Barzan, in the second half of the nineteenth century.[11] This type of conflict is divisive because it promotes tension and rivalry that undermines the creation of solidarity.

Another religious community in Kurdistan with its own identity is Christian. Sizeable Assyrian and Armenian populations still live in Urmia and the surrounding areas northwest of Urmia, but these religious groups are ethnically different from the Kurds. They speak a different language, have their own ethnic identity, and come from different cultural background. Although the Christian groups of Kurdistan were autonomous groups, some Nestorians, from the central Kurdistan were dominated by Kurdish peasants.[12] The Christian groups were dominated and exploited by the Kurdish landlords.[13]

The conflict between Kurds, Assyrians, and Armenians has never been resolved. During the time of centralized control, the tension has been either absent or hidden, and during periods of weak centralized government control, group conflict has intensified as each group fights within the realm of the group's religious-cultural identity. The tension and conflict have obscured the development of a common national goal. In 1915, certain Kurdish tribes supported the young Turks in organizing the deportation and massacres of Armenians within the Christian community. This persecution effort was extended to Jacobites, Assyrians, and Nestorians, who fled to the British and French mandates of Iraq and Syria.[14]

In addition to language differences, religious conflict, and ethno-political problems, Kurdistan continues to suffer from tribal segmentation. Although detribalization factors, such as the mechanization of agriculture, introduction of modern education, and the spread of information technology have culminated in a decline in tribalism in Kurdistan, tribalism continues to persist. Tribal rivalries have been critical in inhibiting the development of a Kurdish political and national consciousness that could serve as a means for the realization of the Kurdish national aspirations. For decades, these Kurdish tribes have rivaled one another. Each has attempted to defeat the other and prevail autonomously, typically through alliance with external forces. Consequently, disruptive tribal conflicts revolve around power struggles between rival Kurdish leaders. In order to achieve its political objectives, a group may initiate inter-clan marriage, a custom that cannot be refused and involves a small dowry. Inter-clan marriages are primarily devised to weaken a rival tribal group. Apart from such marriages, preference is given to a close member of the family, since this strengthens the cohesion of the clan.[15] There has never been a strong nationalist ideology to forge national unity, to foster social cohesiveness, organize mass support for the Kurdish national cause, and lead a programmatic action-driven political liberation struggle appealing to all regionally aggrieved Kurdish and non-Kurdish social forces.[16] The fragmented state of affairs in Kurdistan illustrates this point. As Nezan Kendal argues:

> Tribalism seems to have been the main barrier to the emergence of a national consciousness: even the powerful grip of religion upon the Kurdish people was merely one of its corollaries. We believe that this same feature was mainly responsible for the failure of nearly all the revolts and insurrections aimed at setting up an independent and united Kurdish state, which broke out in the early 19th century and which all eventually collapsed due to betrayals, switching of allegiances, divisions amongst the Kurds themselves, and the tribal ideology.[17]

Kendal feels that tribalism cultivates its own values, which are devised to secure its own self-preservation by virtue of its social organization and rugged mountain locations, isolating villagers from the cities and educational centers. Tribal life, which depends on pastoralism, does not necessitate a need for education. The mountain tribes do not have much contact with the outside world. These people live in isolation and cope with the aggressive and piti-less forces of nature and are primarily driven by the passion of self-preserva-tion. The strengthened unity among the tribal members based upon blood ties is crucial. It is the continuity of this bond that enables them to protect their herds and defend the tribe against intrusion by others.[18] Numbers are crucial in defining tribal objectives. Intermarriage plays a key role in fostering the perpetuation and continuity of blood ties and the strengthening of tribal unity. In this societal setting, the community leader is revered, respected, followed, and never questioned by the followers. He becomes the source of truth for the community. Manfred Halpern refers to this as a relationship of emanation that "involves an encounter in which one treats the other solely as an extension of one's self. The other accepts the denial of his own separate identity because of the mysterious and overwhelming power of the source of this emanation — a yielding which is rewarded with total security."[19]

This emanation relationship, which is one of the leading characteristics of Middle-Eastern politics, prevails in Kurdistan. The tribal leader, or a religious shaikh, lives in an emanation relationship. Respect for him and submission to his will defines the leading feature of the Kurdish socio-political structure. The leader is the soul of the people. When he dies, they die with him.[20] He is above criticism from the community, and all ideas, policies, and orders flow from the top to the bottom. There is no autonomous thinking; all ideas and tactics emanate from the leader. Although the followers of the Kurdish lead-ership may conflict and compete with one another in horizontal societal rela-tions, vertically they are bound by legal subordination and devoted submis-sion to the leadership. If an independently minded individual or an alternative political organization challenges this relationship of emanation, they hasten their own destruction.

These theoretical assertions can be verified by a few examples. The lead-ership of Mulla Mostafa Barzani illustrates the emanation relationship. Mr. Barzani was a dedicated and respectable leader. He was guided by determi-nation and a burning passion for the liberation of his people. For almost fifty years, he wandered throughout the mountains, fought the enemies of the Kur-dish people, and confronted the destructive slash and burn policies of the Kur-dish tribes. He conducted the wars of attrition, as well as guerrilla wars.[21] Af-ter the collapse of the short-lived Kurdish Republic of Mahabad, he was forced to seek political asylum in the Soviet Union. Barzani, along with five hundred Peshmerga, launched the lengthy fourteen-day march of 350 kilo-meters toward the Soviet Union, arriving on 16 June 1947, where he spent eleven years in exile.[22] He never abandoned his political conviction regarding the Kurdish liberation struggle. His followers were prepared to sacrifice their lives for him. His bravery, steadfastness, and courageous political stand in defense of Kurdish rights created the hero-image in the hearts and minds of his followers. During the late 1960s and early 1970s, the Kurdish liberation movement's momentum was due to Barzani's military and political victories, not nationalist sentiment. According to Martin Van Bruinessen, Barzani "became a legendary super-hero, whose feats were sung and told in all corners of Kurdistan . . . his heroics gave the Kurds something to be proud of. The admiration, pride, and loyalty the Kurdish people felt toward Barzani strengthened Kurdish identity."[23]

Mythical perceptions of the Kurds mirror their deeply rooted traditional notion of mysticism based on emanation relations. Mr. Barzani used to smoke utilizing the cigar wood, a long ball pen-like instrument used for filtering purposes. He alternately used two of them and would place them in his headscarf for safekeeping. Abraham Unisi quoted the Kurds saying that the cigarwoods appeared to be an anti-tank or anti-aircraft weapon. Unisi attempted to explain that this was not true, both of the instruments were cigar woods, which Barzani alternated. The Kurds refused to accept Unisi's explanation and continued to refer to them as anti-aircraft or anti-tank weapons.[24]

The Kurds believe that leadership is inspired and led by God. During the 1974–75 conflict with Iraq, I listened to many mythical and mystical stories in Nagadeh of Western Azerbaijan where Mr. Barzani's headquarters were located. I was told by his followers, including Barzani's closest associates and medical doctors, that there were only two great heroes in the world: Mr. Barzani and the Shah of Iran. I could not believe what I had heard. Barzani may be one of the great heroes, but what about the Shah? The Shah cruelly ruled as dictator of the Iranian people, as well as the Kurds. He ordered the hanging of Gazi Mohammad, the leader of the Kurdish Republic of Mahabad.[25] Actually, Mr. Barzani was Gazi's general.

The Kurdish liberation struggles are not only radically different from the other political movements, but they also lack a political program, ideology, and direction, which foster further fragmentation and divisiveness. Kurdish liberation movements are bound by debilitating contradictions. They are deeply rooted in the Kurdish alienating mode of behavior. The traditional political culture of seize-and-loot has largely been abandoned, but still plays a critical role in the politics of factionalism and alienation.

The Kurdish political culture is much more compatible with the Iranian mode of thinking than with the Iraqi and Turkish mode. As mentioned in the introduction, the Kurds have been part of the Persian culture and civilization throughout the country's long history, and they have occupied key administrative positions that have played a critical role in shaping and molding Persia's political destiny. Although Kurdish ethnic nationalism in Iran, based on McDowall's argument, is weaker than in Iraq and Turkey, Kurds first expressed themselves fully in Iran. This took place when Iran had been occupied by allied forces during World War II, and the Iranian leader, Reza shah, had been forced into exile in 1941. The allied countries assisted his son, Mohammad Reza, to succeed his father to the throne. A power vacuum was created that provided fertile soil in which the seeds of Kurdish political ideas were cultivated. Unfortunately, these ideas never developed political maturity largely due to the limitations of tribal culture that continue to characterize Kurdish political thinking. Before the Soviet Red Army reached Urmia, the capital of Western Azerbaijan, tribal forces had looted and burned the bazaar of this city. They captured the weapons left behind by the fleeing Iranian soldiers. In the Kermanshah and Sanandaj areas, looting and plundering of the villages of both Kurds and non-Kurds was also the order of the day.[26]

The Kurdish tragedy is that the conflict involves the central government in Tehran, and is also apparent within the Kurdish group itself, as well as with the non-Kurdish groups. Kurdish political history embodies the empirical evidence to support the claim of enmity of one group against another. The Committee of the British Chiefs of Staff warned the British officers in Iran that the goal of the British government was to protect the territorial integrity of the Iranian central government, not support the reactionary Kurdish movement. The intervention of the British forces in the endless Kurdish personal and tribal conflicts was not in the best interest of Great Britain, though the British were concerned with Soviet policy relating to Kurds in the region.[27]

Internal Kurdish disunity is an extremely devastating contradiction. If the tribal mentality is an obstacle to the realization of the Kurdish national aspirations, could it also be the agent of social transformation?[28] Facts based on a class analysis do not provide a positive answer to this question. All national liberation struggles, including social revolutions, have enjoyed popular support and have been carried out by class alliances. The Iranian Revolution of 1978–79 was initiated by a popular front based on conflict between the ruling elite that controlled the military and political apparatuses, and the people who protested the abuse of power. The Kurdish movement, by virtue of its internal disunity, lack of national class solidarity, and failure to reach out, defies this empirical evidence.

Gazi Mohammad's dream of an independent Kurdistan was frustrated and eventually failed to materialize, primarily due to internal rivalry among tribal leaders and the withdrawal of Soviet support, though the Kurdish leaders blamed it exclusively on the Soviet Union. On 11 December 1946 when the

Mahabad Republic Collapsed, General Barzani had this to say: "It was not the Kurds who were defeated by the Iranian army, but the Soviet Union that was defeated by the United States and Great Britain."[29] Although, this may be true, it is reductionism. The impression is that the Soviet or the Western World's main objective is to liberate the oppressed forces from domination. Liberty is not a gift to be given, it must be taken. This is, first and foremost, the task of the Kurds themselves. This view fails to attack the internal divisive factors that are responsible for hindering Kurdish progress. *Nishtman* (fatherland), a Kurdish magazine, a progressive publication of Komala (or JK Society), succinctly states the problem:

> You, the Aghas and leaders of Kurdish tribes, think for yourselves and judge why the enemy gives you so much money . . . they give it because they know it will become capital to delay the liberation of the Kurds and hope that in a few years this capital will create intrigues detrimental to the Kurds.[30]

Tribal chiefs, Aghas, and Shaikhs are responsible for the existence of strife and disunity among the Kurdish people. It is sad to see how tragically Hama Rashid Khan, a Kurd, seized Baneh and Saggiz in western Azerbaijan and burned Baneh's one thousand houses to the ground.[31] In February 1942, Ali Agha Amir Asad of Dehbukri, who was concerned with Hama Rashid's aggressive move and possible Soviet interventionism, sided with the central government in Tehran. In turn, he was appointed the governor of Mahabad and returned to Mahabad with a car, special driver, and a substantial amount of money. McDowall claims that this power and prestige aggravated further jealousy and rivalry by pitting Asad against his estranged brothers and the leading tribal chiefs: Garayni Agha of Mamash and Abdallah Bayazidi of Mangur.[32] Gazi Mohammad, the great nephew of Gazi Fattah, and the most highly respected personality of Mahabad, who had previously attempted self-rule for Mahabad, bitterly protested Ali Agha Dehbukri's appointment as governor of Mahabad. While Ali Agha Dehbukri showed loyalty to Tehran, his brothers sided with the Soviet Union. Whereas, Gazi Mohammad sought the Soviet Union's support for the Kurdish political cause, his brother, Sadr Gazi, served as deputy in the Iranian parliament from Mahabad; others simply followed both.

Gazi Mohammad, who in 1946 assumed the leadership of the short-lived Republic of Mahabad, had a difficult time persuading the tribal factions in the Mahabad and Urmia regions to set aside their hostilities and unite in defense of the Kurdish political cause. The effort failed because tribal Aghas refused to abandon their long-standing historical enmities. Only Garayni Agha, chief of the Mamash tribe, Abd Allah Bayazidi, chief of the Mangur tribe, and Amar Khan Shikak[33] (who joined Gazi Mohammad through Soviet persuasion), pledged to comply with Gazi Mohammad's call for unity. Based on Archie Roosevelt, Jr.'s account, Bayazidi Agha of Mangur and Garyni Agha's son, Mom Aziz, chief of the Mamash tribe, openly opposed Gazi Mohammad. The Soviets threatened retaliation if they continued opposition. When Mom Aziz refused to comply, the Soviets had Barzani attack him, which forced Mom Aziz to flee to Iraq. The only tribes left for Gazi Mohammad to rely on were the Gawrik of Mahabad and the Zarza of Ushnavieh.[34]

This state of affairs, coupled with Gazi's own miscalculated dependence on the Soviet Union for the success of the Kurdish liberation struggle in Iran, cost not only the lives of Gazi and his closest associates, but also the defeat of Kurdish aspirations for an independent state. According to leading experts on Kurdish affairs, upon the Imperial Army of Iran's entrance to Mahabad on 17 December 1946, the tribes not only refused to fight, but (Shaikhs of Shikak, Harki, Mamash, Mangur and others) conveniently switched their loyalties, supporting the invading army of the Shah.[35] Following the collapse of Mahabad, the tribal leaders remained loyal to the central government. With the fall of Azerbaijan and the Kurdish Republic of Mahabad, a period of consolidation and stabilization, accompanied by systematic repression, began. This was short lived for soon Mossadeg's democratic movement began to disrupt it. This structural/political challenge to the Shah's government once again gave the Kurdish progressive forces a chance to revitalize clandestine political activities. The peasants in Bukan in western Azerbaijan revolted against police brutality and the oppression of Kurdish feudal lords. However, this movement, which spread to the areas between Bukan and Mahabad, was crashed by the alliance of the Kurdish feudal class with the Shah's army, again Kurds killing Kurds and many joining Jashism.

Jash is a Kurdish word which means a donkey foal.[36] Since a foal cannot continue to live without dependence on its mother, the implication is that a Kurdish Jash's wisdom is politically no better than a donkey foal. Dependence on the government betrays the Kurdish Jash's own race and identity. Jashs are more dangerous to the progressive Kurdish faction than regular governmental forces. They are paid by the central government to be secretive informants on dissident Kurds. They are familiar with the logistics and strategies of guerrilla warfare and the tactics of mountain fighting. More importantly, they are armed with false consciousness and have no political motivation. As such, it is a class in itself, but not yet for itself.[37] It is a class that is not aware of its own political interests and, therefore, not ready for change. They resemble the lumpen proletariat, ready to undermine and sabotage the Kurdish movement. Thus, Jashs are undependable, indecisive and changeable, vacillating in their support between the government and the insurgents.[38]

If lumpens can be seen as strikebreakers, Jashs can be seen as killers. During the 1960s, based on my own observation, many Kurdish teachers worked for the Shah's secret police, SAVAK. In this era, extractive sum notes were posted on the doors of Kurds in Pearanshahr located in western Azerbaijan on the northern border of Iraq. The recipient of such a note faced dangerous consequences if he did not make the requested payment. Kurds were terrified by this terror campaign. However, it is difficult to determine whether this was the political plan of government-led Jashs, designed to intimidate and divide the Kurds thereby forcing them to support the central government, or simply the work of the KDPI (Kurdistan Democratic Party of Iran). Some of the Jash leaders were armed and paid by the central government to join government forces in tracking the *chatehs* (a Kurdish word for guerrillas) in the mountains of Pearanshahr. This matter was further complicated when General Oveisi, the Shah's leading command General of Gendarmery (Rural Police), was stationed in Jaldian at one of the triangle military bases (Passveh, Pearanshahr, and Jaldian), thirty-four kilometers from Pearanshah, the northern Iraqi border. During six months of butchery of the Kurdish people in this area, the Khans, tribal leaders, Jashs, and mercenaries sided with the notorious imperial Gendarmary commander in pursuit of the Kurdish guerrillas. The extent of this bloodshed was stupendous. Ironically, based on information given to me by highly respected local Kurds, the Barzani leadership supported the General's massacre in Kurdistan.

For A. R. Ghassemlou, the KDPI's young revolutionary leaders, such as Sharif Zadeh, Abdullah Muini, and Mala Avara, were caught between the Shah's army and Barzani's forces and murdered. In 1968 when Suleiman Muini, the older brother of Abdullah, attempted to escape to Iran, he was arrested by Barzani and executed. His body was sent to the Iranian government and was displayed in several Kurdish border cities in Iran. More than forty Iranian KDP militants were either killed or arrested and turned over to the Iranian authorities by Barzani's men.[39] Again, Kurds were killing Kurds, either directly or in cooperation with the regional forces of aggression.

Ghassemlou's argument supports the indications of divisiveness in Kurdish politics. The Kurds lack international support and their nationalism is weakened by tribal loyalty and internally mutual enmity. They do not possess a national political approach to deal with the dominant socio-structural issues in the region. The Kurds of Iraq in the north refused to defend the Republic of Mahabad because of their dislike for the Barzanis, another manifestation of the internal divisiveness apparent among the Kurdish groups.[40] In reality, the tribal refusal (centered on fragmentation and rivalry) to fight for the realization of the Kurdish political aspirations was largely responsible for the collapse of the Mahabad Republic.

The lack of organizational unity among the Kurds is one of the most critical factors crippling Kurdish liberation objectives. In Iraq, the Iraqi Kurdistan Democratic Party (KDP) and the Patriotic Union of Krudistan (PUK) engage in continual conflict. The former is led by Barzani, and the latter is commanded by Jalal Talabani. These two leaders are long time rivals, pursuing differing political and ideological patterns of persuasions. However, both rely on tribal and foreign forces for support, and often engage in armed conflict with one another. As Mehrdad Izady maintains, a bloody confrontation between these two parties in 1978 resulted in the elimination of approximately eight hundred of Kurdish top military leaders and guerrillas. They were either killed, executed, captured, or turned over to the Turkish or Iraqi governments.[41] Although the PUK claims to have a progressive agenda, Jalal Talabani, an educated man and the leader of the PUK, has repeatedly called Barzani a reactionary tribal man. Yet, Mom Jalal launched bloody attacks on the Socialist Party of Kurdistan (SPK) and the Iraqi Communist Party (ICP), leading to the split of a formerly united movement.

Rasul Mamand and Mahmud Osman, former allies of Mustafa Barzani, formed the so-called United Socialist Party of Kurdistan, in a predominantly agrarian Kurdistan where tribal values, though declining, are still prevalent.[42] This is one of the most critically defining contradictions of the Kurdish political front. Yet, this is happening despite the failed socialism in the former Soviet Union. This mode of thinking clearly shows that political wisdom among Kurdish leaders is in short supply, lacking completely, or not based on historical and empirical experience. When socialism failed in the former Soviet Union, in spite of the existence of the Red Army, a nuclear arsenal, and a highly educated society, one wonders how the Kurdish socialist movement in a religious Muslim society will succeed. Whereas the Soviet Union was highly secularized, the Kurds are peasant-based and traditional with tribalism, primordial values, traditional cultural norms, and a predominantly illiterate Kurdish population prevailing.

According to Izadi, the SPK has also participated in conflicts with the Iraqi Komala, which like the Iranian Komala, has suffered from internal hostilities and contradictions. In 1985, a bloody conflict broke out between the KDPI and Komala when Iranian forces attacked both parties.[43] It becomes obvious that the Kurdish parties are not fighting for the cause of Kurdish liberation, but are at war with each other, and the losers are the Kurdish people.

The Kurdish Democratic Party (KDP), which was created in 1946 and assumed an active political life in the 1960s, made an enormous contribution to the political awakening of the Kurdish forces, thanks to the intellectual and political insights of Ibrahim Ahmad, a lawyer from Sulaymania. Unfortunately, Ibrahim Ahmad, the political nerve center of the party, was ousted by

Barzani in 1964 and forced into exile in Iran, along with the armed peshmergas loyal to him. In 1965, Ahmad returned to Iraq and joined the Patriotic Union of Kurdistan (PUK), led by his son-in-law, Jalal Talabani, a well-educated lawyer. He was fully aware of the political reality of the world system and was critical of Barzani's policies. It was unacceptable for Barzani to tolerate Talabani, who posed a threat to Barzani, referring to Barzani as tribal, feudal and reactionary.[44]

In order to counter Barzani's revenge, Talabani negotiated an alliance with Baghdad in 1966. Although this action was taken primarily for the purpose of political and military survival, it was a major blow to the Kurdish national unity. The timing was politically suicidal for Talabani. He allied himself with the same forces that were fighting the Barzani led peshmargas struggling to liberate Kurdistan. However, this political honeymoon did not last long. In 1970, Barzani forced the Iraqi government to sign an autonomy agreement with him, and Talabani's alliance with Iraq thus proved to be nothing but an anti-Kurd struggle. According to Izadi, Talabani was forced to join Barzani until 1975, which marked the final defeat for Barzani and the KDP led national liberation struggle (discussed in the next chapter). Reliance on the perpetuators of oppression for liberation proved to be not only false, but also wishful thinking. For Izady, this state of affairs seems to be a normal political process, as it has been with other countries.[45] He is correct, but his argument holds only for those forces that had won their liberation struggle and formed a government. In reality, the power struggle starts only in the post-liberation transitional era. The Kurds, having no state and no country, have declared war against one another before achieving any political end. This critical factor hinders the realization of Kurdish political aspirations.

As documented, the Kurds are the major killers of the Kurds. The international political environment is confused by the competing and conflicting tribal values and political-economic interests of the Kurds. As the *New York Times* noted, should the Kurds be defended from Saddam Hussein, or from themselves? The United States committed forces to the protection of the Kurds in northern Iraq by creating and enforcing a security no-fly zone. Without prior notification from Mr. Barzani, the United States then discovered that the KDP of Iraq has extended an alliance invitation to Saddam Hussein. How can this arbitrary action be evaluated when it defies all existing logic of the liberation struggles?

The conflict between Mr. Talabani, the PUK leader, and Mr Barzani of the KDP, ignited over money, power, and resources, which were controlled by Mr. Barzani. Mr. Barzani denied Mr. Talabani a share in the millions in revenue obtained from the Turkish traders who deliver goods to northern Iraq. In December 1994, Talabani forces seized the commercial center of Erbil. To counter this invasion, Barzani's forces surrounded the area three months later.[46] In order to recapture Erbil, the KDP leader entered into a purported temporary arrangement with Saddam Hussein. When Mr. Barzani was questioned regarding this alliance, he responded, "I have a natural right to ask Iraq for help," and, "It was Iraq's natural right to intervene against the Patriotic Union of Kurdistan."[47] Applying the same logic, can it be argued that Iraq had a natural right to defend its right of national sovereignty and territorial integrity against the Kurdish separatist movements? What about the destruction of four thousand villages and the elimination of countless Kurdish civilians by the Iraqi government? Why did Barzani soon forget about Iraqi's atrocities? Was Mr. Masud Barzani unaware that his unholy alliance with Saddam Hussein would result in the elimination of additional Kurdish forces?

Based on the *Washington Post's* report, this alliance resulted in the elimination of approximately four thousand Kurds.[48] Is this a natural right? If so, then why is Mr. Barzani fighting Iraqis? Mr. Barzani's associate, Mr. Ahmad, the Governor of Dohuk Province since 1991, announced that there would be no objection if a mediating party could solve their problems.[49] According to the *Denver Post*, a forty-five year old mother of four who left her home and fled to the Iranian border stated that Masud Barzani had sold the Kurds to Saddam Hussein and left them without a destination.[50] Mr. Barzani blames these atrocities on Talabani, the leader of PUK, arguing that he allied with Saddam Hussein in order to counter the Talabani-Iranian's alliance. Yet the KDP-Iraqi leadership, as well as Talabani, has repeatedly resorted to political machinations of this type. I was told by the KDP Iranian Kurds at Oshnavieh, the western Kurdish border city between Iraq and Turkey, that Barzani's forces were hired by the Iranian government to liberate this Kurdish city from Iranian Kurdish domination. This clearly demonstrates the perverse relationship characterizing the Kurdish struggle; the KDP Iraq battled the Iranian Kurds in favor of the Iranian government.

The Jash record of the Kurdish leadership in association with tribal forces, such as the Zibaris, Surchis, and Baradosti, who had consistently battled Kurdish rebels in favor of dominant regional realities, is empirically validated.[51] It can be inferred from this negative state of affairs that Kurdish leadership is contradictory and manipulative. Self-regarding policies have damaged the Kurds and impeded their liberation struggle; their adversaries have proceeded against them. Kurdish leaders quickly retort that disreputable policies and conflicting alliances have made the continuity of the Kurds possible. There may be some truth to this, but such tactical policies are costly and bloody; it is the Kurdish people who fight, die, and pay very heavily for such alliances.

The Iranian and Iraqi Kurdish situation is also characterized by the politics of fragmentation, manipulation, and separatism as evidenced with the Turkish Kurds. In 1908, the first Kurdish organization was formed under the influence of European nationalistic ideas. The Kurdish Society for Mutual Aid and Progress was rooted in the liberal environment created by the revolution of young Turks. The principal founders of this organization included prominent Kurdish families: Mohammad Sharif Pasha from the well-known Baban family, Amin Ali Baderkhan, the Baderkhanian clan leader in Istanbul, and Shaikh Sayyid Abdulgader, the son of the popular Shaikh Ubbeydallah of Nehri. They supported the Ottomanist ideals of the Young Turk's movement, and they disliked the liberalism of Kemalism that led to the formulation of political nationalism.[52] The Kurdish Society for Mutual Aid and Progress made great strides towards establishing a sense of Kurdish identity. They constructed a publishing house that published a journal and initiated a Kurdish school.

However, this movement toward the creation of Kurdish identity was short-lived, attributable to the competing rivalry between Baderkhanian and Shaikh Abdulgader. The latter, according to McDowall, created his own journal called *Hitavi Kurd* (Kurdish Sun)[53] Disunity dominated the aspirations for the realization of Kurdish cultural identity. This Kurdish organization created by Shaikh Abdulgader was reformist in nature and sought to achieve Kurdish cultural desires within the prevailing Turkish political framework. In reality, the organization did not care much about the common Kurdish people.

In 1912, Kurdish students created an organization referred to as *Hevi*, meaning hope, to replace the former Kurdish society. The students intended that this new organization would be less aristocratic and more nationalistic. Jamil Pasha played a dominant role within this organization, owing his name and fame largely to the Ottomans. Other members of this organization came from "Ottomanized Notables." Unfortunately, their attachment to the Kurdish cause was superficial nationalism, as they were out of touch with common Kurdish people. This organization lost its validity with the outbreak of war in 1914 because members were drafted for war. According to Bruinessen, after the war, rival leaders of the Hevi organization were competing over the attainment of support from foreign governments. Mohammad Sharif Pasha sought assistance from the British, and the Baderkhans contacted the Russians in an effort to secure support.[54]

By the spring of 1919, three modes of thought dominated the minds of the Kurdish leadership: pro-Turkish, pro-allies, and the desire for independence proclaimed by the Dersim Kurds.[55] By 1919–1921, Mostafa Kamal, the emerging nationalist hero of Turkey, offered a stronger appeal to the common Kurds than the so-called Kurdish nationalist organizations. Ata Turk had promised Kurds and Turks the granting and full realization of equality. He did gain the confidence of some tribal forces, but other forces relied on the British.[56] However, the forces that relied on the British failed to understand that the British were pitting the Armenians and Kurds against one another and both groups against the newly founded Turkish state (Turkey). This condition of false consciousness precluded Kurdish recognition of the British time-honored divide and rule policy. Britain's goal was to defend the oil rich regions of Mosul and Iraq from the Kemalist forces. In order to achieve its colonial aspiration, the British promised the Kurds either full autonomy or independence. Ataturk proposed a referendum to determine the destiny of the region in conflict.[57] Realizing that Turkey could win, the British rejected the Turkish call and promoted internal rebellion within the Kurdish forces. Seemingly unaware of Britain's insidious strategy, the Kurdish leadership was manipulated by false and deceptive promises. Khalil Bader Khan, one of the Kurdish chieftains, maintained, "We are wholeheartedly for the British. We desire to live under the British mandate. If Great Britain helps us, we, in turn, will be a buffer zone between Iraq and British enemies: Russia and Turkey. Additionally we will cooperate with Armenians as well as Christians."[58]

This naiveté has undermined nationalistic and liberation struggles. The rival Kurdish political leaders have always, with very few exceptions, sided with the colonizing powers, while claiming to liberate their people from the so-called internal colonizers. This view is further enforced by another political organization in Turkey, the Kurdish Ta'ali JamiYati: "England is our only friend, and the Kurds have resolved to have no other protector than England."[59] Some observers believe that Shaikh Said's revolt, seen by the Kurdish forces as nationalistic, was promoted by the British in order to weaken Ataturk's nationalism for the purpose of controlling the oil resources in the region (Said's movement is analyzed in Chapter V in the section on the Kurdish struggle in Turkey). Britain's control of the region's oil validated the aforementioned claim, which Britain claimed as conspiracy theory and false hypothetical assertions. .

Ocalan's PKK provides an exception to the movements and organizations heretofore discussed. The PKK coalesced upon sentiments of nationalism and the ideals of class struggle. Sadly, this organization was responsible for annihilating village guards, many Kurds were sandwiched between Turkish forces and PKK fighters. Turkish forces hired the village Kurds to work for the security of the Kurdish villagers, and the PKK attacked them; Kurds killing Kurds. The devastating activities of the PKK alienated the Kurds in the countryside. Villagers and peasants were not united with the realization of the common good.[60] It can be clearly determined that Kurdish tribal culture is largely responsible for the politics of fragmentation, disunity, and captivation, rather than emancipation.

NOTES

1. Reo M. Christenson, Alen S. Engel, Dan N. Jacobs, Mostafa Rajai and Herbert Waltzer, *Ideologies and Modern Politics*, 2nd ed. (New York: Harper & Row Publishers, 1975), 6.

2. Ibid.

3. Bernard Susser, *Political Ideology in the Modern World* (Boston, Massachusetts: Allyn & Bacon, 1995), 17.

4. Ibid., 17.

5. Nicos Poulantzas, *Political Power and Social Classes* (London: New Left Books, 1974), 214.

6. Excerpts from Blinsksy's "Open Letter to Gogol," 1847.

7. David McDowall, *A Modern History of the Kurds* (London: I. B. Tauris and Co., 1997), 10–11.

8. Ibid., 10.

9. Ibid., 11.

10. Ibid.

11. Ibid., 11–12.

12. Martin Van Bruinessen, *Agha, Shaikh and State: The Social and Political Structures of Kurdistan* (London: Zed Books Ltd., 1992), 106–107.

13. Ibid., 107.

14. Gerard Chaliand, *The Kurdish Tragedy*, trans. Philip Black (London: Zed Books Ltd., 1994), 16.

15. Ibid., 21.

16. Ibid.

17. Nezan Kendal, "The Kurds Under the Ottoman Empire," in *People Without a Country: The Kurds and Kurdistan*, ed., Gerard Chaliand (London: Zed Press, 1980), 23–24.

18. Ibid., 24.

19. Manfred Halpern, cited in James A. Bill and Robert Springborg, *Politics in the Middle East*, 4th ed. (Harper Collins College Publishers, 1994), 152.

20. Ibid.

21. Derk Kinnane, *The Kurds and Kurdistan*, (Oxford: Oxford University Press, 1964), translated to Persian by Abraham Unisi, Negah Publishers, Tehran 1372, 8–9.

22. Chris Kutschera, *Le Mouvement National Kurde* (Paris: Flemmarion, 1979), translated to Persian by Abraham Unisi (Tehran, Iran: Negah Publishers, 1373), 227–28.

23. Bruinessen, *Agha, Shaikh and State*, 316.

24. Yunis, introduction to the translated version of Derk Kinnane, *The Kurds and Kurdistan*, 9–10.

25. Nagadeh, western Azerbaijan, personal discussions, 1974–75. During this time the Kurdish forces were located in Nagadeh and I played a key role in assisting their accommodation, as I was mayor of the city at this time. I was fully exposed to the

Kurdish tragedies and problems. I have worked with the Kurds and I am fully aware of their problems, tragedies, and deprivations. The Kurds are a people greatly at risk.

26. McDowall, *A Modern History,* 231–233.

27. Kutschera, *Le Mouvement,* 196.

28. McDowal, *A Modern History,* 231; Kutschera, *Le Mouvement,* 200–203; Kinnane, *The Kurds and Kurdistan,* 68–69; Gerard Chaliand, "Minorities Without Rights," in *People Without a Country: The Kurds and Kurdistan,* ed. Gerard Chaliand (London: Zed Press, 1980), 15–17.

29. Kutschera, *Le Mouvement,* 225.

30. Cited by McDowall, *A Modern History,* 238.

31. Ibid., 233.

32. Ibid, 235–36. See also Kutschera, *Le Mouvement,* 200–201.

33. McDowall, *A Modern History,* 238.

34. Archie Roosevelt, Jr., "The Kurdish Republic of Mahabad," in *People Without A Country, The Kurds and Kurdistan,* ed. Gerard Chaliand (London: Zed Press, 1980), 147–48.

35. Ibid., 148; Chaliand, *The Kurd's Tragedy,* 76; Kinnane, *The Kurds and Kurdistan,* 129; Kulschera, *Le Mouvement National,* 224; A. R. Ghassemlou, "Kurdistan In Iran," in *People Without A Country,* ed. Chaliand, 121; Edgar O'. Ballance, *The Kurdish Struggle: 1920–94* (New York: St. Martin's Press, Inc., 1996), 32. For Ghassemlou, The Kurdish tribes have naturally opposed the central government, and were restless under Gazi Mohammad's rule. Because of Gazi's proximity to the Soviet Union, they did not trust him. Therefore, the tribes generally sided with the Iranian Army. Gerard Chaliand, ed., *People Without A Country,* 150.

36. Bruinessen, *Agha, Shaikh and State,* 40–41.

37. It is a Marxist notion that when a class suffers from false consciousness, it will not fight to defend its own interests which are taken away by exploitative measures.

38. Bruinessen, *Agha, Shaikh and State,* 40.

39. Ghassemlou, "Kurdistan in Iran," in *People Without A Country,* ed. Chaliand, 124–125.

40. O'Ballence, *The Kurdish Struggle,* 34–35.

41. Mehrdad Izady, *The Kurds, A Concise Handbook* (London: Crane Russak, Taylor and Francis International Publishers, 1992), 214.

42. Ibid.

43. Ibid., 212–213.

44. Ibid.

45. Ibid., 213.

46. Steven Lee Myers, "A Failed Race Against Time: U.S. Tried to Head Off Iraq," *New York Times,* 5 September 1996: A-11.

47. Douglas Jehl, "Some Iraquis Are Still Dying Inside the Kurdish Regime," *New York Times,* 8 September 1996: 14.

48. Johathan C. Randal and John Mintz, "Kurdish Feuds and Surrogate Powers," *Washington Post,* 1 September 1996: A-34; see also Chris Hedges, "Baghdad's Move Puts the Future of Kurdish Haven in Doubt," *New York Times,* 4 September 1996: A-6.

49. Stephen Kinzer, "Key Kurd Says Deal with Iraq Is Stopgap," *New York Times*, 5 September 1996: A-11.

50. Dougles Jehl, "50,000 Fleeing: Iraq's Kurd's City Abandoned and Without a Fight," *Denver Post*, 10 September 1996: A-3.

51. For a detailed analysis of the Kurdish leadership's Jash record, see Jonathan C. Randal, *After Such Knowledge, What Forgiveness?* (New York: Farrar, Straus and Giroux, 1997), 226–228. Chapter 8 provides excellent documentation of the Kurd's abuses toward other Kurds. It reflects the tragedies that are unique in the history of liberation struggles.

52. Bruinessen, *Agha, Shaikh and State*, 275–276.

53. McDowall, *A Modern History*, 94.

54. Bruinessen, *Agha, Shaikh and State*, 276.

55. McDowall, *A Modern History*, 125.

56. Bruinessen, *Agha, Shaikh, and State*, 279.

57. Ibid., 274–75; see also McDowall, *A Modern History*, 128–29.

58. Kutschera, *Le Movement National*, 56.

59. Cited by McDowall, *A Modern History*, 129.

60. Ibid., 421–423.

Chapter Five

The Kurdish Movements in Contradiction

A. SIMKO AND GAZI MOHAMMAD'S MOVEMENTS IN IRAN

Ismail Agha Simko, the son of Mohammad Agha Simko, was the leader of the Shikak tribe, composed of two hundred families in 1918.[1] In the 1900s, factional politics characterized this tribal group in Azerbaijan. In the northern section of Iran, the Shikak, Zarza, Mangur, and the Mamash were rival tribal groups. Neither of these tribes had a solidarity unit. The internal factionalization, that defined the Shikak tribe led by Simko, was evident in Simko's own family. Based on local accounts, Amar Khan was reported to be Simko's uncle, although others believed that he was Simko's cousin, yet, Amar Khan posed a serious threat to Simko.

According to McDowell, the divisions were so devastating that one brother sought support from the Turks, another brother sought support from the Russians,[2] and often either one sought support from the local authorities. Due to a weak central government, a chaotic situation dominated Persia. In the aftermath of World War I, the country was suffering from a structural crisis. By virtue of its internal contradictions reinforced by World War I, the Qajar dynasty was structurally incapacitated. This is substantiated by Theda Skocpol's theory that revolutions can not occur as long as the centrally controlling repressive system is in power. Revolutions take place when a rupture develops between the ruling classes due to a crisis caused by a war, foreign invasion, and location in a geographically disadvantageous region in the international arena.[3]

Unquestionably, Persia was conducive to revolutionary movements. The Anglo-Russian Treaty of 1907 divided the country into two spheres of influence. The Russians acquired the north and the British occupied the south.[4] This event along with the ineffectiveness of the Qajar shahs and Persia's concessions to the British had triggered the constitutional revolution of 1906–1908. The British never allowed the new shah to implement the democratically formulated constitution modeled after northern Europe. While the forces of nationalism battled the foreign domination, the British tried to shelf the newly formulated democratic constitution. The struggle between the democratic forces of Iran and the pro-dictatorship and anti-democratic British forces continued until the last shah of Oajar, Ahmad Shah, was forced from the throne by the masses. It was hoped that the constitution of 1906–1908 would encourage democratic forces. However, that hope was shattered when the British supported the new monarch who continued to contain democracy and promote absolutism.

In reality, autonomy has no political value under a dictatorship. This was never understood by Simko and subsequent Kurdish leaders. The creation of a banditry, forceful confiscation of Kurdish and non-Kurdish property, looting, plundering, and the exertion of a violent dictatorship of the so-called Simko-created autonomy had no relationship to nationalism. As Susser argues, nationalism in its excessive form promotes fascism based on the criterion: "are you one of us or not?"[5] This accurately describes the political environment created by Simko. He took advantage of a structurally incapacitated and weak central government of Iran, and in the summer of 1919 attacked and conquered Rezaeih (now called Urmia), the capital of western Azerbaijan.[6] His forces looted and plundered the city, violently assaulting the Armenian and Assyrian inhabitants. Simko's lack of interest in inclusionism is reflected in his treacherous murder of Marshimun, the spiritual leader of Nestorian and Assyrian Christians, in February of 1918, which provoked the uprising of some six thousand armed Assyrian forces. Yet, with Turkish support, Smiko managed to defeat these forces in a brutal battle. This minority group was almost extinguished. The British assisted the resettlement of the forty thousand survivors in the newly created kingdom of Iraq.[7]

Corrul Filipov, a Ruissian army officer, led the governmental forces. Russian Cossack forces successfully attacked Simko in the Shapour area, north of Urmia, but did not eliminate Simko (during this era all heads, chiefs, and administrators of Iran were foreigners and especially the Russians played a dominant role in the creation and command of the army). According to Kutschera, Filipov negotiated an agreement with Simko who pledged non-interference in the Rezaeih areas. Although this agreement extended throughout 1920, the following year on 6 October, Simko broke the agreement and attacked Mahabad. This was the largest insurgency.[8] Five hundred and fifty gendarmes were assigned to defend Mahabad. With a force of over two thousand horsemen, Simko massacred the government forces with extreme brutality and cruelty. His forces plundered the city, Kurds were killing Kurds.

According to Kutschera, although Simko was considered by some Kurdish notables to be the father of Kurdish nationalism, Kurds usually(and correctly) spoke of him bitterly. Indeed, Simko's struggle was not devised for the purpose of Kurdish liberation; he was an ambitious, self-seeking, and self-perpetuating leader who cultivated the seeds of separatism in Azerbaijan where his atrocities have not been forgotten. He created a negative image of the Kurds as looters, robbers, and killers.[9] Fereshteh Koohi-Kamali speaks of Simko as "the most outstanding Kurdish chief" who created "an autonomous Kurdish government."[10] Koohi-Kamali fails to realize that Simko undermined the meaning of the Kurdish liberation struggle. He was used by the Russians and the British to blackmail Iranians for the extraction of oil concessions. Simko, blinded by the tribal political culture mentality, failed to calculate a change in policy in 1921, a military coup that brought to power the Reza shah, a British agent. The British had two basic policy objectives. First, they wanted to contain the Bolsheviks, and second, they wanted to create a stable environment for British access to Iranian oil. Yet, by virtue of tribal affiliation, Simko miscalculated these newly emerging policies.

In 1921 Simko said, "I and Sayyad Taha (his advisor and a close relative) promise to you (mainly Great Britian) that if the British government gives us arms and ammunition we can eliminate the Turkish nationalists and occupy Ankara . . . and in a short period of time, force Iranians out of Sanandaj."[11] According to Kutschera, the French government firmly believed that Great Britain subsidized Simko's struggle. Consequently, the French never did respond to Simko's demands.[12]

Rezakhan replaced the last Qajar shah in 1923, declaring himself the Shah of Iran in 1925. It was Rezakhan, a commander of the Cossack forces, who finally defeated Simko in 1922. Simko fled to Turkey and then to Iraq. In 1924 Rezakhan pardoned him, but Simko continued his tribal based separatist struggle. However, he was killed in an ambush by Rezakhan's forces in 1930.[13]

Simko's struggle was incompatible with national liberation movements that were fought against dominant colonial powers and was not consistent with any revolutionary theoretical framework. Simko, instead of being an instrument of liberation, provided the means for the implementation of foreign imperial ideals. He lacked a defined ideological objective, political organization, or political party institution to convert theoretical knowledge into political action. A sense of unity or solidarity was not on Simko's agenda. He never hesitated to plunder the Kurds, as he did in Mahabad. He failed to realize that a liberation movement without a grass roots support system and an inclusive solidarity base is doomed to failure.

Gazi Mohammad came from a well-known and highly respected family with a history of bravery, struggle, and nationalism. Since 1830 the family was committed to the cause of Kurdistan, with nearly all of the Gazi family sacrificing their lives for the liberty of Kurdistan. As Kutschera writes, in 1830 Shaikh Al Mashaikh, the great grandfather of Gazi, organized a movement against the British government around Divan darreh, north of Sanandaj. The goal was liberation for Kurdistan.[14]

The Second World War, the struggle against fascism, began in September 1939. The occupation of Iran by allied forces in 1941 created a politically and militarily incapacitated central government. Reza shah, who was against the Soviet Union, was reluctant to join allied forces against fascism. Given Iran's vitality to deliver U.S. and U.K. supplies to the USSR, and Reza Shah's suspected pro-German feelings, he was forced to abdicate his position on 20 August 1941.[15] The collapse of the central government thus provided a golden opportunity for the forces seeking liberty and freedom. Mahabad became the nerve center of Kurdish nationalism, which came to be exclusionist, not inclusionist. The Kurds in Iran pursued their cause independently of other oppressed and aggrieved forces. The Kurds of Mahahad failed to overcome their parochial values, especially their self-centered autocratic desires. Yet, these Kurds are bright, kind, and politically conscious, and are radically different from Harki Kurds, who have yet to abandon their tribal/traditional culture and fragmentationist values.

In September of 1942, due to the active political climate in Mahabad, the city became the center of political activism, and the Komala J. Society (Jiani Kurdistan, Rebirth of Kurdistan) was established, a politically progressive and nationalistic party. It was led by the middle class intelligentsia and attracted popular support in the urban and rural areas. This political organization welcomed cross-party links between the Iranian, Iraqi, and Turkish Kurds. The goal was to create political solidarity and class unity. To a large extent, its platform transcended tribal cultural idealism and adopted liberation nationalism. The organizational members of the J.K. came mostly from a petty bourgeoisie class. Rahman Zabihi, the party secretary, came from a poor family and lived with his family in a modest one room.

The party possessed a progressive social outlook.[16] It published a progressive magazine called in Kurdish, *Nishtman*, which means "fatherland." It openly attacked the Aghas and Kurdish tribal leaders whom the J.K. held responsible for the failure of the Kurdish liberation struggle. The magazine also sharply criticized religious clergies, considering them obstacles to Kurdish progressive socio-political and structural reformation.[17] Although Kutschera does not see Komala's organization as progressive, claiming that members came from a bourgeoisie tribal upper class, the party had a nationalistic vision, and incorporated a radical theoretical framework and the values of *Hewa* (Hope). The party was composed of progressive intellectual thinkers with a Marxist orientation.[18] If Hewa contained Marxist tendencies and its members came from the urban educated and enlightened middle class intellectuals, as Kutchera claims, then how could the organization have sought an alliance with the Komala? It was one in the same with the Komala. and that is why the two allied together. However, the party's ideals were still incompatible with the rural tribal political culture, which the Soviets and Gazi Mohammad were aware of. In order not to pose an alienating threat to the landed classes, religious, and tribal forces, the Soviets might have advised Gazi to moderate the platform of Komala. For Komala, it was suicidal to alienate Gazi Mohammud, the most popular and reputable political figure. Therefore, Gazi was invited by the Party to accept its membership, and in April 1945, he became Komala's president. After Gazi assumed the presidency that year, he suggested changing the name of the party, Komala, to the Kurdish Democratic Party of Iran (KDPI). This led to the dissolution of Komala and the incorporation of its members into the KDPI, the newly structured party.

The political objectives of this party endorsed by popular and notable Kurdish forces included the following:

1. Autonomy of Kurdistan within the framework of Iran.
2. The utilization of the Kurdish language as the administrative, educational, and official language.
3. Supervision of the Kurdish socio-political affairs to be vested in the Kurds.
4. All state administrators must "be of local origin."
5. The creation of a single law to "safeguard both landlords and peasants."
6. Cooperation, fraternity, and unity with the Azerbaijanian people.
7. Furtherance of the spiritual and material well-being of the Kurds and nationalization of its natural resources.[19]

These political objectives reflected the reformist nature of the KDPI and its call for Kurdish unity and inclusion. It further emphasized the unity and solidarity with Azerbaijani's. By no means did it represent a revolutionary movement. So what triggered the declaration of an independent Republic of Mahabad? The Tudeh party was a highly organized and influential political institution in Azerbaijan and was fully supported by the Soviet Union. The party's goal was to create a government reflecting Soviet-style socialism. When Azerbaijan was declared an independent Republic on 20 November 1945, the KDPI leader, Gazi Mohammad, was deeply influenced and responded by declaring the independence of the Kurdish Republic on 22 January 1946. At a national gathering in Chwar Chera Square (meaning a square with four lights), Gazi Mohammad proclaimed the establishment of the Republic of Kurdistan in Mahabad. On 11 February 1946, Gazi officially became the president of this newly created Republic.[20] The official territory encompassed 80 kilometers with boundaries including the areas of Mahabad, Bukan, Nagadeh and Ushnavieh.

Mahabad was the nerve center of the Kurdish nationalism and political awakening. The Kurdish language was adopted and the KDPI published journals and periodicals such as *Kurdistan, Halala* (tulip), *Havar* (crying), *Nishtman* (fatherland), and *Grougali Mindalan* (children's magazine) were published. According to Ghassemlou, the lands of those landlords allied with the central government were confiscated and distributed among the peasants. The top administrative jobs previously occupied by top officials of the central government were given to the Kurds. Peshmerga Kurdish forces took over military affairs from the Iranian army. For the first time, the Kurdish flag symbolized the Kurdish independent Republic.[21] However, the KDPI failed to implement an agrarian reform as the Tudeh party did in eastern Azerbaijan under Pishavari's leadership.

It could be argued that these events represented a politically revolutionary transformation. If so, why was the Republic short-lived, almost eleven months? The answer to this includes the internal and external factors that have been analyzed extensively in the previous chapters. Here the focus will be centered on these critical factors which have not been discussed.

Gazi's cabinet included thirteen ministers: Haji Baba Shaikh, Prime Minister; Safe Gazi, Defense Minister; Manaf Karirmi, the Secretary of Education; Mohammad Amin, Advisor to the Interior Minister; Mohammad Ayyobbian, Ministery of Health; Abdul Alrrahman Ilkhanizadh (a landlord) advisor; Ismail Ilkhanizadeh (a landlord) Ministery of Roads; Ahmad Elahi, Ministey of Economics; Karim Ahmadean, Ministry of Post Office; Mostafa Dawoodi (businessman) Ministry of Commerce Department; Mulla Hossein Majdi, Supreme Court Justice; Mahmood Valizadeh (businessman), Ministry of Agriculture; and Sadiq Haidary, Ministery of Propaganda. Additionally, Mulla Mustafa Barzani became a general of the armed forces, and three officers, Safe Gazi, Amankhan Shikak, and Hama Rashid were appointed as marshals, and Ziro Beig Harki received the rank of colonel.[22]

With the collapse of the Azerbaijan Republic, the Kurdish Republic understood that the Soviet Union had withdrawn from its commitment to the liberation struggles of both movements. Hence, on 16 December 1946, Gazi Mohammad, Safe Gazi, and Hajibaba Shaikh the Prime Minister, surrendered to Major General Homayouni, the Shah's General. After peaceful negotiations they were allowed to go back to Mahabad. Mulla Mustaf Barzani, Gazi's general, begged Gazi to leave with him from Mahabad. But Gazi, like Socrates, desired to remain in Mahabad, at any cost. Mahabad collapsed on 17 December

1946. Gazi Mohammad, along with his brother Sadr Gazi, and his cousin Safe Gazi, were tried secretly on 1 Januray 1947. In the dawn of March 31, all three Gazi's were hung in the same square where Gazi had declared the independence of the Mahabad Kurdish Republic.[23] (See pictures on pp. 70–72.)

The reasons for the collapse of Mahabad Republic were manifold. The political immaturity and political miscalculation were important factors. Gazi and his delegates visited Baku in September of 1945, and were advised by Bagherov, the Soviet negotiator, that the time for an independent Kurdistan was not ripe. For Bagherov, the liberation of Kurdistan was contingent on the victory of all oppressed forces in Iran, Iraq, and Turkey; liberty won in one place would be lost in another area. It would be advantageous for the Kurdish people to remain a part of Azerbaijan Republic until the unity of all Kurds, as well as other oppressed people, was achieved.

Gazi and his advisors failed to realize the true political intentions of the Soviet Union. The Soviets were war-torn and war-weary in 1945. They had lost thirty-three million Soviet citizens in the defeat of fascism and were economically devastated and physically exhausted. With these distressing circumstances, it was inconceivable that the Soviet Union would consider another major military confrontation with the West over Iran, let alone the Kurdish or Azerbaijan Republics; although, the Soviets would not hesitate to annex eastern and western Azerbaijan, if possible. The Soviet's critical objective was to obtain an oil concession in the northern part of Iran by using the two separatist movements to achieve this goal. Contrary to Soviets expectations, the unity between the independent Republic of Azerbaijan under Pishavari's leadership and the Mahabad Republic under Gazi, was unrealistic to expect. Certainly, the Soviets were aware of the conflict over land and territorial disputes between the Kurds and Azari speaking Turks. This included other non-Kurds, both minorities and majorities, in western Azerbaijan, especially in Rezaieh (Urmia), where the Kurds, as opposed to Shi,i Muslims, Armenians, and Christians were a minority Sunni population. Nevertheless, the territory was claimed for the Kurds, and the majority of Azerbaijanians were "aliens and had no rights to Urmia."[24]

The issues of land and territory are extremely divisive, undermining the development of mutual understanding and creation of national class solidarity. Hashimov, the Soviet counselor, tried unsuccessfully to mediate these divisive issues. Soviets, along with the KDPI and the Tudeh party, had miscalculated the will, intention, and comparative advantages of the United States. The United States was emerging as a new superpower and was fully determined to embark on the post-Cold War nation building. All subsequent containment policies of the United States, such as the Marshall Plan, military build up, and support for the highly centralized military governments reveal this intention. The Soviets had no choice but to leave Iran. The Soviet withdrawal on 10 May 1946 resulted in the inevitable collapse of both Republics. The political immaturity of the KDPI became apparent when it failed to understand the rational for the Soviet withdrawal from Iran, and failed to understand why the Turkish-appointed ministers had been forced out of the government in the Azerbaijan Republic in Tabriz (the capital of the Republic). Gazi failed to read the United States' policy of commitment to the national sovereignty of Iran, announced openly on 27 November 1946, by the American Ambassador to Tehran.[25]

The failure was further rooted in the Kurdish exclusionary mode of thinking. The Soviet consulate advised Gazi Mohammad to join the movement with the Azerbaijan Republic, whose leading party, the Tudeh party, was progressive: Gazi chose not to. The conservative forces of Mahabad had been frightened by the progressive nature of the Azerbaijain Republic, and therefore, did not want to enter into this union.[26] Once again, the Kurdish movement's conservatism and isolationist tendencies contributed to its defeat.

Moreover, from the outset, serious fractional tensions prevailed within the party leadership. Ziro beig Harki was at odds with Shaikh Abdullah, who conflicted with Gazi. Additionally, many Aghas, shaikhs, and landlords considered the Mahabad Republic as an extension of the Soviet Union, and did not want to lose their privileged link with the central government. Before the collapse of the Republic, several of the Kurdish chiefs offered their support for the central government. Hama Rashid, one of the three marshals appointed by Gazi Mohammad, volunteered to defect if appointed by the central government as *Bakhshdar* (head of the district) of Baneh City, north of Kurdistan.[27] With the exception of Gazi Mahammad, who believed in the nationalist Kurdish cause, the remaining nerve center of the movement was irresolute. It suffered from the false tradition of tribal consciousness, the defining internal cause of the collapse of the Republic.

Fereshteh Kohi-Kamali also identifies the lack of unity and cohesive leadership within the party. The establishment of the Republic "created enormous problems: the backwardness (economic, social, cultural, and political) of Kurdistan was probably the main internal cause of its failure."[28] Kamali suggests that the conflict among the tribal chiefs was a major contributing factor to the downfall of the movement. However, she fails to distinguish between Simko's and Gazi's nationalism and fails to point out that national liberation struggles cannot succeed without the support of a united front. These empirically established facts do not conform to the theoretical expectation of the national liberation struggles. Although the Kurdish authors speak of the political inexperience of the Kurdish leadership, the crucial question is when will the Kurdish leadership learn from their past mistakes? The Kurds have been struggling for over a century and the "inexperience" thesis is not validated empirically. Kurdish leaderhip suffers from false consciousness. The Kurdish struggle is used as an instrument for the realization of internal and external objectives. They have been the agents of their oppressors. Consequently, they have been unable to succeed with their liberation objectives.

By 1952, Dr. Mossadeq'a progressive political mobilization efforts inspired the nationalization of Anglo-Iranian oil companies. Mossadeq's nationalistic movement culminated in the structural breakdown of the autocratic central government. This liberalization environment provided another chance for the KDPI to reorganize itself. In August 1952, out of five thousand Mahabadians who supported Dr. Mossadeq's reform movement in a referendum, only two voted for the central government.[29] However, this time "the operation of Ajax," sponsored by Britain and the United States, cut-short Kurdish hope. Although sporadic movements occurred throughout Kurdistan, the Shah's government backed by the center of the world system, maintained full control of Kurdistan. The Shah's control lasted until the 1978–79 Iranian Revolution. The parochially-minded tribal leader's interests superseded the Kurdish national liberation aspirations, and they gave their support to the Shah's central government.

According to Nader Entessar, Salar Jaf and his brother Sardar Jaf, prominent figures in the Jaf tribe, were given important governmental positions. The Shah's 1960–1963 white revolution claimed land reform as its major component, but the Jaf's land holdings were not distributed to the Kurdish peasants. The Jaf and the Ardalan tribes, backed by the central government, played a critical role in containing the Kurdish rebellion. This situation was further aggravated by Mulla Mostafa Barzani's movement against Iraq's Bathist party during the 1960s. At its inception in 1961, the movement attracted substantial material and emotional support from the KDPI, whose assistance (until 1966) made a great contribution to the continuity of Barzani's struggle against Baghdad, the capital of Iraq.[30]

In response to this movement, the Shah's autocratic government formulated a two-fold policy objective. In order to weaken the Bathist regime of Iraq (which was seen as a threat to Iranian monarchy since its overthrow of the Hashemite monarch), the Shah's government offered assistance to Barzani. The calculated goal was to create dependence on the Iranian government and to contain the Kurdish movement in Iran by breaking down the prevailing solidarity between the KDP and KDPI-Iraqi forces. The result was the freeze thesis imposed on the Iranian KDP.[31] Barzani advised the Iranian Kurds not to disrupt the aid to Barzani from the Shah's government. Any Kurdish KDPI member who refused to follow this self-defeating thesis was considered to be an enemy of the Kurdish revolution. This thesis eventually undermined Kurdish solidarity between the Iranian and Iraqi Kurdish forces.

The disappointed Iranian KDP insurgents, who previously were fighting for Barzani's cause, returned to Iran and resumed their rebellion against the Shah's autocratic government in the regions of Baneh, Mahabad, and Sardasht. The guerrilla insurgency effort began in the winter of 1967 and lasted eighteen months. However, the Shah's army surrounded these progressive forces and Barzani's forces blocked their escape. Each of the key leaders of this insurgency, Sharif Zadeh, Abdullah Muini, and Mala Avara, were murdered. Others like Suleiman Muini, and Abdullah, Muini's older brother, were arrested and executed by Barzani. More than forty Iranian Kurdish insurgents were killed or arrested by Mustafa Barzani's forces and handed over to the Iranian autocracy to face the death penalty. In the cities of Nagadeh and Mahabad in western Azerbaijan, Suleiman Muini's dead body was placed in a truck for public viewing for a full day in spring of 1968.[32] These circumstances defied the spirit of the liberation struggle and proved once again how the Kurds were repeatedly victimized by their selfish, parochially-minded, and shortsighted leaders.

Internal contradictions led to the structural incapacitation of the Pahlavi Dyansty, culminating in the Iranian Revolution of 1978–1979, and provided the Kurds with another golden opportunity. Due to the opportunistic nature of the Kurdish leadership, many Kurdish scholars anticipated that because of the failure of the previous movements, the leadership would have gained the maturity and wisdom to act wisely. This did not occur within the leadership division. The reductionistic experience model attributes the success or failure of a revolutionary movement to an experience vs. inexperience thesis. It ignores the world context, political consciousness, ideological factors, national solidarity, class alliances, and the political objectives of the movement. The inexperience thesis is mute to internal contradictions of Kurdish society. One of the key contradictions existed with the feudal lords who, for the purpose of their own class interest, invariably sided with reactionary central governments. The thesis also ignores the fact that tribal and parochial forces act as obstructionists, blocking the realization of Kurdish political aspirations. Furthermore, the Kurdish leader's reliance on external forces and their inability to forge national unity and class alliances creates a legitimization crisis. These variables are the critical factors.

The validity of this hypothetical construct can be proven. Although Ghassemlou was an educated intellectual with a modern vision of the western values of coalition building, compromise, multiculturalism, pluralism, democratic socialism, social justice, and democracy, his leadership was not an improvement over Gazi Mohammad and Barzani's leadership. Precisely, it proved to be disastrous. However, this does not mean that the Kurdish left was politically correct. The Kurdish Marxists applied Marxism to a predominantly Muslem, peasant-based, isolated, and underdeveloped Kurdish society, making the same mistakes as the Bolsheviks did in 1917. Nonetheless, this criticism of Ghassemlou holds. Ghassemlou's greatest political mistake was his suicidal move at Nagadeh, a city in western Azerbaijan with a majority population of non-Kurds. He had been advised by regional and local forces to avoid an armed march by the Kurdish Peshmarges (KDPI forces) because the action could provoke agitation and retaliation. His subsequent action triggered the Kurdish and Turkish confrontation that resulted in the massacre of Kurds, as well as Turks, in Nagadeh, oppressed forces killing the oppressed, a calamity unprecedented in the history of the national liberation struggles.

This miscalculated strategy by a western-educated intellectual defies the logic of class alliance and national solidarity formation. Instead of coalition building and the creation of national unity with non-Kurds, who have been as much oppressed and fettered as the Kurds, he forced Kurdish sympathizers into an alliance with the government. With this type of divisive strategy, Ghassemlou was struggling to create "democracy for Iran, autonomy for Kurdistan."[33] The Kurdish left felt that Ghassemlou's actions conflicted with his theoretical conceptions. He propagated democracy for Iranian, Iraqi, Turkish, and Syrian Kurds. But like his predecessor, Mustafa Barzani, Ghassemlou heavily relied on the world system for liberation. Therefore, the result was a disastrous defeat.

Another influential leader in Kurdistan was Shaikh Azaddin Husseini, who according to the Kurdish left and Sipah-i Pasdaran-e Inqilab Islami (the Islamic Revolutionary Guard), established close relations with the Shah's Savak. Based on document 26 and letter number 50/6/22–1/7/64 issued to the Shah's secret police, SAVAK Azaddin had been appointed as the Friday prayer at Mahabad. But his religious qualifications regarding this position were questioned by other prominent Kurdish religious leaders. According to the aforementioned letter that was signed by the head of the Iranian SAVAK, General Naseery, Azaddin Housseini was well qualified. The protest of other religious forces against his appointment was the result of ongoing differences and conflict among the religious leaders. Since Housseini was a respected personality, SAVAK saw no reason to remove him from the position assigned to him by the order of his majesty the Shah.[34]

If this document of SAVAK cited by the Office of the Islamic Revolutionary Guard and the charges made by the Kurdish left are valid, then the Kurdish liberation movement is nothing more than an instrument of tribal and parochial-minded leaders who have used brave and innocent, but aggrieved Kurdish forces for the realization of their own short-term objectives. It is not surprising that the liberation movements have all collapsed and have led to further antagonism, factionalism, and frustration. Mom Jalal's (the leader of

PUKS) letter addressed to Shaikh Ottman Nagshbandi supports this calim. Mom Jalal accused Mom Barzani as a "Kurd killer and treasonous of the Kurdish revolution. Barzani's criminal hands are tainted with the blood of Kurdish heroes . . . Molazem Hasan, Khoshnav, Kok shasvar, Shaikh Jalal, Kakeh Ali . . . Shaikh Houssein Babeh Shaikh . . ." He added that it was time that Kurds stopped killing other Kurds.[35] Yet, sadly, unity and solidarity among the Kurdish factions remains to be seen. Kurds continue to kill other Kurds. This is a radical departure from the intent of national liberation struggles.

Again, this reflects an important contradiction that undermines the Kurdish liberation struggle. As mentioned earlier, Jash politics divide and block Kurdish unity and destroy liberation aspirations. Ironically, Jashism has been sharply criticized by Kurdish leadership, yet the Kurdish leaders subscribed to the same notions. Self-interested and self-perpetuating policy agendas are extremely destructive to the Kurdish liberation objectives.

While the base of the movement in Kurdistan, especially in the rural areas, is predominantly composed of parochial, traditional, tribal, and loyal patron-client relations, the political superstructure includes traditional and modern-minded leaders who assume a contradictory position. The modern-minded leaders attempt to lead and liberate the mass base of the liberation movement; the traditional-minded leaders are more appealing to the masses. Consequently, when secular leaders enter a class alliance with the traditional forces the political objectives of the movement stagnate. Both traditional and secular-minded leaders then must rely on external forces to secure their position. Historically, external forces have played a critical role in perpetuating Kurdish misery and have contained the liberation struggle. The Kurdish leaders have relied on hostile external forces in their struggle to override the influence and power of rival Kurdish leaders. With the help of external forces, Kurds kill Kurds. This is the most devastating result of the reliance on external forces, resulting in de-mobilization and fragmentation of the Kurdish people.

The Kurdish movement is exclusionary and has created a hostile environment, replete with unsympathetic social forces. The Kurdish leadership has failed to enter into a coalition with non-Kurds or other social forces. It is difficult to differentiate friends and enemies of the Kurdish people. This is vitally important if a liberation movement is to succeed.[36] The Kurdish movement has failed because a self-created and self-perpetuated hostile environment has surrounded the leadership. The leadership has not attempted to change this reality and has not been willing to enter into class alliances with other progressive and non-Kurdish forces

From 1990–1993, all highways in western Azerbaijan (Mahabad to Urmia, Piranshahr to Nagadeh, Mahabad to Bukan, Saggiz, Miandouab Nagadeh to Sardasht) were arenas of struggle between governmental forces and Kurdish guerrillas. The government created daytime watching posts every four or five miles to guard the innocent civilians from indiscriminate attack by the Kurdish rebels. The government forces were in charge of the roads from dawn to dusk; the guerrillas controlled the roads during the nighttime hours. The common people were often looted and robbed by the Kurdish rebels. Hence, peo-

Chwar Chera Square of Mahabad where Gazi Mohammad was hung in the dawn of March 31, 1947. He was the President of the short lived Republic of Mahabad (1946–47).

On the gallows at the Chwar Chera Square of Mahabad is Abul Gassem Sadr Gazi who was hung with the two other Gazi's in the dawn of March 31, 1947.

محمد حسین خان سیف کا طهی

This is Mohammad Houssein Khan Safe Gazi, on the Gallows, Gazi Mohammad's
Secretary (Defense Minister) of Defense, Mahabad Chwar Chera. March 31, 1947

ple rarely could travel during the night hours. This behavior has no place in national liberation struggles. It is attributed to the shortsighted and alienating policies of the Kurdish leadership.

Unfortunately, Ghassemlou was only interested in negotiating an amnesty for his fighters, not a political settlement, and was eventually assassinated in Vienna. As the KDPI-RL noted, Ghassemlou was a victim of his own political mistakes. Many observers see the Kurdish struggle, not as a liberation movement or a quest for cultural and political autonomy, but as a secessionist movement. Clearly, the Kurdish liberation struggle in Iran has deviated from the theoretical and empirical expectations of national liberation struggles.

B. MULLA MOSTAFA BARZANI'S UPHEAVAL IN IRAQ

The history of political movements in the northern part of Iraq and in Kurdistan, especially in the district of Barzan, illustrates Barzani's bravery and courage. This history also bears witness to the bloody liberation struggles aimed at the realization of the Kurdish people's political rights. Barzan is known as the birthplace of Kuridsh nationalism and the subsequent liberation movements.

Barzani possessed strong commitment to the Kurdish cause, as tough as the mountains of Kurdistan. However, his liberation struggles were contradictory. They did not conform to the theoretical and practical expectations of national liberation movements fought out by the dominated forces throughout history. While liberation struggles seek liberation from the repressive dominating colonial powers, Mr. Barzani sought alliance and support from the forces that had perpetuated Kurdish oppression and captivity. He failed to realize that the external forces he unequivocally relied on did not welcome Kurdish autonomy and independence. These claims are empirically validated by the political events in Kurdistan.

Following the 1930 bloodshed in Sulaymania, national consciousness was on the rise among the newly emerging educated intelligentsia. The educated and politically conscious forces challenged the Kurdish upper class landholders, who by virtue of their own dominant class position, always sided with the ruling class, the oppressors of the Kurds. A Kurdish political organization did not exist to mobilize the Kurdish forces into political action. This encouraged the intellectuals and dissenters to join the Iraqi Communist Party (ICP). The ICP formed in 1934 and promoted the cause of all nationalities. The party condemned governmental atrocities inflicted on the Iraqis and Kurdish minorities, and in 1935, the party openly supported Kurdish independence. However, given the backwardness of Kurdistan and the deeply rooted tribal culture and provincial values of Kurdish society, the success of the party was compromised. The ideals of this party still remain to be realized.[37]

The Brayatic (brotherhood) was formed and led by Shaikh Latif, son of Shaikh Ahmad. Members came from notable urban classes and many were religious dignitaries. Radicals and leftists formed Kargar, an association of progressive individuals linked with the Iraqi Communist Party (ICP). These combined parties did not have adequate membership, and in 1941, the two organizations fused to form Hewa, the Kurdish word for "hope." Hewa now had a membership of fifteen hundred and was the organizational base of the Kurdish leader, Mulla Mostafa Barzani. Barzani and his brother, Shaikh Ahmad, were sentenced to house arrest in Sulaymaniya. In 1943, Barzani was able to escape to Barzan where he would begin his political activities.[38]

Although well versed in guerrilla war tactics and a first-hand witness to the bloody outcome of the 1930–1931 liberation struggle, Mulla Mostafa Barzani learned almost nothing from it. In the 1931 rebellion, his brother, Shaikh Ahmad Barzani, attacked Iraqi bases at Barzan and Margasour while Shaikh Mahmood's forces caputred the city of Kharmal within ten miles of the Halabja and Shaneder districts. Unfortunately, this bloody victory was short lived. The British air force, in cooperation with the Iraqi army, entered into battle defeating Shaikh Mahmood and Shaikh Ahmad Barzani's forces.[39] Shaikh Mahmood communicated the following in a letter to the colonial British office in Baghdad:

> The crime that took place in Sulaymaniya could be seen as unprecedented in the history of the Kurdish people. Indeed, the British army committed the most horrible and savage crimes against the Kurdish people . . . [40]

Mulla Mostafa Barzani either ignored the crimes inflicted on the Kurdish people, or he simply did not understand the intentions of a brutally colonizing imperial power. He failed to realize that Britain, as a colonial power, pursued a divide and rule strategy that intended to captivate, not liberate, its colonies. National liberation movements in colonized and imperialized zones are vivid illustrations of this type of British aggression. In reality, the British Empire did not give liberty as a gift to its colonies, and liberation struggles have been necessary to incapacitate the dominant colonial hegemony.

Mulla Mostafa Barzani's optimism envisioned Great Britain as a savior, not a colonizer. In a letter to Sir Kinahan Cornwallis, the British Ambassador to Baghdad, Barzani wrote: "Whatever your orders, I shall obey them as a child would the orders of a compassionate father . . . our friendship for the merciful British government knows no bounds."[41] There is no empirical evidence that Britain was a compassionate father or a merciful friend to the colonially dominated and captivated people. Ambassador Cornwallis' response to

Barzani's letter reveals Mr. Barzani's unrealistic thinking. Cornwallis communicated that Barzani would accept Baghdad's terms and discontinue unlawful activities. Barzani was further warned that if he continued his illegal activities he risked serious consequences.[42] The statements made by Ambassador Cornwallis resonate with the colonial domination mentality. From Ambassador Cornwallis's point of view, Barzani's efforts to liberate his people from oppression and to enable them to realize their national rights is illegal, but British supported Iraqi state terrorism was legitimate and acceptable.

State-sponsored terrorism exercised by dominating powers is well documented. Consider, for example, the overthrow of Dr. M. Mosaddeg (1953), a legitimately chosen premier of Iran; support for apartheid in South Africa; events in Latin America, support for dictators in the Middle East; and the direct colonial control in India. Barzani failed to realize that when there is a conflict between colonial economic rights and human rights, the former is given priority. Barzani also miscalculated British policies in the Middle East. Based on a cost and benefit analysis, it was logically impossible for the British to side with Barzani forces at the cost of millions of Arabs. What the British wanted was cheap labor, cheap raw materials, consumers, oil and co-operative leaders, who would willingly accommodate British demands. Occasionally, British policy did mirror a degree of latitude for Barzani's cause, but it was politically motivated. The British used the Kurdish movement as a political arm to maintain its exploitative colonial interest, and to extract additional resources from the region. It was illogical for the British to act otherwise. Unfortunately, Mr. Barzani never abandoned his loyalty to the British. The accuracy of this analysis is proven because after decades of struggle, the realization of the Kurds' legitimate rights still remains to be seen.

According to Edgar O'Ballance, in October 1943, in spite of the defeat of the Biroki's revolt in Turkey, Mulla Mostafa Barzani opted to continue his guerrilla insurgency movement in northern Iraq. This intimidating insurrection forced the Iraqi government to react, but Barzani's forces trapped the Iraqi military unit in the area of Diyana. This provoked the British-Indian occupational forces to counter the threat. Meanwhile, the British colonizing authorities compelled Barzani to negotiate with the Iraqi government. He disagreed with the dictated terms under which he was required to stop the insurgency, but was offered, in return, a choice of going to Iran or staying in the northeast of Sulaymaniya.[43] These terms were typical of a colonial power solving a political problem. In a sense, the terms represented a demand for Barzani's unconditional and peaceful surrender, and plainly indicated British sentiment regarding Kurdish nationalism. What did Mr. Barzani learn from these events? Based on the evidence presented above, Mr. Barzani learned nothing about the motives of the British colonial power.

What about Barzani's relationship with the Hewa party? Hewa had adopted anti-British policies, yet according to Chaliand, Barzani heavily relied on the British for international recognition. Chaliand's reasoning is problematic. Barzani might have received international recognition if the British really had been concerned with the Kurdish cause. How does the bombing of the Kurdish villages result in Kurdish liberation or the recognition of their legitimate demands? Chaliand's argument is inconsistent with the theories of national liberation struggles. Hewa was aware of the imperialistic British policies in the region and the rights of the oppressed people. Yet, the party's leadership never believed that the British priority centered on its own imperial and colonial interests. Perhaps, from Barzani's point of view, the British were more reliable than Jash tribal leaders. However, both proved they were the enemies of the Kurdish people. Barzani's ultimate defeat was caused by the British and his old tribal enemies: the Baradustis, Surchis, and Zibaris. Mahmud Agha Zibari, Mr. Barzani's father-in-law, sided with the Iraqi government against Barzani's forces. Thus, the British and Iraqi and tribal triangle's unholy alliance defeated the 1945 phase of the Kurdish struggle in northern Iraq. Barzani and his fighters were forced into Iran, where the Mahabad rebellion was in the making.[44]

In Mahabad, Mr. Barzani, by virtue of his attachment to the British, was treated suspiciously since the Kurdish leadership in Mahabad perceived him as a British agent. However, since Gazi Mohammad was in need of organized defense forces, he had no other choice, but to cautiously welcome Barzani and his nine thousand followers in November of 1945. As mentioned earlier, on 22 January 1946, Gazi Mohammad declared Kurdish independence at the Chwar Chera Square of Mahabad (Chwar Chera is a Kurdish word for "four lamps," which the city square still has). Following Gazi Mohammad's presidency of the Kurdish Republic of Mahabad, Mr. Barzani was appointed as chief commander of the armed forces of the Republic with the rank of general, a title he kept for the remainder of his life.

The new government of Gazi Mohammad controlled a small territory that included Bukan, Mahabad, Nagadeh, and Ushnavieh. In order to expand the territory of the Kurdish Republic of Mahabad to the south, General Barzani was dispatched to the south to fight the Iranian army in Saggez, Baneh, and Sardasht. If successful, this operation would liberate Paveh, Sanandaj, Kermanshah, and the surrounding Kurdish speaking areas.[45] On 24 April 1946, General Barzani's troops ambushed and inflicted major causalities on the Iranian army, north of Saggez in an area called Gara Ava. Twenty-one soldiers of the imperial army were killed, seventeen were injured, and forty were captured and sent to Mahabad.[46] Barzani's plan to incorporate the south in the newly formed Republic was short lived. Under Anglo-American pressure, the

Soviet's withdrawal from the northern part of Iran on 10 May 1946, brought the Mahabad Republic to an abrupt end. Gazi officially surrendered Mahabad, the capital of the Kurdish Republic, and the three Gazis, Gazi Mohammad, Safe Gazi, and Sadr Gazi, were executed and their bodies put on display for a full day.[47]

General Barzani observed these events. He was also fully aware that the Imperial Iranian Army, in its incapacitated form without British and American support, could not defeat the Republics of Azerbaijan and Mahabad. George Allen, the American Ambassador, in his policy statement on 27 November 1946, declared: "The United States of America supports the full sovereignty of Iran." This statement validates the claim that external forces were responsible for the dissolution of the Kurdish attempt for a homeland.

Again, General Barzani did not learn his political lesson from this tragic event. Based on Chris Kutschera's argument, on 20 December 1946, General Barzani visited Major General Homayoni of the Imperial Army of the Shah, and informed him that he wanted to return to Iraq, if the British guaranteed his safe return and immunity.[48] The evidence supports the claims that Barzani's defeat was caused by the British support of the Iraqi government, and in Barzani's revolts of 1930–1945 and Gazi Mohammad's short-lived Republic, reactionary tribal forces and imperial interventionism played a critical role. The British refusal to secure Barzani's return to Iraq after the collapse of the Kurdish Republic of Mahabad indicates British support for Iraq and demonstrates that the British no longer required Kurdish support. Evidence from confidential British documents discloses how the British only intended to use the Kurds as a policy instrument towards the realization of their own colonial interests in the region.

General Barzani, having reached a dead-end in his armed struggles for Kurdish liberation, was forced into exile in the Soviet Union. Barzani and his small fighting unit of five hundred men walked 350 kilometers in fourteen days to the Aras River, and then on to the Soviet Union. During the journey he fought pro-governmental tribes, as well as the Iranian Army. In June 1947, Barzani reached his destination in the Soviet Union, where he and his forces spent eleven years in exile.[49] These tragic and bloody encounters illustrate the extent of Barzani's incessant struggle, his people's pains and sufferings, and the heroic resistance of the Kurdish people to political discrimination, domination, and oppression.

Although General Barzani's exile to the Soviet Union was seen as a victory by those who stood by the status quo, the Kurdish underground political struggle continued, though it repeatedly experienced bloody confrontation and suppression. In General Barzani's absence, there was a void in the leadership of the Kurdish movement. Several dedicated Kurds embarked on the reorganization of the Iraqi KDP (Kurdish Democratic Party), initially founded in 1946 by General Barzani while he was in Mahabad. But as Mc-Dowall notes, the party could not abandon its parochial values until the 1970s. The party failed to adopt social and economic programs because the party did not want to alienate tribal forces and landed classes.[50] The socio-economic interests of tribal chiefs and Aghas blocked aspirations for change. The influence of these classes contributed to the defeat of the Kurdish liberation struggle, and this explains why the Iraqi Communist Party (ICP) criticized the KDP for its "petty bourgeoisie Kurdish nationalism."[51] The Iraqi KDP was further criticized by the ICP for its exclusive and separatist policies since the party did not identify with the oppressed masses, but advocated sectarianism. It was seen as an instrument of imperialistic forces using the false assurances of independence to conceal their hegemonic intentions.

Other criticisms from the Iraqi ICP alleged that the Iraqi KDP failed to realize that without liberating Iraq from imperial domination, freedom would not exist in any other place.[52] This criticism is supported with factual evidence. How is it possible to have democratic autonomy in an unfree and undemocratic country? It was this negative state of affairs that eventually led to further restructuring of the KDP, resulting in the convening of the second Kurdish congress in 1951. In this congress, Ibrahim Ahmad, just released from jail, was chosen as Secretary General. It was under Ahmad's leadership at the third convention of 1953 that the party adopted a leftist position. The party supported land reform, supported the workers' and peasants' rights, and advocated the creation of the workers' association. However, the party did not support a class struggle because this dynamic was far from maturation in Kurdistan, and the influence of the landed class was very strong.[53]

The Iraqi KDP was a victim of its own internal contradictions. Reliance on the costly and unaffordable political support from the tribal chiefs and the landed class, forces that have always been on the side of the status quo and have resisted socio-economic and political structural reforms, was unfortunate. Furthermore, the party adopted a progressive platform to incorporate leftist alternatives, which was unacceptable to the traditional operative forces throughout Kurdistan. The party also lacked organizational leadership capabilities.

However, the Kurdish struggle, with the incapacitation of the monarchical political structure, reasserted itself. On 14 July 1958, the forces of General Gasem overthrew the monarchy and declared Iraq a republic. Ismet Sheriff Vanly calls Gasem's coup d'etat a revolution. In practical terms, it was not a revolution at all. It did not alter the socio-political structure of Iraq, but only changed the regime. Kurdish enthusiasm was primarily due to the inclusion of Article 3 into the provisionally formulated constitution. Article 3 maintained:

Iraqi society is based on complete cooperation between all its citizens, on respect for their rights and liberties. Iraqis and Kurds are associates in this nation; the constitution guarantees their rights within the Iraqi whole.[54]

General Gasem's policies led to the legalization of the Iraqi KDP and the declaration of general amnesty for all Kurdish prisoners and exiles. Banned under monarchism, the Kurdish press, including the publications *Khebat* (struggle), *Jin* (life), *Hetaw* (sun), and *Azadi* (liberty) were freed.[55] General Barzani wired congratulations to Gasem and sought his consent to return to Iraq from exile in the Soviet Union. Gasem granted Barzani's return, and Barzani was given a heroic welcome. Baba Ali Shaik, Mahmud's son, was included in General Gasem's cabinet. And the KDP Secretary General, Ibrahim Ahmad, pledged the party's support for Gasem's regime.[56]

These politically based reform measures, however short-lived, raised Kurdish optimism to the point that it referred to as a revolution. Again however, the Kurdish leaders failed to calculate the political meaning of these temporary concessions. As Hamdi argues, the agreement for General Barzani and his associates to return to Iraq and the recognition of Kurdish rights in the provisional constitution was politically motivated. The goal was to create a political balance of power by bringing the Kurds to the side of the new regime, thereby neutralizing the political pressure of Arab nationalism inspired by Jamal Abdul Nasser of Egypt. The British Ambassador's report to the United Kingdom's Foreign Affair's Ministry further illustrates the shortsightedness of the Kurdish leaders. The following is an excerpt from the British Ambassador's confidential correspondence with the British foreign ministry:

... Gasem's support for the Kurds is to prevent Iraq from falling into the United Arab Republic. . . . It is clear that as of now General Barzani has given up the ideal of an Independent Kurdistan. . . . It is crucial to emphasize that the support of tribal chiefs for Barzani is temporary whenever they realize that Barzani's policies are not for their interests, they will stop backing him up . . . we are scrutinizing Gasem/Barzani alliance very precisely. But we are of the conviction that this alliance will not last long, because Gasem's shift either from the left to right or vice versa will be critical . . . of course the Soviet Union will not support General Barzani, for such a support will be contingent on the Kurds advocacy of the Arab nationalism.[57]

Kurdish leadership once again sided with the reactionary forces, proving its shortsightedness. The Kurdish political intellectuals were against the KDP's alliance with reactionary forces. Both the ICP and Arab nationalists accused the KDP of preferring an alliance with reactionaries rather than with the progressive Iraqi forces, who had struggled for a democratic, inclusive,

and accommodative Iraq. They charged that the KDP always allied with un-
favorable forces that undermined the realization of the democratic rights of
the oppressed social forces.

Ibrahim Ahmad's position was not exclusionary. He was fully aware that
Arab nationalism also had an important political role to play. However,
Ibrahim Ahmad's views were not acceptable to General Barzani. As a result,
Barzani ousted Ahmad and replaced him with pro-Communist Hamza Abd
Allah in January 1959.[58] Ibrahim Ahmad was a highly educated intellectual.
He spoke fluent Kurdish, Arabic, Persian, and English. When the newscast-
ers visited his home, they found that his library contained books by Marx,
Lenin, Sartre, Bertrand Russell, and Dostoevsky. It was Ahmad who trans-
formed the ideological stand of the KDP to a Marxism-Leninist orientation.
The leftist critique of Ahmad accused him of advancing nationalistic ideals
and incorporating Baathist and Gasemite ideals.[59] This criticism can be substantiated by his pledged support to Gasem's regime and his proximity with
Arab nationalism.

In March 1959, General Barzani's forces helped Gasem suppress a major
uprising in Mosul. It was led by Arab nationalists and Baathist officers, who
were disillusioned with his policies. Barzani's forces took advantage of this
event, and entered into battle with feudal lords who had sided with nationalists against Gasem's regime. While Kurds and Communists received the
credit for repelling the revolt against Gasem, the latter used these forces to
eliminate the nationalists and Baathists from the armed forces and government.[60] Hence, a triangle between the KDP, the ICP, and Gasem developed,
which enabled Gasem to successfully deal with the major threats to his
regime. However, this alliance was temporary, unusual, contradictory, and
precarious. The ICP of the northern section of the Iraqi Communist party was
dominated by Kurdish progressive forces that possessed direction, conviction, and a genuine ideology of liberation.

The political agenda of the ICP was incompatible with General Gasem's reactionary and military thinking and Barzani's attachment to tribal values. The
alliance broke down when the Kurdish tribal chiefs revolted in Rawanduz
against Gasem's regime in May 1959. The agrarian reforms of 30 September
1958 and the ICP's firm support of the peasant's land rights frightened them.
This uprising was quickly defeated by governmental/Barzani supporters,
forcing twenty thousand to flee to Iran and four thousand to flee to
Turkey.[61]This incident led to the split between Barzani and the Communists.
Certainly, the growing influence of the ICP among the oppressed forces of
Kurdistan might have posed a serious threat to Barzani's leadership.

Barzani attributed this rupture with the Communists to their attempt to as-
sassinate him.[62] Was this an excuse on Barzani's behalf to expel the Commu-

nists, or was it due to the growing and appealing popularity of the ICP-based Kurdish movement? According to Kutschera, this rupture was provoked when the Barzani supporters began to question Kurdish peasants. The peasants were asked whether their loyalty was with the Kurds or Communists.[63] Apparently, the assassination threat led to Barzani's repressive action. The communist movement was neither acceptable to the British, the United States, or Gasem, nor to the tribal supporters of Barzani. When Hamza Abdallah attempted to defend the Communists, General Barzani removed Hamza from his position as KDP General Secretary and reappointed Ibrahim Ahmad. Gasem, threatened by General Barzani's growing power, joined his natural allies, the rightist forces, including Arab nationalists and Barzani's traditional rival enemies. He banned political parties and armed the feudal lords (the Kurdish Aghas) to attack Barzani's family and Kurdish KDP leaders. Kurdish language newspapers were prohibited and KDP leaders were arrested. Ibrahim Ahmad, the editor of *Khebat* and the KDP Secretary-General was brought to trial. This military dictatorship forced General Barzani to seek refuge in Barzan. Following these repressive measures, a pro-government journal published articles demanding complete assimilation of the Kurds; the Arabization of a distinct and unique culture.[64]

In Kurdistan, the clash between the Barzani and Zibari Kurds, led to the defeat of the latter, resulting in a chaotic situation in the region. This was used as an excuse for governmental interventionism, and on 13 September 1961, Gasem's regime began bombing Barzan and Kurdistan. However, the Iraqi KDP did not join Barzani's northern rebels until March 1962. The debate within the party involved Barzani's and the Iraqi CP's marginalization. The hope was that Barzani's marginalization would result in the KDP's prevalence as a people-based organization whose political objective would be Kurdish liberation.[65] Ahmad felt that it was a peasant and tribal war imposed on the party and considered a lost cause from the outset.

The question became whether to participate in the struggle and become an ally of General Barzani and the tribal forces under his control or passively surrender. Again, it must be emphasized that the tribal values of the movement impeded the realization of the Kurdish aspiration for liberation. McDowall quotes Sa,ad Jawad:

> Had the KDP remained true to its championship of Kurdish national aspirations, it would never have submitted to the tribal leadership, and thus ruined its chances of leading the movement.[66]

It follows that in the absence of an organized political party infrastructure, the defeat of the movement was inevitable. Thus, General Barzani and his forces had no choice but to seek refuge against the Iraqi army in the Zakho Mountains.

The KDP finally entered the struggle in March 1962. General Barzani limited the KDP to the southern regions since his own area of influence was the north.[67] General Barzani, who in theory was the KDP President, refused to identify himself with the KDP or any other political organization and declined political debates, which are critical components of democratic thinking. He failed to realize that the clash of dissenting ideas not only culminates in truth, but also solidifies the strategic foundation of a guerrilla war. His traditional background was fertile ground for the development of authoritarianism.[68] Hence, Jalal Talabani and Ibrahim Ahmad, both lawyers, educated, and well-traveled assumed the leadership of the KDP, opposing Barzani's traditionalism and tribal authoritarianism. Barzani never relinquished his loyalty to Great Britain, never understanding the imperialistic dynamics responsible for the tragedies inflicted on the Kurds. This criticism is substantiated by the British Ambassador to Turkey who maintained, "The people of Kurdistan are dissatisfied with the 14 July 1958 Iraqi government. The British government, by offering them some sort of autonomy, can use them for its future purpose."[69]

Was Barzani aware of the British intentions, or was he an imperial agent? It is difficult to ascertain, but as McDowall points out, Barzani rarely spoke of Kurdish rights. He was primarily obsessed with land reform laws and the conflicts promoted by Gasem, and the fact that Barzani "still seemed to want a deal with the British."[70] This argument is validated by confidential British documents. When the British Ambassador visited Barzani, Barzani's brother, Shaikh Ahmad, complained about the events that took place during the British presence in Iraq. He stated that "he [Ahmad] has always attempted to cooperate with the Britains . . . but his reward was twelve years captivity at Basreh's prisons." General Barzani then expressed his hope that their meeting will be a beginning of new relations between the Kurds and Great Britain.[71] To thank the British Ambassador for his visit, General Barzani revisits the British Ambassador on 28 February 1960. This behavior reflects Middle Eastern cultural practices. Visits, especially by a dignitary are reciprocated as an indication of respect for the person making the initial visit. However, during this visit, General Barzani complained about the Zibari Kurds, his traditional tribal rivals.[72] A conclusion that can be drawn from this inconsistent behavior is that the Kurdish struggle, by virtue of its domination by tribal leadership, is not only contradictory, but also a radical departure from the theoretical expectations of national liberation struggles.

In spite of his weaknesses, Barzani emerged from the Kurdish insurgent struggles as the symbol of the Kurdish resistance and as the leader of their liberation struggle. The 1962 liberation struggles proved advantageous for the Kurdish people because of the Peshmergas' dedication to the cause (Barzani's rebels) and to a greater degree, the contradictions permeating Gasem regime.[73]

Gasem's regime was war-torn, economically devastated, and the high level of unemployment induced discontent. These factors led to the destruction of Gasem's regime, toppled on 8 February 1963, during which General Gasem was executed.

Following Gasem's execution, the Kurds negotiated with the Iraqi regime that emerged from the coup. On 10 February 1963, the KDP formally recognized the coup. The party made political demands on the coup leaders, such as an official declaration of autonomy, initiation of a cease-fire, compensation for those who had been injured in a war, punishment and removal of authorities responsible for torture of the Kurdish people, and the release of war prisoners.[74] The party failed to understand the nature of the status quo-oriented new administrative forces. The KDP did not learn from the tragic struggles and repeated deceptions perpetrated by Iraqi leaders. The party cared very little about a bloody Communist witch hunt and opted to remain idle. The ICP members were arrested and many of them were executed without a trial.

Kutschera maintains that the coup was responsible for the death of one thousand Communists. During the course of the Communist witchhunt, a military curfew controlled the poor residential areas so that mobilization in favor of the opposition would be curtailed. According to Kutschera, the number of prisoners was so high that in the ministry of oil, all but two employees had been arrested. Not realizing that the Kurds may be the next victims, General Barzani declared a cease-fire and conveniently watched the slaughter of the progressive democratic forces. He did not take any action, hoping that the coup leaders would treat his forces differently, respecting Kurdish autonomy. Another miscalculation! This decision led to the elimination of seven thousand ICP members and the creation of a mass grave for 280 massacred civilians.[75]

The constructive aspect of KDP policy was to dispatch Jalal Talabani to Cairo, Egypt to meet with Jamal Abdul Nasser, who had semi-officially recognized the validity of the Kurdish struggle for autonomy. Contrary to the desires of Iraqi leaders, Nasser supported the Kurdish movement, compelling the Ba'ath leadership on 9 March 1963, to recognize Kurdish rights on the basis of "decentralization" instead of "autonomy." However, the concept of decentralization was not acceptable to KDP intellectuals who devised a counter plan in late April, prioritizing Kurdish rights. The KDP wanted the oil fields of Kirkuk, Khanigain, and the northwest to be included within the autonomous area, and the Kurds would receive a proportional share in oil revenues.[76]

General Barzani did not like the KDP's position on the negotiated issues, or Jalal Talabani, who was the dynamic brain of the party. In fact, Mr. Barzani saw Talabani's policies as a threat, for they tended to undermine General Barzani's own position. Barzani openly criticized Mr. Talabani during the most difficult and critical time of the Kurdish struggle. According to McDowall, if the Kurds had been united, they might have achieved a better arrangement. The divisiveness was critical in inviting governmental forces to capture Barzan and then advance further north.

The war actually started on 10 June 1963, during which hundreds of people were massacred in Sulaymania. This assault intended to crush the Kurdish movement militarily, an Iraqi mistake to provide a military solution to a political problem, and to actualize Arabization as a solution. These objectives were erroneous, antagonistic, and further promoted politicization and radicalization, rather than provide a solution. This was a consequence of the coup-born government's search for a hasty solution. Nonetheless, the Baathists pursued the policy objectives aggressively.

The coup-born government was overthrown in November 1963. The new strong man was General Aref, who had been in touch with General Barzani prior to the coup. He repeated the same deceptive promises uttered by the previous leaders to Barzani. Barzani responded to the decpetion by declaring a cease-fire without notifying the KDP leaders. General Barzani's poor judgment was bitterly criticized by Ibrahim Ahmad and Talabani. The agreement was negotiated unilaterally, and excluded the notion of self-administration, let alone autonomy, which constituted the heart of the Kurdish struggle. Worse yet, the Barzani/Aref agreement undermined the basic tenets of the Kurdish struggle. Aref had promised to punish Barzani's opponents, and Barzani, in turn, had declared that an attack by the Kurdish insurgent forces against Aref's government would be seen as an attack on him. Barzani also noted that if abolition of the KDP would serve the interests of the Iraqi government, he would support it.[77]

It is at this time that a rupture developed between the KDP intellectuals and Barzani's traditional base. While the KDP pledged to follow the ideological imperatives of national liberation struggles, Barzani's forces relied on the conservative, religious, and tribal forces. This divisive mode of thought continued to the tragic end of the Kurdish movement in 1975. The Ahmad-Talabani faction was committed to the cause of liberation, at least in the form of political autonomy; the Barzani alliance clearly chose the perpetuation of the status quo in the interest of the Aghas, tribal leaders, and religious forces.

The KDP also suffered from inconsistencies in pursuit of its political objectives. Because of the absence of political consciousness, the party glorified General Barzani, whose base was more solid in terms of mass mobilization, due to support from the Aghas, tribes and religious strata. In reality, the party fully relied on Barzani to pursue the realization of Kurdish freedom. According to McDowall, the KDP had elevated Barzani to the level of an heroic leader symbolizing the Kurdish uprising. Although the Ahmad-Talabani faction was the intellectual backbone of the KDP, they did not choose to implement a different, but empirically valid approach to achieve Kurdish freedom. The KDP leaders, by surrendering to Barzani, strengthened his position. In McDowall's words "the cause had miscarried," especially when General Barzani arrested the Ahmad-Talabani delegates to Barzani's Sixth Congress held at Gala Diza in July 1964. Ibrahim Ahmad-Talabani and four thousand men were forced into Iran where they remained in exile until 1965. This led to the marginalization of the KDP intellectuals and domination of the party by parochialism and personal-based leadership.[78] The party lost its intellectual base and critical autonomous thinking was suppressed and replaced with authoritarianism. This shortsightedness of Barzani hindered not only Barzani, but also the Kurdish people. In reality, the honeymoon was short lived, since Aref's new provisional constitution did not include what the General expected.

Hostilities began again in April 1965, though scattered clashes had been taking place throughout 1964. Many Kurds participated in this struggle. What is surprising with regard to the KDP leader's contradictory position, is that the Ahmad-Talabani forces, after living almost one year in Iran, came back and supported the Kurdish national struggle. During this struggle, the Kurds were encouraged when the newly appointed civilian prime minister, Bazzaz, recognized the Kurdish political demand. Supporting General Barzani in his struggle to succeed, as the Ahmad-Talabani group did, and simultaneously waging a war with Barzani demonstrates the Kurdish movement's tragic internal divisiveness and rivalries.

As mentioned, in April 1965, the Ahmad-Talabani forces assisted General Barzani in the Iraqi assault on Kurdistan, and in January 1966, they joined the enemy, the Baghdad government. They organized with the help of government militias groups consisting of approximately twenty thousand men.[79] They were popularly called the "1966 Jashes" because they joined the pro-government Jash Kurds to fight General Barzani's forces. These "1966 Jashes" were the counter weight to Barzani until 1970. The Ahmad-Talabani group justified this defection on the grounds that Barzani's movement was of a tribal nature representing the Agha and landlord classes. For Ahmad and Talabani autonomy could only be realized with the defeat of these classes. A contradictory position demands a justification in contradictory terms. Ahmad and Talabani failed to comprehend how autonomy could be realized within a dictatorship that had inflicted repeated assaults on Kurds. How could autonomy be granted from the Iraqi government when it had denied autonomy to General Barzani? Why should one believe that autonomy would be granted to the Ahmad-Talabani group? General Barzani felt that the Ahmad-Talabani group was a new breed of mercenaries. They were agents for any one who pays,[80] forgetting conveniently that he, too, did exactly the same with Gasem and Aref. It is reprehensible that Barzani sought support from the Shah of Iran, and then in return would halt any support to the movement of the Irani Kurds. General Barzani arranged the murder of two members of the revolutionary council, S. Moini and K. Chowbach, who wanted to organize a guerilla front in Iran from bases in Iraq.[81]

The armed struggle continued until 15 June 1966, resulting in Barzani's victory. By retaining Hendrin Mountain, the Kurds were able to control the Hamilton road that was the lifeline of supply to the Barzani forces from Iran. The Iraqi debacle at the Hendrin battle led to the resumption of negotiations on 29 June 1996. A cease-fire agreement was reached and Prime Minister Bazzaz, as mentioned earlier, officially recognized Kurdish national rights and Kurdish was recognized as an official language. The Bazzaz agreement consisted of twelve articles. The most important of the articles were: Parliamentary Electoral Democracy, General Amnesty, Kurdish as an Official Language, and Maintenance of the Peshmergas until the Normalization of the Situation. Unfortunately, this did not secure lasting peace. In fact, as Kutschera argues, the Kurds had won the war, but lost the peace.[82]

The Baathist, with the support of the army, launched a successful coup in July 1968. To consolidate their position, they promised to carry out Bazzaz's declaration. Toward this end, the Baathist government nominated a number of Kurds to the cabinet. Talabani remarked about the new government: " . . . the first ruling Arab political party . . . to extend its hand to the Kurdish people directly, sincerely and hopefully," glorifying it naively as the first to "recognize the national rights of the Kurdish people."[83] Wasn't Talabani aware that he and his groups were being used as a means to have Kurds kill Kurds? It was clear from the outset that Baathists were buying time to consolidate their power base. At this point, General Barzani, with the Baath leaders in power, had completely forgotten the concept of autonomy. Barzani's priority was to assault the Ahmad-Talabani forces, the so-called "Jash 66" (meaning donkey foals). They came predominantly from tribes who were hostile to Barzani. For General Barzani, the precondition for negotiation with the Baath's regime was to stop all support for the Jash 66 group. Hence, Barzani's peshmargas clashed with the Jash 66 forces and prevailed. Yet, for the purpose of weakening General Barzani's position in the north, the Iraqi government not only encouraged the KDP dissident group, Jalal Talabani and Ibrahim Ahmad, but pressured them to attack Barzani's forces.

Although the Baathis promised to carry out the Bazzaz's declaration and appoint two Kurds loyal to General Barzani as government ministers, General Barzani ordered an attack on Kirkuk's oil installations in March 1969. Baghdad retaliated by sending four divisions to Kurdistan. The army carried out a number of operations against civilians.[84] On 19 August 1969, the Iraqi army in Dakan suffocated sixty-seven women and children who had taken refuge in a cave. In September 1969, the army surrounded the village of Serija in Zakho and then completely destroyed it.

The Iraqi government was fully aware of the escalating cost of the war. This concern was aggravated when the Iraqi government discovered that Barzani was supported by both the CIA and the Iranian government.[85] Again, Barzani's struggle is subject to question. In a sense, this revelation about Barzani-CIA cooperation supports the conspiracy theory claiming that Barzani was the agent of the oil corporations, and, at this period of time, the tool of the CIA. In order to protect their corporate interests and undermine the Soviet influence in the Middle East, the imperial forces would do all they could to destabilize Iraq and weaken it militarily. This policy still continues to dominate the agenda of imperial powers. The Iraqi government was fully aware of the political meaning of the conspiracy theory. Therefore, the government of Iraq chose to negotiate, although there was some opposition from within the military. Nonetheless, Saddam Hussein, then Vice President of Al-bakr, negotiated an accord with Barzani in Kurdistan on 11 March 1970. This agreement led to the adoption of the following fifteen articles:

1. The Kurdish language shall be, along with the Arabic language, the official language in areas with a Kurdish majority, and will be the language of instruction in those areas and taught throughout Iraq as a second language.
2. Kurds will participate fully in government, including senior and sensitive posts in the cabinet and the army.
3. Kurdish education and culture will be reinforced.
4. All officials in Kurdish majority areas shall be Kurds or at least Kurdish speaking.
5. Kurds shall be free to establish student, youth, women's and teacher's organizations of their own.
6. Funds will be set aside for the development of Kurdistan.
7. Pensions and assistance will be provided for the families of martyrs and others stricken by poverty, unemployment or homelessness.
8. Kurds and Arabs will be transferred to their former place of habitation.
9. The Agrarian reform will be implemented.
10. The constitution will be amended to read "The Iraqi people is made up of two nationalities, the Arab nationality and the Kurdish nationality.
11. The broadcasting station and heavy weapons will be returned to the government.
12. A Kurd shall be one of the Vice Presidents.
13. The Governorates (provincial) law shall be amended in a manner conforming with the substance of this declaration.

14. Unification of areas with a Kurdish majority as a self-governing unit.
15. The Kurdish people shall share in the legislative power in a manner proportionate to its population in Iraq.[86]

Following this accord, the Iraqi leaders honored what they had guaranteed. They released political prisoners and declared amnesty for all Kurds. Saddam created a committee composed of four Kurds and four Arabs. It was charged with the implementation of the 11 March 1970 manifesto that was to be completed within years. However, five Kurds were appointed as cabinet members, and three Kurds became Governor General of Erbil, Dohuk, and Sulaymaniya. The KDP was legalized and the Iraqi supported Jash 66 group was dismantled, and the government allocated sixty million dollars to the reconstruction of the north, which started immediately. In addition, the government started the implementation of the 1959 Agrarian Reform Law, amended the constitution to include the statement that "the Iraqi people is made up of the Arab and the Kurdish nationalities," and financed six thousand peshmargas to serve as a border guard. These steps taken by the Iraqi government indicated that Iraq intended to implement at least some of the basics of the 11 March 1970 agreement.

Nonetheless, contentions surfaced between the KDP and Iraq involving the Kirkuk region. The Kurdish leadership wanted the region to be autonomous Kurdish areas, which Iraq objected to. In reference to article 15 of the agreement, Iraq wanted to postpone the census for dispatched regions originally planned for December 1970 to Spring 1971, although they intended to apply the 1957 census to Kirkuk.[87] This was not acceptable to General Barzani. Another problem was the governmental refusal of Habib Karim, the KDP nominee for the vice-presidency of the republic. The Iraqi government rejected Mr. Karim's nomination on the grounds that he was not an Iraqi Kurd, but an Iranian. The government wanted either General Barzani, or his son, Idris Barzani, nominated for the vice-president's position. The situation further intensified on 29 September 1971 by an assassination attempt on General Barzani.[88] This served as a triggering factor in derailing the 11 March 1970 agreement. The relevance of this fact is ambiguous since assassination attempts are normal political factors, even within the most politically stable countries. General Barzani blamed the assassination attempt on the Iraqi government, ignoring the fact that neither the Shah of Iran, Israel, Turkey, nor the United States, wanted peaceful relations between Barzani and the Iraqi government. The possibility can not be excluded that these countries were involved in an attempt to promote or perpetuate the hostilities. The contending issues could have been easily and diplomatically re-negotiated. However, the General demanded more concessions in addition to the 11 March 1970 agreement and sought aid from the United States and Israelis.

The conclusion of an Iraqi-Soviet treaty in April 1972 created the perception of a regional threat for the externally supported reactionary puppet regimes in the Middle East. They, along with the United States, saw the Soviet Union as a major threat to its regional imperial interests. The Shah of Iran, who had been disappointed by the March 1970 accord and intimidated by the Soviet treaty, immediately resumed generous military and economic support to the Barzani forces. The Iranian government always looked at the Kurds as a "card to be played."[89] General Barzani's forces were used as a tool of policy to weaken the Iraqi government.

The nationalization of oil by the Iraqi government in June 1972, which enhanced Iraq's economic revenues, heightened concern in the United States. The United States, sharing the Shah's concerns, was determined to pursue the destabilization policy in Iraq hoping that if the Baath regime was toppled, the new government would allow the United States access to Iraqi oil fields. Again, General Barzani repeated his political ignorance by relying on the United States, the same tragic mistake he made when in the past he depended on the British. Once again he failed, either due to the lack of political knowledge or an inability to learn from past miscalculations. Barzani failed to realize that the Kurdish national liberation struggle would not be won by support from external forces. Barzani's blind faith and pathological attachment to the United States masked the possibility that the CIA used Barzani forces as an instrument for weakening a pro-Soviet regime in Baghdad. The CIA had little concern for Kurdish autonomy. Support for this claim is reflected in the following memo of the CIA, dated 22 March 1974, quoted in the Pike Report presented in the United States House of Representatives:

> . . . Both Iran and the U.S. hope to benefit from an unresolvable situation in which Iraq is intrinsically weakened by the Kurds' refusal to give up their semi-autonomy. Neither Iran, nor the United States would like to see the situation resolved in one way or another.[90]

According to Kissinger, this policy was "merely an instrument to dissuade Iraq from any international adventurism."[91] Barzani accepted the United States and Iranian advise to take to the mountains. The CIA paid Barzani sixteen million dollars and the Shah supplied him generously with weapons and money. Barzani also received indirect aid from Israel. During the 1967 Arab-Israeli war, he was paid a stipend of fifty thousand dollars to undermine the united frontal capability of the Iraqi army on the Israeli front.[92] During the 1973 Arab-Israeli conflict Barzani declared a symbolic solidarity with Baghdad, even though he was seriously considering an attack on the Iraqi army. To confirm that his decision was in accord with American policy, he discussed his plan with Kissinger and was advised to abandon his plan for an attack. In

June 1973, General Barzani held a brutally revealing interview with the *Washington Post*. Barzani said:

> We are ready to act according to the U.S. policy if the U.S. will protect us from the wolves. In the event of the sufficient support we should be able to control the Kirkuk oil fields and confer exploitation rights on an American company.[93]

This statement by General Barzani is clear evidence of the instrumentality of the Kurdish struggle. The General insinuated that he was ready to fight if he was so ordered by the United States, despite any negotiated agreement with Baghdad. In reality the Iran, Israel, and the United States alliance, all three potential enemies of Iraq, had already pulled the trigger. The movement's subordination to an external power undermines any hope for liberation. It alienates nationalists and progressive forces that constitute the heart of the national liberation struggle. This was the case with the KDP leaders who attributed the movement's failure to Barzani's dictatorial and pro-tribal attitude. In early 1974, several KDP central committee members defected from the movement and accused General Barzani of rejecting democratic practices and kidnapping and executing a number of Kurdish leaders. He was also accused of exercising "an excessive personality cult."[94]

Barzani's blind and pathological attachment to foreign aid compromised the movement's stated objectives. General Barzani aggravated Kurdish problems. It would be a mistake to ignore the fundamental errors committed by the Kurdish leadership. The Kurdish liberation movement was a movement by the CIA, for the CIA, and of the CIA. The tribal mode of thinking converted the Kurdish national liberation struggle into a Jash-CIA sponsored movement whose objective was to promote the foreign oil agenda. Thus, the Kurdish leadership inflicted as much devastation on the Kurdish people as did on its enemies. The Kurdish struggle deviated from the theoretical and practical tenets of national liberation struggles.

Having exhausted their options, the Iraqi government attempted to declare a unilateral autonomy with or without[95] the Iraqi KDP, and to bring the dissenting Kurds to the fold of government sympathy. The unilaterally declared autonomy law in 1974 by the Iraqi government was not acceptable to Barzani. Why didn't General Barzani accept the 1974 autonomy law? According to Kurdish observers, there were two reasons. First of all, the law did not include Kirkuk, although Sulaymania, Erbil (the Kurdish regional capital), and Dohuk were incorporated into the autonomous area with Erbil. Second and most importantly, the CIA, Israel, and the Shah of Iran did not want Barzani to accept the terms of the autonomy law.[96] Baghdad desperately needed this rejection. It forced the government of Iraq to launch a massive offense against the Kurds.

It must be noted that it was not that Barzani disliked the achievements of the Kurdish struggle, but he was obliged to act in accordance with the wishes of the Shah, Jashism, and the CIA. General Barzani's oldest son, Ubayad Allah, had the following to say in response to this claim:

> [Barazni] does not want self-rule to be implemented even if he was given Kirkuk and all of its oil. His acceptance of the [autonomy] law will take everything from him, and he wants to remain the absolute ruler.[97]

This remarkable assertion proves the contradictory nature of the Kurdish movement. General Barzani said later, ". . . were it not for the American promises, we would never have become trapped and involved to such an extent."[98] Unfortunately, by virtue of his deeply seated internalized tribal values, the General never realized that the CIA, Israel, and Shah were another triangle of Jashism primarily concerned with their own socio-political and security interests. In McDowall's words, Barzani remained "an innocent abroad."[99] He failed to discern that this imperial bound triangle did not have any desire for the creation and implementation of Kurdish autonomy.

The general also never departed from his role as an instrument in imperialistic strategies. He pointed out that his forces were critical in the military and political equation of the Middle East, and asked that the West advise him in what role he had to play. It is ironic that the General promised the West that "he would prevent the Kurds in Iran and Turkey from agitating for independence."[100] This was a pledge to demobilize Kurdish forces. The General instilled a cohesive and intense nationalism in Iraq, where he decisively alienated the progressive forces from the Kurdish struggle. In Iraq, the forces of nationalism directly targeted the Kurdish leadership as the agent of imperialism. It was how the war of 1974–75 started, and this war proved to be a disaster to the Kurdish people. The Kurdish movement was thus defeated by its own leadership. The crucial contradiction of the Kurdish movement was that while the Kurds, as an oppressed people, were struggling to realize their liberation, the leadership relied on imperialist support, and the Iraqi government, as an oppressor, enjoyed the overwhelming support of progressive forces, including socialist countries.

Another devastating contradiction lies in the reactionary nature of the General's movement. The Kurdish leadership betrayed its own liberation cause. To receive weapons and support from the Shah of Iran, the Kurdish forces did not hesitate to deliver to the Shah the Iranian Kurds who opposed him and had sought refuge in the Iraqi-Kurdistan. The movement from its beginning to its tragic end was used by imperialist powers and their agents as a political instrument toward their hegemonic ends. Neither the United States, the Shah of Iran, nor Israel were interested in Kurdish autonomy. All three desired a weakened and internally destabilized Iraq. Additionally, the Shah of Iran wanted a redefinition of its contested border with Iraq, hoping that the Kurdish struggle would weaken the Iraqi Baath regime. The objectives of these reactionary forces were achieved at the cost of Kurdish blood.

President Boumedinne of Algeria, backed by Anwaral-Sadat of Egypt and King Hussein of Jordan, supported the adoption of a resolution on the Iran-Iraqi border, known as the Algiers Treaty. On 6 March 1975, at the OPEC conference in Algiers, Saddam Hussein and the Shah of Iran signed the treaty. Iraq agreed to recognize the Thalweg line of Shatt al-Arab as a defined boundary between the two countries, a demand that occupied the political agenda of the Iranian government in its conflict with Iraq. In exchange, the Shah agreed to discontinue aid to the Kurds.[101]

The Kurdish struggle was a winning card for the Shah of Iran. Immediately after the agreement, the Iranian forces were pulled out of Kurdistan, halting supplies to Barzani. However, at the Shah's request, Baghdad declared a cease-fire as an opportunity for Barzani's forces to surrender or seek refuge in Iran. Thus, blind optimism and faith in imperial powers coupled with the leadership's shortsightedness brought the Kurdish liberation struggle to an end. Barzani, the ironed-will Kurdish hero, either consciously or unconsciously, utilized a tactical guerrilla approach that benefited imperialism and its regional agents. This strategy did not liberate the Kurdish people as intended. It proved that the national liberation struggle could not be won by reliance on imperial powers. Although General Barzani died in 1979, the Kurdish struggle continued to live, in spite of conspiracy-based treason. As General Barzani himself stated, "my personal role is finished . . . but putting an end to the Kurdish life is impossible . . . other leaders from within the Kurdish people will rise and continue the struggle."[102] Barzani was correct on this claim. On 1 June 1975, Talabani formed the Patriotic Union of Kurdistan (PUK) in Damascus, Syria. It included two other groups; the Komala with a Marxist-Leninist orientation and the socialist party of Kurdistan, which joined together to organize a new party. This newly formed party (PUK) led by Talabani issued a statement attributing the collapse of the Kurdish struggle to "the inability of the feudalist, tribalist, bourgeois rightist, and capitulationist Kurdish leadership."[103] The PUK committed itself to the acquisition of autonomy for the Kurds and democracy for Iraq, and asked all progressive forces to join the PUK in an attempt to overthrow the Iraqi regime. Thus, in 1976, the PUK initiated its operations in Kurdistan. Idris and Masud, sons of the late General Barzani, attempted to organize the KDP-Provisional Leadership (KDP-PL) Party.

Unfortunately, the Kurdish political movement involved conflict between the Kurdish leaders. The leadership failed to achieve a united liberation front against its enemies. In the aftermath of Barzani's departure, the conflict became internal. The PUK Peshmargas fought with KDP-PL forces, and the new opposition leaders, in spite of their sharp criticism of the late General Barzani's tactics, imitated his divisive approach to the Kurdish liberation struggle. Based on McDowall's analysis, Talabani, writes to his headquarters saying,"Iraq, Iran, and the KDP-PL are all enemies for us."[104] Talabani further subjects the PUK-peshmergas commander, Ali Askari, to sharp criticism for his failure to crash the KDP-PL forces. Contrary to his written communication, it was revealed that Jalal Talabani was holding secret negotiations with the Shah's Secret Police. According to McDowall, the irony is that the Shah's secret police wanted the two new Kurdish parties, the PUK and the KDP-PL, to unite as an effective front against the Iraqi government. Yet, the PUK leadership promised cooperation with the Shah's secret police only if SAVAK abandoned its support for Idris Barzani and the KDP-PL forces. This was the same group who had ambushed PUK Peshnargas on two separate occasions: July 1976 and January 1977.[105]

Further factionalization took place within the Kurdish political movement. In November 1979, the KDP-PL, at the ninth congress in Iran, stated its intentions to switch from the KDP-PL to the KDP. This party did not abandon its traditionalism, and retained the previous orientation and ideology. In order to obtain support from the Iranian revolutionary leadership and strengthen its forces against the Talabani-PUK faction, the KDP-Idris Barzani group sided with Tehran, attacking the KDP-Iran. Seeking autonomy from the emerging revolutionary Iran, the KDP-Idris Barzani group played a key role in defeating the Kurdish insurgency in Iran, despite PUK support for the Iranian KDP. The truth of the matter is that in 1981, at the peak of the Iran-Iraqi war, Talabani supported the Iranian KDP leader, Ghassemlou, not because of Ghassemlou's political conviction, but to off-set Iranian support given to the Idris-Masud Barzani led KDP-Iraq. Ghassemlou, in spite of his intellectualism and a modern, westernized education and doctorate degree from Czechoslovakia, depended on the Iraqi government to launch guerrilla attacks against the Iranian revolutionary government.

Kurdish leaders who have conveniently ignored the political meaning of dependency have perpetuated the captivity of their people. The KDP and the PUK distrusted one another. According to Chaliand, Idris led KDP-Iraq felt that PUK's leadership was negotiating with Iraq to gain superiority over the KDP-Iraq from the very beginning of the PUK's formation. Instead of uniting against their common enemy, the party peshmergas in 1978 violently attacked one another in the Badinan area. Many Kurdish activists, including Ali Askari, were killed. This was another example of Kurds killing Kurds.[106] The Kurdish organizations are ineffective due to their internal divisions and subordination to foreign powers. It was the Communists who maintained their commitment to the Kurdish struggle, but were ignored by the Kurdish leaders. Kurdish leaders preferred to accommodate the aggressive imperial forces.

The Kurdish leaders continue to rival one another and remain disunited. They frequently lend support to regional or external forces to defend their own stated purpose. In April 1983, the KDP, ICP, and KSP (Kurdish Socialist Party), attacked the PUK in Erbil. The PUK launched a counter-attack in May of the same year and inflicted serious damage; fifty Communists were killed and seventy were captured.[107] In December, following this attack, the PUK and Baghdad concluded a cease fire agreement designed to create a united national government. This PUK-Iraqi alliance also included the ICP, who had been attacked in May of 1983. Surprisingly, from December 1983 to October 1984, the PUK supported the Iraqi government's war against Iran.

The Iraqi-KDP lost its legitimacy because of its alliance with the Iranian government. The Iranian government had clashed with the Baghdad assisted KDP-Iran. The PUK lost its support due to the party's arbitrary cooperation with the anti-Kurdish liberation Iraqi government. In additions to these problems, three thousand Talabani supporters defected to the Idris-Barzani led KDP. The Talabani led PUK lost Syrian and Libyan support because of its alliance with Iraq. Talabani was criticized for the betraying of the Kurdish struggle. An isolated Talabani sought reconciliation with Iran and the Idris-KDP, which culminated in the 1986 agreement among the competing factions: the KDP, PUK, and the ICP. A joint statement called for a united front against the Iraqi government. By 1986, the KDP led by Barzani and the PUK led by Talabani, received financial and military support from the Iranian government against the Baathi's regime in Iraq.[108]

In November 1986, the PUK and the KDP-Iraq agreed to an accord with the Iranian government in Tehran. This agreement was strengthened after the perpetration of violent assaults on five thousand civilian Kurds in March of 1988. This event mobilized a Kurdish front apart from the PUK and KDP-Iraq. The formation included the socialist party of Kurdistan, the ICP-Kurdish branch, and the popular democratic party of Kurdistan. The front inflicted heavy casualties on the Iraqi forces.

In August 1988, a cease-fire agreement between Iran and Iraq frustrated Kurdish aspirations for liberation. The agreement abruptly ended Iranian support and freed the Iraqi army front. Supported by the Kurdish Jash group, the Iraqis responded by launching a full attack against Kurdish forces, which resulted in the destruction of 478 villages, the gassing of seventy-seven other villages, and the displacement of 100,000 Kurds. The West, the so-called champions of human rights, supplied Saddam Hussein with chemical weapons. The United

States sold "sensitive equipment" to Iraq hoping to defeat the Iranian revolution. The success of the Iranian revolution would have threatened the interests of imperialistic forces in the region. Unfortunately, neither the Iraqi leadership nor the Kurdish forces understood (or ignored) the imperialistic intent.[109]

Saddam Hussein's miscalculation led to an invasion of Kuwait in January 1991. Huessin's forces were defeated by the American-led coalition. This in turn led to the re-assertion of Kurdish insurgency. This time, the Jash group supported the Kurdish insurgency and launched an effective assault on major cities. The Kurds captured Kirkuk on 19 March 1991. The United States after "Operation Desert Storm," sought to mobilize the Kurdish opposition and the Shai,i Muslims, for the purpose of eliminating Saddam Hussein. But concerned with the disintegration of Iraq, Washington supported a non-interference policy regarding Iraqi's internal affairs, and promised Turkey and the Saudis that it would not support the Shai,i Muslims or the Kurds. This plegde encouraged a counter offensive intended to expel the Kurdish rebels from occupied territories, especially in Kirkuk.

The result of this assault on the Kurds created a massive influx of refugees. The United States once again left the Kurds to their fate. Barzani's successor did not learn from the Kurd's bitter experience and the imperialistic political design. In 1994, the KDP and PUK forces resumed the violent and bitter rivalry. This clash left five hundred Kurds dead and thousands displaced. The rivalry conflict was so intense that the KDP and PUK sought meditation from the Iraqi government, which they had fought against for years.[110] Fighting with the Iraqi government and seeking mediation solutions from the same government defies the logic of national liberation struggles. Thus, the contradictory nature of the Kurdish struggle prevents the realization of Kurdish autonomy.

C. THE KURDISH STRUGGLE IN TURKEY: ABD ALLAH OCALAN

The Kurdish political tragedy in Turkey differs considerably from Iran and Iraq's treatment of the Kurds. In Iraq, the internal factionalism and external interventionism served as critical factors in shaping and defeating the Kurdish movement. According to Ismail Besikci, the Kurdish struggles in Iran, Iraq, and Turkey were defeated by imperialism.[111] When questioned in 1973 about the liberation of Kurdistan resulting from the autonomy granted by Iraq, Barzani expressed his displeasure, "It is not us who decide, our decisions are made for us . . . ."[112] This statement supports Besikci's thesis, but ignores the intertribal rivalry and divisive factionalism that prevents the Kurdish liberation.

As mentioned in the previous section on Iraq, the Kurdish movement in Iraq was organized and led by external forces. However, Besikci fails to explain why the Kurdish leaders in Turkey did not learn from Iran and Iraq's tragic experience. The question remains unanswered: Why did the Republic of Mahabad collapse without the firing of a single shot? Besikci's analysis is reductionistic since it blames the perpetuation of Kurdish problems on external forces, in spite of the validity of imperialism as a critical variable hindering the realization of Kurdish aspirations. These oversights limit Besikci's analysis. Imperial and colonizing forces have always prioritized their own interest. Divide and rule policies and human rights activities, such as the quest for liberty and democratic values is commonly used to promote opposition forces. Once puppet regimes are created and socio-economic and political domination are achieved, justice, human rights, and democratic aspirations are conveniently abandoned. Human rights are used as foreign policy tools. The Kurdish leadership has generally allied with the aggressive forces, failing to identify the dynamics of the world system that create hopelessness, discrimination, and destruction of humanity in the form of wars, coups, and regional and racial conflicts. Besikci has ignored this manifestation of false consciousness, which has victimized the Kurdish people more severely than imperialism and its local/regional agents. The Kurds kill each other more systematically than do their oppressors. Tribal culture promotes false consciousness that, in turn, allows jealousy, tribal rivalry, and hatred to dominate the Kurdish political struggles. Feudal and tribal ideologies have paralyzed Kurdish national liberation struggles. It is the politically consciousness united front that forms the heart and soul of the national liberation movements.

An examination of the important Kurdish revolts in Turkey is imperative to understanding the Turkish historical setting. In February of 1925, one of the most important revolts was led by a religious leader, Shaikh Said of the Nagshbandi brotherhood. The religiosity of his movement was instrumental in the mobilization of the tribal forces. He was in favor of the Sharia-based government (Quranic law), and intended to defend Islam against the secular government of Ataturk. The abolition of the caliphate in March of 1924 provided the impetus for this uprising. Hoping to restore the caliphate, those who joined the Shaikh's uprising were defending Islamic values against the Turkish leadership's "irreligious policy measures."[113]

Kurdish observers identify the Shaikh's revolt as nationalistic. But in reality it was rooted in a religious nationalism. McDowall noted that Shaikh Said failed to promote the Kurdish cause among the Khurmak and Lawlan tribes, although he had a degree of success with the Zaza-speaking tribe and other tribal chiefs. The warring factions could not be persuaded to abandon their hostilities and participate in Shaikh Said's uprising. The movement also failed to attract strong urban support. The Kurds of Diyarbakir declined involvement in the revolt. In other Kurdish cities, such as Elazig, the Kurds attacked the Shaikh's rebels, who captured the city and resorted to ". . . excessive looting and pillage."[114] Notwithstanding Shaikh Said's strong religious belief and a fierce nationalism, his strategy of alienation, instead of mobilization, was instrumental in the defeat of his own struggle. Ironically, looting and pillage have no place in the Islamic Sharia, and must be attributed to the demobilization and alienation of religiously minded Kurds.[115]

It is claimed that Shaikh Said's revolt was inspired by the British military advisor in Istanbul,[116] and the movement was defeated by the Turkish army. Shaikh Said managed to escape but was caught while crossing the Murad River north of Mush on 14 April 1925, betrayed by the Jibran tribal chief.[117] On 28 April 1925, Shaikh Said and forty-seven of his associates were tried for treason in a pretentious government trial, and on the morning of 29 June 1925 they were hung in Diyarbakir.[118]

Kurdish liberation struggles have been hindered by the Kurdish reliance on colonial powers and regional governments, and also hindered by the culture of rivalry and fragmentation. Zaza-speaking Kurds supported the revolt because of Shaikh Said's religious influence. Others like Jibran Aghas, namely Qasem Beg, betrayed Shaikh Said because of tribal interest and convenience. The Alavi Kurd's support of the Turkish secular government stemmed from their conflict with the Jibran tribe, and as a reaction against the Sunni ideology of the movement, which was hostile to Shi,ism and afforded protection by the law of Ataturk's secular government. The creation of an autonomous or independent Kurdistan under the leadership of the Sunni Shaikhs was an advantage for the Alavi Kurds.[119]

The lack of tactical and strategical planning was another disadvantage. It is impossible for tribal armies to fight against an experienced, sophisticated, and modern army equipped with communication networks and rapid military deployment machinery, a fact that Kurdish leadership has ignored. The particular motivating goal of the Shaikh Said's revolt was to restore the caliphate, jettisoning the nationalistic goal of securing Kurdish liberation.[120]

Shaikh Said's rebellion provoked the Turkish government to commit ruthless atrocities against he Kurdish people. Villages were burned and demolished, and the villagers massacred." People were denied access to food sources. Kurds not directly involved in the rebellion were slaughtered also, prompting populations to flee from Turkey. Kurdish religion was suppressed and their Tekiyes and pilgrimage sites were closed down. However, in spite of the state-sponsored terrorism against the Kurds, Turkish assimilation policies, and the forced deportation of the Kurds to the west of Anatolia, the Kurdish movement continued.[121]

The dissenting forces regrouped under the leadership of General Ihsan Nuri Pasha, previously an officer in the Ottoman army. This rebellion was supported by the Kurdish intellectuals living in exile in Syria and Lebanon. They organized a new party, the Khoyben party, led by Jaladat Badr kahn, to incorporate all previous parties, and created a planned, trained, and organized military power to discourage tribal uprisings. Although the intention was to organize a nationalistic liberation movement, Khoyben, from the outset, sought cooperation from tribesman and can be described as a traditionally motivated rebellion. The perception that Ihsan Nuri Pasha's movement was secularly nationalistic can be repudiated.[122] He joined forces with several tribes fighting the Turkish army in the Mount Ararat area where he worked closely with the Jalali chief, Ibrahim "Bro" Haski Talu. According to McDowall, Talu cooperated with the Turkish government in 1925 to defeat Shaikh Said's uprising. However, this act of treason did not insure Turkish protection for Talu, because the Turkish government had a general deportation policy launched against the Agha class. Talu escaped to Ararat in 1925 and was followed by Nuri in 1928.[123]

Entessar's argument that Nuri's revolt was nationalistic is erroneous. Quite the contrary, it fully coincided with tribal values and was not a politically independent revolt. American and Italian expertise trained Kurdish military forces. In a sense, Ehsan Nuri's Ararat movement relied on mercenary forces. Nuri relied on Reza Shah's support in Iran. Reza Shah, the king of Iran, in conflict with the Turkish government, used Nuri's revolt as a way to force Turkish concession to his territorial claim.

By the fall of 1929, Nuri's forces controlled an area stretching from Mount Ararat to the northern part of Bitlis and Van, and unable to contain the Kurdish revolt, the Turkish authorities decided to negotiate. By 23 January 1932, Turkey and Iran signed an accord that gave Turkey Iranian territories in the vicinity of Mount Ararat and in the Van area. Iran's Reza Shah discontinued support for the Kurds, which resulted in the defeat of the Kurdish rebellion in the summer of 1930.[124] Following this tragic defeat, some leaders of the rebellion fled, while others were captured and executed. According to Entessar, "In Van a hundred intellectuals were sewn into sacks and thrown into the lake."[125]

The violent barbarism inflicted on the Kurds continued to intensify. In the aftermath of the rebellion, Kurdish villages were bombed, Kurds were deported, and the Kurdish Shaikhs and Aghas were exiled. The Turkish government legally sanctioned these acts of savage repression against the Kurds. A law published officially in the *Turkish Journal* maintained that no one would be punished for crimes committed against the Kurdish people. Article I of Law no. 1,850 reads:

Murders and other actions committed individually or collectively, from the 20th of June 1930 to the 10th of December 1930, by representatives of the state or the province, by the military or civil authorities, by the local authorities, by guards or militiamen, or by any civilian having helped the above or acted on their behalf, during the pursuit and extermination of the revolts which broke out in Ercis, Zilan, Agridag (Ararat) and the surrounding areas, including Pulumur in Erzincan province and the area of the first Inspectorate, will not be considered as crimes.[126]

This law revealed the savage pacification of Kurdistan and the devastation of the Kurdish regions. The Turkish Prime Minister, Ismet Pasha, said: ". . . only the Turkish nation is entitled to claim ethnic and national rights in this country. No other element has any such right."[127] This declaration was echoed by Ismet Pasha's Justice Minister, Mahmud Esat Bozhurt: "We live in a country called Turkey, the freest country in the world . . . I believe that the Turks must be the only Lord, the only master of this country. Those who are not of pure Turkish stock can have only one right in this country, the right to be servants or slaves."[128] Both statements indicate the contradictory Turkish policy regarding the Kurds. First of all, the "freest" country on earth cannot be free if it suppresses its own people, since racism and freedom cannot coexist. A democratic system cannot be exclusionary, and the Turkish treatment of the Kurds has been exclusive, not inclusive. The Kurdish deprivation of their own culture, language, and tradition is incompatible with democratic norms. It reflects an apartheid system that victimizes minorities like Armenians, Kurds, and Shi,i Muslems. The Turkish government systematically failed to learn from the historical evidence. Forced assimilation is not a solution for national solidarity, and the continued repression of the Kurds cannot indefinitely secure Turkish unity. Turkey's "democratic" character is jeopardized by these exclusive policies.

The Kurdish leadership suffers from its own tribally defined ideology. Tribal values, lack of unity, and reliance on regional and external and international forces prevent the realization of the national liberation struggles. General Ehsan Nuri Pash was able to fight the Turkish modern army contingent on Iranian support. Based on the Turkish-Iranian Accord of 1932, as soon as the Turkish troops entered Iran, the Kurdish rebels were defeated. Kurdish tribalism has always threatened the achievement of political/class solidarity by the divisive nature of tribal political cultures. McDowall writes that "the lack of homogeneity of the Kurdish forces and the lack of coordinated action seriously weakened the Kurds' fighting capacity. While a substantial number were willing to rise against their Turkish oppressors, tribes could always be found to do the state's bidding, as had been true in the nineteenth century."[129] These tactics continue to dominate the Kurdish political liberation struggles in the twenty-first century.

The movement's asserted nationalism does not live up to its practical expectations. The Kurds of the Dersim area did not participate in General Nuri Pasha's struggle against the Turkish oppressors. The Kurdish reason that "this particularly mountainous and inaccessible region had, until then, kept out of all the revolts . . ."[130] But is this explanation feasible? Does it mean that the Dersim Kurds were immune from the Turkish government because of their location? If the autonomy of the Dersim Kurds was due to the formidable surrounding mountains, why were they the next victim?

The Kurdish left's explanation for the non-participation of the Dersim Kurds in General Nuri Pasha's revolt is inadequate. The Dersim Kurds did not consider General Nuri Pasha's movement as their Kurdish cause owing to their tribal ideology and tribal culture. In a sense, they were victims of false consciousness. The Turkish government, as a result of the law of accommodation formulated on 5 May 1932, initiated mass deportation and assimilation policies directed at the Kurds. This assimilation process was implemented by population displacement. Based on a confidential document prepared by one of the key Turkish politicians, Abdin Ottman, six principal steps were to be taken:

1. Turkey must always be aware of the danger the Kurds, with enemy support, pose to its being.
2. The Turkish farmers must be located in the East with a policy of gradual take-over of the Kurdish lands.
3. Turkey must limit the usage of the Kurdish language. Towards this end, the creation of schools and compulsory instruction of the Turkish language and prohibition of dialogue in the Kurdish language can eliminate this language (meaning Kurdish) in the east of Turkey.
4. In the long run, the creation of linking transportation system and population movement in the east is critical for altering the tribal nature of Kurds.
5. Concessions such as offering land and home for Turkish employees to stay in east Turkey must be carried out. This measure is to diversify the Kuridsh population altering their culture and language.
6. Dispatching reputable governmental employees to the east can accelerate the process of Turkification, culminating in the elimination of the Kurdish identity.[131]

This racist policy did not exclude the Kurds of Dersim. Dersim was to be evacuated because of its strategic importance. In 1936, the governmental policies of population movement and evacuation provoked the Dersim Kurd's resistance. While Dersim Kurds fought the Turkish army with guerrilla warfare, the Turkish army used poison gas, artillery, and air bombardment.

"People were shut up in caves . . . and burned alive by Turkish soldiers. Forests were encircled by troops and set alight to exterminate those who had sought refuge there. There were collective suicides; many Kurdish women and girls threw themselves into the Monzour River. Dersim was entirely devastated."[132]

The rebels refused to surrender and the Turkish government continued to terrorize Kurdish villages.

The rebellion was finally put down in October 1938, culminating in the destruction of Dersim. The political objective of the Turkish army was to eliminate the memory of the bloodshed in Dersim and destroy Kurdish identity. Dersim was placed under a state of siege until 1950. The concepts of "Kurd" and "Kurdistan" were abolished from the Turkish vocabulary, and the use of Kurdish words was prohibited. The Kurds were referred to as "Mountain Turks."[133] Dersim's Kurds paritcipated only when they were attacked. The Kurds failed to understand that the abuse of other Kurds who rebelled against the Turkish government before the Dersim event was a national issue, not confined to one group of one geographic area. It was not formidability and inaccessibility of Dersim that prevented the Dersim Kurds from participation in previous revolts, but the dominance of false consciousness and the lack of national solidarity. The Turkish left has underestimated the value of political awareness.

Following the fall of Dersim, no major upheavals occurred in Kurdistan until late 1950. However, the defeat of fascism and the emergence of the victorious Red Army made a fundamental difference. When the Soviet Union showed sympathy to the Kurdish cause by allowing General Barzani to seek asylum in the USSR, the Turkish authorities became suspicious. The Turkish government knew about the confidential British document regarding the racist Turkish policies. According to the British Ministry of Foreign Affairs in Lebanon, "It is impossible to silence the Kurds. The implementation of racist policies will perpetuate the crisis of the region. The Turkish government, like the Soviet Union, must recognize the rights of minorities and respect the Kurdish language, culture, and tradition."[134] The report maintains that the Turkish minorities, due to Turkish racist policies, will actively defend themselves and their cultural heritage." The foreign ministry argued that the Turks loved militarism and would not tolerate freedom and enlightenment.[135]

The Turks reacted bitterly to the criticism from the foreign ministry. Ismet Inonu, succeeding Ataturk in the late 1940s, decided to contain the external threat by enacting internal liberalization policies. Several parties originated in 1946, challenging the lengthy dominance of the Republican People's Party (RPP), the controlling Turkish party. By 1950, the democratic party gained control and retained its allegiance to realism. The party's democratization and liberalization programs benefited the Kurds, who had massively supported the democratic candidate. The party was now under the leadership of Adnan Menderes, a rich landowner and had served as a Prime Minister under Ataturk's leadership. Under Menderes's leadership, substantial structural reforms were initiated. . Police atrocities decreased, and many of the tribal leaders and Aghas, who had been exiled, returned to Kurdistan and repossessed their lands confiscated by the Turkish government. Roads and hospitals were improved, and the general features of the infrastructure were augmented. The party initiated integrative policies that sought to integrate Kurdish leaders with the government. Many of these leaders were elected to the Turkish National Assembly and some became ministers.[136] As McDowall noted, Islamic values were allowed to capture the heart of national identity. The call to prayer in Arabic was allowed, and the citation of the Islamic Holy book, the *Quran*, was permitted on radio broadcasts.

All these initiatives were good news for the Kurdish faithfuls, who had fought for their restoration after the caliphate, have been abolished. The party also directed efforts to develop the Kurdish east, referred to as *Doguculuk* (Eastism), an area that had been neglected by the previous administration. Simultaneously, the party introduced land reform in 1946, while also asserting itself as the guardian of private ownership. On the one hand, the party wanted to improve the conditions of the peasantry, and on the other hand, it recognized the interests of the landed class. The party did not want to disturb the fragile solidarity between the landlords, Aghas and Sheikas, and the peasants. When the democratic party promised to maintain the bond of solidarity, the peasantry, as instructed by their landlords, supported the reform.[137] The Kurdish people were more inclined to uphold their feudal and tribal connections, rather than support national solidarity.

The Eastists included several deputies and Kurdish activists. They were careful not to polarize their efforts through a reference to Kurds or Kurdistan.[138] There was no indication that the Eastists sought separation, autonomy, or independence; they desired to work within the present system. The main goal was to develop and modernize the eastern Turkish states where the Kurds lived, where socio-political and economic underdevelopment prevailed.

However, Eastism was short-lived. The government authorities, especially the military that had lost its political influence to some degree, were disturbed by the renewed Kurdish struggle in Iraq following General Barzani's return from exile in Moscow in the aftermath of the Iraqi Revolution of 1958. Suspicious of the Eastists, the government arrested approximately fifty in the group, violently dismantled a daily Turkish paper called *Ileri Yurt*, a Turkish word for "forward country," and arrested the publishers. The paper discussed the underdevelopment, lack of infrastructure, hospitals, schools, and other public facilities in the eastern Kurdish states. The Army was resentful of its marginal status and was looking for a scapegoat. On 27 May 1960, the military staged a coup d'etat. By June, the authorities had arrested and then detained 485 Kurdish notables for several months, and fifty-five of the most influential detainees (those who belonged to the democratic party) were exiled to western Turkey for two years.[139] The repressive assimilation and Turkification policies instituted in 1935, once again began. In the forward to M. Sherif Firat's book entitled *Dogu Illeri Ve Varto Taribi*, President Gursel argued that "the Kurds were in fact of Turkish origin, and that there was no such thing as the Kurdish nation."[140] This book was endorsed by Turkey's president, and was written by Mr. Firat, a Kurd, who openly denied his own Kurdish identity. Mr. Firat based his erroneous premise on false and misleading documentation.

In May 1961, in response to military policy of Turkification and denial of the Kurdish identity, major demonstrations occurred in Diyarbakir, Bitlis, and Van. The demonstrators carried banners claiming: "We are not Turks, we are Kurds . . . the Turkish government must recognize our national rights."[141] According to McDowall, the military acted with unremitting violence, leaving 315 Kurds dead and 754 demonstrators wounded. In spite of the atrocities committed by the military government in response to the Kurdish supplication, General Gursel favored a return to the civilian government. He authorized the formulation of a new constitution in 1961, which allowed freedom of expression, thought, association, and publication.[142]

This new liberalization trend encouraged the development of new political parties: the Justice Party (JP), the New Turkey Party (NTP), and the Turkish Workers Party (TWP), which was founded by 15 trade union leaders. In the 1961 elections, no political party won a majority vote, but the Justice Party was able to obtain a plurality. In the elections contested in Kurdistan, the New Turkey Party was the main rival of the Justice Party. Their rivalry and contest resulted in an even split. A coalition government was formed and the presidency was entrusted to the RPP's, Ismet Inonu, who had been replaced by the Democrats in the 1950 elections. Under the leadership of Ismet Inonu, Dr. Yusef Azizoglu, a Kurd, became Minister of Health in June 1962.[143] Azizoglu devoted himself to the development of the backward areas of eastern Kurdistan and built more hospitals and dispensaries in the Kurdish regions than any of the other previous governments had. He gained great popularity and fame in Kurdistan, and was soon accused of "regionalism" by the Turkish assembly, and was forced to resign.[144]

Some Kurdish observers believe that the externally mobilized leftist parties were a result of the relative political freedom permitted during the 1960s and

1970s. It must be noted that after over forty years of political development in the Middle East, no Middle Eastern country currently allows the formation of externally mobilized parties, which would reflect an inclusive strategy. Alternative political platforms are a critical component of democratization. The Turkish constitution of 1961 officially permitted the creation of a socialist party, which is still prohibited (2004) in the Middle East. Accordiang to Nazan Kendal, the Turkish Workers Party (TWP) was instrumental in raising political consciousness by promoting socialistic ideals and democratic values. Nonetheless, Nezan Kendal maintains that the development of political awareness was due to the political struggle of the Kurdish left within the TWP. This suggests that the party was inclusive, a critical political means whereby groups could legally pursue their goals. The party ideologically and dialectically negated Kemalism.

Kendal criticizes the Turkish Communist Party (TKP) because Kurdish national and political questions were never addressed during the fifty years of its existence, although the party claimed to support the right to a group's self determination and condemned the Turkish government's violent policies against the Kurds.[145] Kendal fails to realize that nationality issues in the theory of communism have no meaning. Theoretically, communism denotes an equitable and classless society and the notion of majority vs. minority has no context. The TKP fought against the dominant Turkish bourgeoisie class, and although was communistic principally in theory, was still more progressive than the elite dominated RPP. Chaliand, the intellectual leader of guerrilla movements, writes: "The fact that the Kurds were prohibited from forming a party with regionalist foundations, along with the natural opposition to Kemalist ideology, explains why so many of them joined left wing organizations."[146]

However, Chaliand's thesis is empirically weak since he fails to recognize that leftist parties do not attract members based on subjectivity or lack of a choice. Leftism is the result of conviction and political consciousness that promotes a desire for national class solidarity. Mobilization from the left supports political rights for the dominated classes. The Kurdish political party was paralyzed by its regional emphasis and could not contend with the progressive and inclusive nature of the Turkish leftist parties. The Kurdish political parties with regionalist foundations in Iraq became disastrously reactionary. It is also true that the Turkish leftist parties were limited in their applicability to Turkish society. Ahmet Samim points out that Turkish society was both underdeveloped and incompatible with the European model of parliamentary socialism. The political culture of socialism was limited in Turkish society let alone in Kurdistan, which is still, in comparison to other parts of the country, extremely underdeveloped.

However, in the 1965 elections, the Turkish worker's party scored a staggering victory. By virtue of proportional representation, the party received 300,000 votes and fifteen seats in the national assembly. In the urban areas the support for the party came from the middle class progressives, and predominantly the Kurds, Alavis, and the Shi,i minority in Turkey composed the base of rural support.[147]

In November 1971 at the fourth congress, under pressure from the Kurdish left, the Turkish Worker's Party (TWP), declared, "There are Kurdish people in the east of Turkey . . . the fascist authorities representing the ruling classes have subjected the Kurdish people to a policy of assimilation and intimidation that has often become a bloody repression."[148] This statement was a proven fact and hailed by the Kurdish activists, but the expectation for a reversal of Turkish government policies with only fifteen seats out of 450 was not realistic. This was the party's calamitous miscalculation. Given the Turkish army's apologetic paranoia of the Kurds, the government of Nihat Erim banned the party and arrested the leaders. The leaders of the party were kept imprisoned for twelve years. Their release came as a result of the July 1974 amnesty declared by the government elected to power in the 1973 October elections.[149]

The governmental crackdown on the TWP could not stop the proliferation of leftist parties that had begun before the demise of the party. In the fall of 1974, members of the TWP led by Ms. Behice Boran, revived the party, but it was not the only legal leftist group in Turkey. Before the ban of the TWP, members had created the Turkish Socialist Worker's Party (TSWP), the Socialist Party (SP), and a Maoist Party. These parties had progressive agendas and defended the rights of the people against the class in domination.[150]

Again the complaint of the Kurdish intellectuals was that the parties did not position themselves on the Kurdish political question. If the Kurdish question embraces autonomy or self-determination, these aspirations cannot be realized within a class society defined only vertically. The ideal of liberation from domination is the missing ideological link in Kurdish political thought. To Turkish political authorities the realization of this ideal implies separation.

The Kurdish political leader, Faik Bucak, a lawyer and a member of the Turkish Parliament from Urfa and an Agha himself, created the Kurdish Democratic Party of Turkey (KDPT) in 1965. It was modeled after the KDP-Iraq, which was, as mentioned earlier, a reactionary party. The party was rightist in ideology, appealing to the conservative land-holding Aghas who lived in Ankara. Both Faik Bucak and his successor, Sait Elci, used the KDP-T to promote the conservative interests of the landed class, a further undermining of Kurdish national solidarity. With Bucak's assassination in July 1966, the KDP-T was fractured. A more radical and leftist faction of the KDP-T was created by Dr.

Shivan, who requested Iraqi assistance for his guerrilla movement against the Turkish government. The other Turkish rival faction of the party was led by Sait Elci, but the military coup of 1971 forced him to flee to Iraq. Although the nature of the event is obscured, it is reported that Dr. Shivan and Sait Elci were killed in Iraq

The dissension and rivalry over ideology and tactics was obvious between Dr. Shivan and Sait Elci, another critical variable contributing to Kurdish disunity. Based on Michael Gunter's evidence, Dr. Shivan assassinated Elci and then Shivan was executed by General Barzani. Some observers attribute the murders to the Turkish military intelligence.[151]

Abd Allah Ocalan's political vision led to the creation of the Partiya Karkari Kurdistan (PKK, the Kurdistan Worker's Party). Abd Allah means "servant of God," but Ocalan was widely known as "Apo" out of respect for his leadership. "Apo" in Turkish means uncle, and Apo's followers were known as the "Apocular." Ocalan was a student of political science at Ankara University when the military coup of 1970 took place. He was deeply involved in the activities of the Ankara Higher Education Association, which demanded language and cultural rights for the Kurdish people. According to McDowall, after the amnesty of 1974, Ocalan joined with six other friends to create the Kurdish National Liberation Struggle inspired by Marxist-Leninist ideology. The group separated from the Turkish left and in 1975 withdrew from Turkish territory to the Kurdish areas where they would recruit followers. The forces that joined Apo's movement were different from other Kurdish forces. These forces were victims of the Turkish policy of Kurdish proletarianization in the rural and urban areas. Ocalan, contrary to the policies of the PUK in Iraq or Komala in Iran, skillfully combined the sentiments of nationalism with the idea of class politics.[152] In contrast to the Iraqi's political organization, the followers of Ocalan's political organization came predominantly from the impoverished classes.[153]

The PKK desired to reinvent Kurdish identity. Ocalan's forces had lost their cultural identity, and were a marginalized group who firmly believed that they have been excluded from the country's socio-economic development. Ocalan offered hope and the political means to regain the lost "opportunities for action, heroism and martyrdom."[154] In 1977, the Apocular group met in Diyarbakir and presented a critical analysis of the socio-economic situation of the Kurds. As a reaction to economic retardation and exploitation, they focused their criticism on Kurdish policies of the Turkish government in a revolutionary pamphlet called "Kurdistan Devriminin Yolu," or "The Path of the Kurdish Revolution." The pamphlet defined the Kurdish society as a colonial entity dominated and exploited by Kurdish feudal lords and "comprador bourgeoisie," who cooperated with the ruling classes of the colonizing countries, especially Turkey. The oppressive forces perpetuated the exploitative capital extraction from the Kurdish peasants and working classes. The pamphlet also attacked Kurdish intellectuals for denial of their own national and cultural identity, pretending to be "Turks" rather than Kurds."[155]

The revolutionary goal of the PKK included a two-phased strategy in enabling the Kurdish people to realize their national and democratic rights. The first dimension of the national phase would establish an independent Kurdistan, critical for the realization of liberation ideals. The democratic phase, the second dimension, was devised to solve the contradictions dominating the Kurdish society which included ". . . feudal and comprador exploitation, tribalism, religious sectarianism, and the slave-like dependence of women."[156] The PKK's political objectives sought the creation of a classless society based on Marxist theoretical formulations.

The military coup that took place in September 1980 brought the insurgency activism of the PKK, as well as other political parties, to a temporary halt. Anticipating the coup, the Apocular group withdrew to Syria where they prepared to launch their selective attacks on the Turkish army. Between the military rule period from 1980–83, the PKK adopted a low-key strategy, occasionally attacking the border guards, but this strategy did not stop the Turkish military atrocities. According to McDowall, "following the coup, 1,790 suspected PKK forces were captured," some of whom were members of the central committee.

In the first congress of the party, held in July 1981 at the Lebanese/Syrian border, the PKK was criticized for its tactics and armed clashes with other Kurdish forces, such as the PUK. A strategy was also devised to establish relations with the KDP-Iraq. However, this was contingent on the capacity of the PKK to tolerate KDP-Iraqi forces that were conservative and traditionalist. In the Baghdad/Ankara alliance against the Kurds, Barzani agreed with the Apoculars in July 1983 to use Northern Iraq, provided the two parties (KDP-Iraq and PKK) would not harm each other.

At its second congress in 1982, the PKK forces adopted a strategy focusing on defense, balance of force, and offense.[157] This strategy was based on Mao Tse-Tung approach to revolutionary wars involving an active defense with decisive engagements. Mao Tse-Tung cited Marx as saying that "once an armed uprising is started there must not be a moment's pause in the attack," reactionary forces must not be given a chance to recover. One must not hesitate to move forward even if "locked in a battle with an enemy who enjoys superiority." Even when hard pressed, that does not necessarily mean that "[one] should not adopt defensive measures." Hence, "the defensive continues until an encirclement and suppression campaign is broken, whereupon the offensive begins, these being but two stages of the same thing; and one such enemy campaign is closely followed by another." Mao included that when one's power or strength "surpasses" the enemy, there is no need for the strategic defensive. In this situation the policy must rely on the strategic offensive alone. Such a change "will depend on overall changes in the balance of forces."[158] Following Mao's theoretical formulation, the PKK forces adopted the strategies of the guerrilla war.

The PKK began with an active defense hoping to force out the Turkish army from Kurdistan. The PKK guerrillas skillfully used this Mao Tse Tung's method .of confrontation with the Turkish army, in spite of superiority, numbers, and strength.[159] Although the PKK avoided a direct confrontation with the Turkish forces, it was able indirectly to define the limits of a well organized, highly equipped, trained, and numerically strong army of the Turkish state. However, Maoism strategy is effective only when the guerrillas are supported and sheltered by the people. Although discontent was prevalent in the rural areas, it was not common to shelter the insurgent guerrillas. Slightly more than 3 percent of absentee landlords owned thirty-three percent of the arable land. These landlords were thought to be mediators between the Turkish government and peasantry, but in actuality, the landlords served as government agents who delivered votes of legitimization needed to contain rural insurgency. In Hakkari province, one landlord during the November election of 1983, instructed his peasant followers to support ANAP (the motherland party). The peasants delivered over 5,000 votes, 9 percent of the vote of the province. The peasantry, though disaffected, avoided confrontation with their Agha class.[160]

The PKK's strategy was to alter the conservative rural norms by exterminating the landlords. This was an effective approach in dealing with the landed class that cultivated the seeds of reactionary modes of thinking in rural areas. It was also a challenge to the Turkish army that could not protect its agents. PKK militants ambushed the Turkish security forces, and in October 1984, the PKK following its initial August attack killed three governmental forces members and then ambushed a Turkish army unit killing eight soldiers in Cukurca, Hakkari. The Turkish army mounted a massive retaliatory attack against the Kurdish insurgent forces. In August 1985, guerrilla attacks by the Kurdish National Liberation Front intensified. The PKK's liberation front repeatedly attacked Turkish security forces and their agents. Although PKK forces could not match the highly organized Turkish army, their presence was intimidating.[161]

The PKK was better organized than Talabani-Barzani political organizations. While the PKK fought the landed classes in Kurdistan, Talabani-Barzani forces derived support from them. The feudal Ahgas were KDPI and PUK political component. The PKK had a well-defined political ideology, while the KDP Iraq and PUK did not. Contrary to the KDP—Iraq and the PUK that depended on external forces, especially the United States, in their struggle, the PKK leaders considered it captivation by Imperial forces, not liberation. The PKK was extremely progressive, even though it was not entirely compatible with the tribal/feudal cultures of Kurdistan. This incompatibility and the tribal fragmentation was reinforced by the imperially dominated conservative world system.

Although Ocalan was inspired by the Marxist-Leninist political philosophy, he generally employed the revolutionary theory of Mao Tse-Tung, which favored revolutionary liberation struggles in the countryside where the basis for social revolution can be developed. The PKK adopted Mao's concept of "guerrilla fish swimming in the water of the people."[162] However, the water was not deep enough, as it was in China, to shelter the insurgent Kurdish guerrilla fish. In the summer of 1984, the PKK guerrillas launched their first offensive against Turkish security forces. The PKK's military arm, the Peoples Liberation Army of Kurdistan (ARGK) and its guerrillas, took over the cities of Semdinli and Eruh in the Hakkari province. The ARGK attacked the prison in Eurh and released the Kurdish prisoners. They executed collaborators who were mostly villagers called "village protectors."[163] The villagers were paid to counter and/or contain the PKK's attacks on their villages and governmental concerns. The tribes that offered these village guards included Jirki, Pinyanish, Goyan, and the Mamkhuran, and were either in conflict with the PKK or with the local supporters of the PKK.

From the government's point of view, the casualties were welcomed when Kurds fought against Kurds. The villagers did not have a choice between the pressure exerted by the PKK and the government; those who refused to join government organized village protectors were considered to be PKK accomplices. If they complied with governmental policies, the result was retaliation and elimination by the PKK guerrillas.[164] The PKK guerrillas attacked the government organized village guards, and the government retaliated by attacking the PKK supported Kurdish villages. The ruthless attacks and counter attacks involving PKK forces against the Kuridsh Jash operating under the village guards system defined the nature of the Krudish liberation struggle: Kurds killing Kurds. As the government and village guard militia attacks on the PKK guerrillas intensified in early 1987, the PKK guerrillas were forced into systematic assaults on the village guards Kurds.

McDowall claims that by 1989, the PKK eliminated village guards, Aghas, men, women, and children in the provinces of Mardin, Siirt, and Hakkari indiscriminately and without any conscientious assessment of the guilt associated with the outcome of its insurgency. However, the PKK demonstrated its ability to destroy the network of Jashism. In September 1989, the PKK announced its intention to attack thirteen tribes who collaborated with the Turkish government. The PKK followed with brutal attacks on the tribal leaders by "killing the son and two cousins of Sadun Seylan, chief of the Alan."[165] Seylan owned twenty-six villages and received a monthly payment of $115,000 from the Turkish government to fund the operation of five hundred village guards against the PKK guerrillas.[166] The PKK's impressive assault on the dominant Turkish bourgeoisie class and its comparador class allies in some cases provoked the villages to contain a small attacking unit of the PKK guerrillas. The violence associated with the PKK's actions proved costly; it alienated popular support and provoked the opposition of other Kuridsh political forces. On 20 June 1987, during a PKK attack on Pinarcik (in the province of Mardin), a village that had been accused of collaboration, thirty people (including sixteen children and eight women) were killed.[167]

Human Rights Watch/Helsinski documented the PKK's actions involving the killing of twenty-nine Kurdish civilians indiscriminately: six women, thirteen children, and ten worshippers at a Mosque in Diyarbakir.[168] The PKK ultimately suffered for this needless violence, even though the violence was a reaction to state-sponsored terrorism. Ocalan's liberation struggle was compromised by Mom Masud Barzani's abrogation of the KDP-Iraq's alliance agreement with PKK forces. Barzani accused the PKK of terrorism, a party that "promoted hatred and disgust of all the Kurdish people."[169] This accusation actually cannot be documented because even before the PKK's existence in 1984, Turkey had massively violated Kurdish rights. Turkey, throughout its history, had repeatedly denied socio-cultural rights to the Kurds, attempting to assimilate them forcefully into Turkish-Ataturk ideology.

The PKK is the result of the state-sponsored terrorism. It is the product, not the cause, of Turkey's intolerable Kurdish policies, and economic hardships inflicted on Kurds in southeast Turkey.[170] In addition to the economic problems in Kurdistan, the result of discriminating governmental policies, the Turkish government has continuously and consistently denied the existence of Kurds as Kurds. PKK forces did not create assimilation, dispersement, and forced resettlement policies. The Turkish government wished to create a nation state with a single Turkish language and culture, and used the policies of destruction, evacuation, and forceful assimilation to achieve that end. Turkey first applied this policy to the Armenian minority. In 1915, it exterminated the Armenian people, and in 1920, it expelled 1,200,000 Anatolian Greeks. This racist policy of the Turkish government is known as the "biggest ethnic purification operation of the inter-war period. The Kurds, last of the original local populations, were then also to be deported and dispersed to the four corners of the country."[171]

The de-Kurdification of Kurdistan and assimilation of the Kurds into Turkish politics and culture has been the political plan of the Turkish government.

As the former Joint Chief of Staff, General Gures stated: "The objective is to disperse the maximum number of Kurds," or as President Ozal continued to say: "Scatter them! Scatter them!"[172] Masud Barzani and others who referred to the PKK as violent, should have known about the violent policies of the Turkish government in carrying out a scorched earth strategy on Kurdish lands. According to the *International Herald Tribune,* the state terror in Turkish Kurdistan has culminated in the "scorched earth policy," the destruction of hundreds of the Kurdish villages.[173]

Turkey's *Human Rights Report* further supports the accusation of Turkish terrorism directed against the Kurds. In April 1994, Interior Minister Nahit Mentese maintained that 871 villages and hamlets had been evacuated. By the end of 1944, Mr. Mentese mentioned in a written statement that almost 2,297 villages and hamlets had been either partially or fully evacuated.[174] By 25 July 1995, the *Turkish Daily Milliyet,* reported that 2,664 villages had been partially or fully evacuated, resulting in displacement of some two million Kurds who sought refuge in the slums of major Turkish cities.[175] These examples illustrate the reality of Turkish state terrorism. Mom Masud Barzani and those who argue that Turkish state violations of human rights and terrorism are in response to the PKK violence, have not read Mehdi Zana's book entitled, *Prison No. 5, Eleven Years in Turkish Jails.* In this book Mehdi Zana documents the torture and humiliation inflicted on prisoners by the Turkish state at a time when neither the PKK guerrillas nor terrorist threats existed.[176] The statistics are staggering. Turkey carried out massive violent attacks on those (Kurds and non Kurds) who disagreed with the Kemalist unitary form of ideology. After the coup d'etat of September 1980, 650,000 people were detained, 210,000 of whom were subsequently charged, over 100,000 people were condemned to various sentences, the military courts asked for 6,353 death sentences, 50 people were hung, 171 were tortured to death, 30,000 had to flee the country for political reasons, 14,000 were stripped of their nationality by decree of the council of ministers, and 133,000 books were burned. Another 118,000 people were repelled, 29,000 civil servants, magistrates, policemen, and teachers were sacked; 937 films were banned, and 23,667 clubs and associations were closed down."[177]

Mr. Barzani and mainstream scholars have failed to publicize the tragedy of state-sponsored terrorism, nor have they criticized the abusive tactics of the armed squads of gray wolves who have with governmental approval, terrorized, and executed the Turkish progressive left and Kurdish activists. Theoretically, Kurdish leadership belongs to the Kurds, but in practice, external forces control the leadership. Political and military alliances among the Kurdish forces do not exist or are short-lived. Self-interest dictates the alliance.

A Kurdish observer from the Kurdish library in New York accurately remarked that "they [the Kurds] would sell each other for a quarter." *Radio Free*

Europe reported that the interests of Mom Barzani's KDP lie largely in transit fee, amounting from three to four hundred million dollars annually. The PUK's interest lies in taxes from "much more limited truck traffic carrying" Turkish goods into the north of Iraq.[178] The PUK struggles to close the income gap between the two rival factions, the KDP-Iraq and PUK-Iraq. To accomplish these ends, Mom Jalal is friendly to the Turkish government and to some extent relies on smuggling operations, which have been continuous for more than eight years with the knowledge of the United Nations and approval of the United States of America. "For Turkey and the United States the quid pro quo is active warfare against those Kurdish rebels from Turkey in northern Iraq."[179]Self-interest among the rival Kurdish leaders has been the defining element.

From Apo's point of view, Mom Jalal and Mom Masud are businessmen. They tend to compromise Kurdish national liberation struggle for personal self-interest. With the PKK's presence, both leaders are bankrupt. They have made deals with the oppressors that have jeopardized the Kurdish liberation movement. Referring to a verse in the Muslim Holy book: "Ja,al hagg va za-hagal batel," Apo argues that with the coming of the truth (the PKK forces), the falsehood (PUK and KDP-Iraq) will vanish: truth will prevail over falsehood. For Apo, the Kurdish leaders (PUK and the PKK) instead of explaining the reasons for the oppressed status of Kurds, have focused on self interests. These parties and leaders have been neither nationalist, nor democratic. They have been tribal and feudal-based organizations and have been the primary beneficiaries of socio-political control.[180]

According to *Kurdish Life*, the Barzani and Talabani forces gave support to Turkey's military in its attack on the PKK guerrilla forces in October 1992. This information source also claimed that the PKK forces raided a meeting of KDP and PUK commanders in the Haftanin area in northern Iraq. The documents that were seized indicated that there was a trilateral committee composed of one PUK commander, one KDP commander, and a senior Turkish major who had direct access to the Turkish high command and directed the Peshmergas (Iraqi Kurdish fighters of both parties). Much of the heavy weaponry sent to the peshmergas by Turkey was used by Turkish officers and troops. The captured Peshmerga commanders alleged that the plans for military operations were formulated by Turkish officers.[181] In reality, it was Mom Barzani's 15,000 strong Peshmergas that had attacked the PKK forces. Mohammad Soleivani, Talabani's spokesperson, reported that "we [Peshmerga forces] drive them [PKK forces] to the top of the mountains and Turkish jets blast them there."[182]

Houssein Sinjari, a former KDP-Iraqi minister, said, "I see the future of northern Iraq, within Iraq, but within a federal Iraq." Regarding the Kurds in

Turkey, he commented, "I am happy that the number of people who want separation is decreasing as a result of improving democracy and democratic culture."[183] Mr. Sinjari failed to understand what democracy is. He failed to distinguish between the status of the Iraqi and Turkish Kurds. In Iraq, Kurds are fighting for land rights, while in Turkey, Kurds fight for political and human rights. A democratic arrangement does not show preference for people or culture. He begs the questions: why are the Kurds in Turkey subject to forced assimilation? The genuine meaning of political equality means that everyone must count for one and no one for more than one.[184] The Kurds in Turkey are totally discounted, let alone counted as equals.

Dissension and opposition constitute another feature of democratic thinking, yet Kurds, who claim their cultural identity, language, and tradition are considered separatists and the enemies of the Turkish state. These antidemocratic norms do not exist in Iraq, nor with Iraqi Kurds under Iraqi rule. Mr. Sinjari also fails to realize that in order for democracy to exist, there should be a democratic culture. The concept of social equality defined as a form of material equality and equal access to the means of production does not exist in Turkey, let alone in rural Kurdistan. If by democracy he means liberal democracy, they have failed worldwide to deliver a degree of material equalities. And these inequalities are supposed to be corrected by the liberal state interventionism. Mr. Sinjari should know that under the capitalist system, the main function of the state is to maintain the unequal distribution of power, a characteristic of capitalist social relations.[185] However, in rural Kurdistan, policy actions, such as dam construction and reform programs, have taken place recently, but Kurds remain impoverished. The Kurds have nothing to lose but their oppression. Social inequality stifles democratic values. It is foolish to talk about democracy when Kurdish society cannot claim its cultural values and is ridden with political and social inequalities.

Ertugrul Kurkcu is correct in realizing that the Turkish hegemony is in crisis. The country, by virtue of its policy of exclusivity, does not have real economic power. The Kemalist ideology is the pillar on which the legitimacy of the Turkish republican elite rests. This nationalistic ideology created a nation-state out of the multi-ethnic remnants of the Ottoman Empire. It has suppressed any other ethnic identity. However, the 1984 armed struggle of the Kurdish Workers Party (PKK) supporting Kurdish self-determination, shattered the Kamalist ideology of nationalism. Turkish hegemony is under attack.[186] It is in the process of disintegration and anachronization.

The Kurdish leaders suffer from tribal conflict and rivalry. Kurds killing Kurds is a practice that continues to live. Ocalan's accusation that Mom Talabani led a primitive nationalistic feudalism line is accurate, but Ocalan's own conviction in the wake of his capture is more condemning. He perverted his definition of nationalism in favor of Turkish nationalism. He referred to his own version of Kurdish nationalism as anachronistic. With the assistance and intelligence of the Turkish military, the PUK/KDP Kurdish forces continued assaulting the PKK forces. The Kurdish leaders fail to see themselves as the culprit in their on-going tragedies.

Ocalan, like Mom Jalal and Mom Barzani, was unaware of the contradictory nature of the prevailing conservative world system that has divided the world for over five hundred years. It has never occurred to Ocalan why the Iraqi Kurds are treated differently than the Turkish Kurds. If the external forces can create friction among the Kurdish groups, the Kurdish hopes for liberation will never materialize. This is the divide and rule strategy. The United States as the leader of the world system, prepared to intervene in Kosov, but is unwilling to intervene on behalf of the Kurds, also in the NATO areas and under very similar circumstances.[187] Turkey is a member of NATO and is a serious violator of Kurdish rights. Turkey as a NATO member commits murder, destruction, and permits the abductions of the Kurds. This state-sponsored terrorism continues to receive military, economic, and political support from Washington. Ocalan has ignored the conflicting and divisive policies of the world system. Ocalan, likeMom Barzani and Mom Jalal, made a radical turnaround and sought asylum from the same world order responsible for the regional conflicts and the destruction of the Kurdish people's ideals and aspirations. Kurdish leaders struggle for an independent Kurdistan, their hearts belong to Kurds and Kurdistan, while their heads belong to external forces.[188] If Ocalan understood the captivating nature of the world system, he would not have sought political refuge status from Italy. In October 1998, Turkey forced the Syrian government to abandon its harboring of the PKK forces operating from Lebanon and Syria since the military coup of 1980 in Turkey. By mid-November, Ocalan fled to Rome where he sought political asylum, but instead he was arrested.[189] He failed to realize the motives of Washington and the Israeli Mosad. Mark Parris, the United States Ambassador to Turkey, admitted that Washington had exerted pressure on many countries to have Ocalan returned to Turkey.[190] The United States thus blocked Ocalan's extradition. "We welcome Ocalan's arrest as an important step in the fight against global terrorism," said James Rubin spokesman for the U. S. State Department." The United States designated the PKK as a terrorist organization under the 1996 Anti-Terrorism and Effective Death Penalty Act.[191] The Kurdish activists in Moscow went on a hunger strike calling the action against Ocalan an international conspiracy. The Kurdish leadership was blind to the world system and its oppressive strategies, or simply lacked the political maturity required to assess the situation.

Third world formations are dominated by the world system, technologically in all cases, materially in the majority of cases, and in terms of market relations, metropolitan capital has always been distinct winner; even where the localities have their own capital and their own commodities like the OPEC countries. This is further complicated by political dependence on the world system. In the case of the oil producing Arab countries, "they are unable to defend the one cause they call their own—the Palestinian cause."[192] Since 1948, PLO forces have been continuously subjected to the state-sponsored terrorism that has been organized, subsidized, and led by Zionists. At its peak, the movement radicalized and politicized the entire region. The suicide bombers were an outgrowth of this movement. According to Middle-Easterners, the horrifying event of 2001 September 11th was linked to the radicalization of the region largely promoted by the Zionist hunger for land and its massacre of Palestinians on their own soil.

The world system has supported Zionist violence. Environmental destruction, exploitation, terrorism, child labor, prison labor, and now child prostitution have been the contradictory elements of the world system. This is a system that depends on wars of aggression, political violence, bloodshed, and hegemony for its existence. The World Wars I and II, Vietnam War, War of 1812, Mexican War, Spanish War, Gulf War, Afgani War, Iraqi War, fascism, and communism have all involved terrorism. War is considered good for the economy. What type of system relies on permanent conflict? Mr. Ocalan should have done some research on this system before attempting to act against it.

As documented in this book, the Kurdish leaders have been part of this system. This is not to suggest that the world system is invincible and liberation from it cannot be achieved. Evidence from the national liberation struggles and the factual history of social revolutions suggest otherwise. The problem is that the Kurdish movements have deviated from the theoretical model of political liberation movements.

The alliance between Israel, Turkey, and the United States and the regional cooperation from Mom Barzani and Mom Jalal, forced Syria to stop its support of the PKK in 1998. Ocalan left for Moscow hoping to use Russia's influence to obtain support from the Hague, but the Netherlands declined. Subsequently, he flew to Athens where the Greek Foreign Minister came under intensified pressure from the U.S. government to reject Ocalan's request. On 1 February 1998, Ocalan arrived in Nairobi, the base of CIA operations. On 14 February 1998, CIA-Mosad forces abducted Ocalan while he was on route to the airport to fly to South Africa. He was delivered to the Turkish commandos, who were waiting for him at the airport.[193]

Ocalan was jailed on Imrali Island, thirty-five kilometers from Istanbul. He was kept there for ten years with limited access to his lawyers. On 31 May he appeared in court; but with no solid defense. Ocalan, surprisingly, made apologetic defense for his action, calling the so-called Kurdish liberation struggle a "mistake." He failed to take the opportunity to explain the Kurdish cause to the world. He said nothing about thousands of Kurds killed or their disappearance while in police custody, nor did he mention the millions who had become homeless, tortured, jailed, and intimidated. In spite of his apologetic position, Ocalan on 29 June 1998 was found guilty of treason and sentenced to death.[194] Until this point, pressure from the European Union had prevented his death sentence. Turkey wanted entry into the European Union, but had a record of serious human rights violations, especially regarding the Kurdish minority, either in the form of destruction of their homes, villages or torture and disappearances. The Turkish government's elimination of the Kurdish rebel leader would have meant suicide. Hence, thanks to the European Union, Turkey failed to carry out Ocalan's death sentence.

It should be emphasized that with Ocalan's capture, the PKK plunged into a leadership crisis. But does this mean that the Kurdish movement is dead and that the so-called unity forces have won? The answer to this question is an emphatic "no." Unity created by force cannot endure. Although apartheid in South Africa, and military dictatorships in Latin America, Iran, and the Soviet Union lasted for some time, all these countries paid a heavy price socially, politically, and economically.

The causes of violent movements are frustration, alienation, strains, exigencies, class system, discrimination, and the desire for freedom. People like Edwards, Pettee, and Sorokin attribute political violence to the repression of human values. Arendt sees the causes of revolutionary violent movement in the repression of aspirations for freedom. Marx attributes class conflict to economic inequalities.[195] Ted Robert Gurr's groundbreaking study in *Why Men Rebel* proves that the majority of the people cross-nationally are dominated with the aforementioned variables. The Kurdish region of Turkey is economically devastated. The people are deprived of their cultural values, treated as criminals, and are subjected to assimilation and Turkification.

In terms of social services, they are the most deprived minority in the world. The Turkish military continually dictates: You are either Turks or nothing at all. This encourages mounting rage and deprivation, which will always seek an outlet. According to Gurr, "The primary casual sequence in political violence is first the development of discontent, second the politicization of that discontent, and finally its actualization in violent action against political objects and actions."[196] In Turkey, the Kurdish forces have become radicalized and politicized and discontentment has reached its heights. The instigating condition for participation in violent action is already in place. This heightened violent state of affairs is further aggravated by the availability of comparative knowledge on one's own socio-economic and political status, via the information superhighway. It is impossible in this information age to suppress knowledge or exercise coercive socio-political control indefinitely. The period of social control is over. Humanity, though ushering in a new era of dawning hopes, faces limited resources that cannot be wasted in conflicts involving senseless ideologies.

Military conflict in the containment of the PKK's separatist strategy was extremely costly. It was a drain on Turkey's economy, education, and social programs. "By 1999 it was costing the state ten billion U.S. dollars annually in military terms alone . . . it had also cost Turkey greatly, worth eight billion dollars annually, double its value only seven years earlier, but in 1999, tourism had decreased 30 percent."[197] The conflict also tarnishes the international image of the Turkish government. The Germans did not want to travel to Turkey, not because of the fear of the on-going war, but because of the Turkish human right's violations against the Kurds.[198] If not solved, the Turkish/Kurdish problem will undermine the realization of its asserted democratic values. In the aftermath of Ocalan's capture, the PKK has forsaken the concept of "Kurdistan" and opted for the pursuit of Kurdish rights.[199] The PKK, with its rebel leader incarcerated, recently dispatched a delegation to Turkey to negotiate the concept of self-administration, attempting to seek Kurdish rights within the Turkish whole. Unfortunately, the delegation members were all incarcerated. The PKK is planning to send in new delegations. However, according to *The Kurdish Life*, this new future peace delegation may also end up "in the company of their incarcerated kin."[200]

The Turkish system is suffering from a severe political crisis, recognized by the sharpened gap between conflicting forces: military versus civil, religious versus secular, Turkish versus Kurdish and Sunni versus Alavi. These clashing factors are not conducive to the promotion of the country's unity in Ataturk's fashion. Together they may well undermine Ataturk's legacy of a united Turkey. In conclusion, it is apparent that the Kurdish movements suffer from a lack of unity and solidarity, key components of national liberation struggles.

NOTES

1. Chris Kutschera, *The National Movement of the Kurds* (*Le Mouvement National Kurd*), *Joonbish Mell Kurd* (Persian), translated into Farsi by Ibrahim Unisi (Tehran: Negah Publisher, 1373), 59.

2. David McDowall, *A Modern History of the Kurds* (London: I. B. Tauris, 1996), 215.

3. Theda Skocpol, *The States and Social Revolutions: A Comparative Analysis of France, Russia, and China* (London: Cambridge University Press, 1979), 18–24,41.

4. Ervand Abrahamian, *Iran Between Two Revolutions* (Princeton, New Jersey: Princeton University Press, 1982), 96.

5. Bernard Sucessor, *Political Ideology in the Modern World* (Boston: Allyn and Bacon, 1995), 231.

6. Ibid.; Kutschera, *The National Movement of the Kurds,* 60.

7. O'Balance, *Kurdish Movement,* 7; Gerard Chailand, *The Kurdish Tragedy* (London: Zed Books, 1994), 73–74. See also Kutschera, *National Movement of the Kurds,* 60.

8. Kutschera, *National Movement of the Kurds,* 60–66.

9. Ibid., 61–62.

10. Fereshteh Koohi-Kamali, "The Development of Nationalism in Iranian Kurdistan," in ed. Philip G. Kreyenbroek and Stefan Sperl, *The Kurds: A Contemporary Overview* (London: Routledge, 1992), 175.

11. Quoted by Kutschera, *The National Movement of the Kurds,* 67.

12. Ibid.

13. Ibid., 67–72.

14. Ibid., 194–95.

15. A. R. Ghassemlou, "Kurdistan in Iran," in *People Without a Country: The Kurds and Kurdistan* (London: Zed Books, 1980), 118; Koohi-Kamail, "Development of Nationalism," 177.

16. McDowall, *Modern History of the Kurds,* 236–38; Kutschera, *National Movement,* 205.

17. McDowall, *Modern History of the Kurds,* 238.

18. Kutschera, *National Movement,* 206–07.

19. Ibid., 208–09; McDowall, *Modern History of the Kurds,* 240–42; for detailed information see, Ghassemlou, "Kurdistan in Iran," 118–19.

20. O'Balance, *The Movement of the Kurds,* translated by Ismail Fattah Gazi into Persian (Tehran: Negah Publishers, 1377), 61; Ghassemlou, "Kurdistan in Iran," 118–19.

21. Ghassemlou, "Kurdistan in Iran," 119. The Kurdish flag adopted the colors of red, white, and green. As Ghassemlou describes the Kurdish flag: "The flag was decorated with a sun surrounded by corns of wheat with a quill in the middle; the sun for freedom, the quill to undermine the importance of your actions."

22. Kutschera, *National Movement,* 212.

23. Ibid., 223–225.

24. Ibid., 213–217. Kutschera cites Ziro Beig, a Harki Kurd and Colonel appointed as Marshal by Gazi, saying that the aliens of Rezaieh did not have any rights to the city. He tried to prove his claim to Hoshemov in the following way: He, the Colonel, picked up a chair and put it in the middle of the room where the meeting was being held, and asked Hoshemov, "This is your room, can I sit in the middle of your room and claim that it is mine? No, it can't be." The implication was that the Azeri Turks, Armenians, Assyrians, Christian Persians, and all Shi,i forces posses the Kurdish lands and must vacate them. This might appear to be a superficial opinion by one Harki tribal leader, but, unfortunately, based on my observation and the repeated wars, and bloody confrontations, evidence is provided supports the divisive and separtist intentions of the Kurdish political movements.

25. Ibid., 225; George Allen announced that he would defend the integrity and national soveriengty of Iran. See also Ghassemlou, "Kurdistan in Iran," 122; *Mojtaba Barzoei, Ovza-e Syasie Kurdistan* (Political Conditions of Kurdistan), 1258–1325 (Tehran, Iran: Nashr-e feker-e now, 1378), 367–385.

26. Kutschera, *National Movement*, 213–217.

27. Koohi-Kamali, "The Development of Nationalism," 178. See also McDowall, *Modern History of the Kurds*, 242.

28. Ghassemlou, "Kurdistan in Iran," 122. See also Koohi-Kamali, "The Development of Nationalism," 178–79.

29. Nader Entessar, *Kurdish Ethnonationalism* (Boulder: Lynne Rienner Publishers, 1992), 26–29. "Operation Ajax," is a well-cited quotation on American intervention in Iran which is extensively documented. For related information on this, see James. A. Bill, *The Eagle and the Lion* (Connecticut: Tragedy Haven, 1998) 92–95, and Chapter 2. Hossein Fardoost Zehoor va Segoot-e Pahlavi, *The Rise and Fall of the Pahlavi Monarchy*, vol.1 (Tehran: Ettela,at Publication, 1991), 176–184. See also Marvin Zonis, *Majestic Failure: The Fall of the Shah* (Chicago: University Press of Chicago, 1991), 105–110.

30. Entessar, *Kurdish Ethnonationalism*, 28; Ghassemlou, "Kurdistan in Iran," 124–125.

31. Ibid., 124; Entessar, *Kurdish Ethnonationalism*, 28–29.

32. Ghassemlou, "Kurdistan in Iran," 124–125; Entessar, *Kurdish Ethnonationalism*, 29; Kutschera, *National Movement*, 430.

33. Cited by Entessar, *Kurdish Ethnonationalism*, 34.

34. Sipah-i Pasdarani-I Inqilab-I Islam Kurdistan (The Islamic Revolutionary Guard) (Tehran, Iran: Daftar-i Syasie Sipah-i Pasdaran-i Inqilab-i Islami, 1980), 21. This source makes a judgment based on Shaikh Azaddin Hosseini's own correspondences with the SAVAK, the Shah's secret police. The translation is that letter:

Dear Kalbasi, the Head of Mahabad's SAVAK,

   I am happy to take this opportunity to offer you my congratulations on the occasion of Eid said Feter (celebration at the end of the month of fasting). I hope you will succeed in carrying out your assignments devised to serve the Shah and promote prosperity of the people.

This letter is from document 22 on p. 121. See also documents 24, 25, 26, 27, and 28 on pp. 121, 123, 124, 125, 126, and 128.

35. Sipah-i Pasdarani-I Inqilab-I Islam, 128–29, document 28.

36. Mao-Tse Tung, *Selected Workds of Mao-Tse Tung*, vol. 1 (Peking: Foreign Language Press, 1977), 13–14. For Mao, political liberation objectives are achieved by knowing who the friends and enemies of the liberation struggle are. The key to revolutionary success is unity with those who sympathize with the liberation cause. Unfortunately, the self-interests of Kurdish leadership has always positioned the Kurdish struggle on the wrong side.

37. Edgar O'Ballance, *The Kurdish Struggle* (New York: St. Martin's Press, 1996), 24–25.

38. Gerard Chaliand, *The Kurdish Tragedy* (London: Zed Books, 1994), 54–55; David McDowall, *A Modern History of the Kurds* (London: T. B. Tauris, 1997), 286–290.

39. V. Hamdi, *Kurdistan and the Kurds in the Confidential Documents of Great Britain*, translated by Behzad Khoshhalli (Tehran: Noor Alam Hamadan Publishers, 1378), 125.

40. Ibid., 126–27.

41. Cited by David McDowall in *A Modern History of the Kurds*. 291.

42. Hamdi, *Kurdistan and Kurds*, 132.

43. O'Ballance, *Kurdish Struggle*, 24.

44. Chaliand, *Kurdish Tragedy*, 55; McDowall, *Modern History of the Kurds*, 292–93.

45. O'Ballance, *Kurdish Struggle*, 28–29.

46. Chris Kutschera, *The National Movement of the Kurds* (*Le Mouvement National Kurd*), *Joonbish Mell-e Kurd* (Persian), translated into Farsi by Ibrahim Unisi (Tehran: Negah Publisher, 1373), 217.

47. Ibid., 225.

48. Ibid., 224–25.

49. See Mortaza Zarbakht, *Az Kurdsitan-e Araq Ta On Sooie Rud-e Aras* (From the Kurdistan of Iraq to Over Aras River: Historical Walk of Barzani to USSR), (Tehran, Iran: Shirazeh Research and Publishers, 1326), 3–27.

50. McDowall, *Modern History of the Kurds*, 296.

51. Gerard Chaliand, ed., *People Without a Country: The Kurds and Kurdistan* (London: Zed Press, 1980), 164.

52. Kutschera, *Kurdish National Struggle*, 246–47.

53. McDowall, *Modern History of the Kurds*, 296–97.

54. Cited by Chaliand, *People Without a Country*, 165; Kutschera, *Kurdish National Struggle*, 249. See also, *Kurdistan and the National Liberation Struggle and the Kurds* (1972), 28–29. The author and publication information for this book remains anonymous. The author supports the leftist position and fears that he could be kidnapped and eliminated.

55. Ismet Sheriffvanly, "Kurdistan in Iraq," in Chaliand, ed., *People Without a Country*, 165.

56. McDowall, *Modern History of the Kurds*, 302–03.

57. Hamdi, *Kurdistan va Kurd*, 145–47.

58. McDowall, *Modern History of the Kurds*, 304.

59. Kutschera, *Kurdish National Movement*, 270–71.

60. Ibid., 256–57; McDowall, *Modern History of the Kurds*, 304.

61. McDowall, *Modern History of the Kurds*,309–310; Kutschera, *Kurdish National Movement*, 259.

62. Claliand, *Kurdish Tragedy*, 56.

63. Kutschera, *Kurdish National Movement*, 259–60.

64. McDowall, *Modern History of the Kurds*, 307–08; Sheriffvanly, "Kurdistan in Iraq," in Chaliand, ed., *People Without a Country*, 165–66.

65. Chailand, *Kurdish Tragedy*, 57.

66. McDowall, *Modern History of the Kurds*, 311.

67. Chaliand, *Kurdish Tragedy*, 57.

68. Kutschera, *Kurdish National Movement*, 264.

69. Cited by Hamdi, *Kurdistan va Kurds*, 143.

70. McDowall, *Modern History of the Kurds*, 311.

71. Hamdi, *Kurdistan va Kurds*, 148.

72. Ibid., 149–50.

73. Chaliand, *Kurdish Tragedy*, 57–58.

74. McDowall, *Modern History of the Kurds*, 313.

75. For further insight, see Kutshcera, *Kurdish National Movement*, 280–283 and Sheriffvanly, "Kurdistan in Iraq," in Chaliand, ed., *People Without a Country*, 167. Sheriffvanly states that 7,000 communist members were killed; Kutschera estimates that 1,000 were killed.

76. Chaliand, *Kurdish Tragedy*, 58; McDowall, *Modern History of the Kurds*, 313–314.

77. Chaliand, *Kurdish Tragedy*, 58–59; McDowall, *Modern History of the Kurds*, 314–17; Kutschera, *Kurdish National Movement*, 311–15.

78. Chaliand, *Kurdish Tragedy*, 59; McDowall, *Modern History of the Kurds*, 316–17; Kutschera, *Kurdish National Movement*, 308–12.

79. Chaliand, *Kurdish Tragedy*, 60; McDowall, Modern History, 319–20.

80. Sa,ad, Jawad, *Iraq and the Kurdish Question, 1958–1970* (London: Ithaca Press, 1981), 37; McDowall, *Modern History of the Kurds*, 319, 325.

81. Chaliand, *Kurdish Tragedy*, 60.

82. McDowall, *Modern History of the Kurds*, 318–320; Kutshcera, *Kurdish National Movement*, 323–325.

83. AlNur, published in Baghdad, sponsored by Ahmad-Talabani, 19 November 1968, qutoed in McDowall, *Modern History of the Kurds*, 325–26.

84. Chaliand, *Kurdish Tragedy*, 61. For a detailed analysis of the Jash group, see Edgar O'Ballance, The Kurdish Struggle, 1920–1994 (New York: St. Martin's Press, 1996), 57–60, 77–78; McDowall, *Modern History of the Kurds*, 325–26.

85. Chaliand, *Kurdish Tragedy*, 61; see also, O'Ballance, the Kurdish Struggle, 93.

86. Quoted by McDowall, *Modern History of the Kurds*, 328. See also, Ismet Sherriff Vanly, "Kurdistan in Iraq," in Chaliand, ed., *People Without a Country*, 168–69.

87. McDowall, *Modern History of the Kurds*, 328–29; Kutschera, *Kurdish National Movement*, 348–49; Sherriffvanly, "Kurdistan in Iraq," in Chaliand, ed., *People Without a Country*, 170–173.

88. Kutschera, *Kurdish National Movement*, 348–352. According to Kutschera, a delegation of nine clergies (*Mullas*) went in two vehicles to the general's headquarters for the purpose of easing the deteriorated relations between Baghdad and Barzani. They were given tape recorders to hide inside their *goorshaghs* (a low back belt that the Kurds wear). However, they were unaware that within the tape recorders explosives had been installed. One of the drivers, apparently armed with a remote control, set off the explosives once the delegation had entered the headquarters. All nine of the clergies were killed, but General Barzani and Dr. Mahmood Uthman were not harmed.

89. McDowall, *Modern History of the Kurds*, 330–331; Kutschera, *Kurdish National Movement*, 353–57; Sheriffvanly, "Kurdistan in Iraq," in Chaliand, ed., *People Without a Country*, 183–86.

90. The Pike Report reproduced in New Yorks's *The Village Voice*, 23 February 1976, quoted by Ismet Sheriffvanly, "Kurdistan in Iraq," in Chaliand, *People Without a Country*, 185.

91. Pike Report quoted in Chaliand, *People Without a Country,* 185.

92. McDowall, *Modern History of the Kurds*, 331.

93. Quoted in McDowall, Modern History of the Kurds, 333. Also see Kutschera, *Kurdish National Movement*, 358.

94. O'Ballance, *Kurdish Struggle*, 94–95.

95. Chaliand, *People Without a Country*, 189; Chaliand, *Kurdish Tragedy*, 62.

96. Kutschera, *Kurdish National Movement*, 366–373. See also the Pike Secret Report to the U.S. House of Representatives Committee on Intelligence in O'Ballance, *The Kurdish Struggle*, 103; Chaliand, *People Without a Country*, 184–85.

97. Quoted by McDowall, *Modern History of the Kurds*, 337.

98. Ibid., 336.

99. Ibid., 336. For an extensive criticism of Barzani, see Chaliand, *People Without a Country*, 189–192.

100. Ibid., 336.

101. Nader Entessar, *Kurdish Ethnonationalism* (London: Lynne Rienner Publishers, 1992) 76–77; Chaliand, *Kurdish Tragedy*, 62–63; O'Ballance, *Kurdish Struggle*, 116.

102. Kutschera, *Kurdish National Movement*, 413.

103. Cited by McDowall, *Modern History of the Kurds*, 343.

104. Ibid., 345.

105. Ibid., 345.

106. Chaliand, *Kurdish Tragedy*, 64–65.

107. McDowall, *Modern History of the Kurds*, 347.

108. Ibid., 345.

109. Chaliand, *Kurdish Tragedy*, 65. See also, O'Ballance, *The Kurdish Struggle*, 169–70, Bruinessen, *Agha, Shaikh, and State*, 43; Entessar, *Kurdish Ethnonationalism* (Boulder, Colorado: Lynn Riennen Publishing, 1992), 136–40.

110. Chaliand, *Kurdish Tragedy*, 70–72.

111. Ismail Besikci, *Masalei-e Kordestan Dar Turkkieh va Iragh* (The Kurdish Problem in Turkey and Iraq) translated by Mohammad Raooph (Tehran, Iran: Hamida Publisher, 1378), 54–68. Ismail Besikci is a sociologist; he is not a Kurd. He is a Turkish scholar spending more than ten years in prison for his publications on the Kurdish people. Born in 1939, he studied at the Department of Political Science at the Ankara University. He wrote his dissertation on the Kurds that was published in 1959. The dissertation was entitled, "The Socio-Economic and Ethnic Foundations of Eastern Anatolia." The Turkish government called it "communist and Kurdish propaganda," which sent him to prison for a period of four years (1971–1974). He was released as a result of amnesty declared by Bulent Eavit, the Turkish Prime Minister. However, further publications put him in prison from 1979–1981, and again for questioning the

validity of governmental ideology, he was imprisoned two months after his release in 1981, and remained incarcerated until May 1987. Amnesty International has labeled him a "prisoner of conscience." See also, Gerard Chaliand, *The Kurdish Tragedy* (London: Zed Books, 1994), 33.

112. Chris Kutschera, *Le Mouvement National* (Paris: Falmmarion, 1979), 364.

113. Caliphate is the name for religious institution and Caliph is the religious leader who presides over it. Ataturk (Father of Turks) by 1929 made serious secular reforms from above. He first asked the Ankara National Assembly to pass a law declaring that sovereignty belongs to the people. This declaration is a radical reversal of the Medieval Islamic Doctrine that sovereignty belongs to God. Following the abolition of traditional Islamic institutions and religious symbols, Ataturk embarked on radical secularization and modernization schemes. He abolished Arabic alphabet replacing it with the Latin script. He started Turkification measures. Ataturk began to suppress popular Islamic symbols such as the Fez, the veil, religious clothing. The traditional calendar was replaced by a new calendar. All of his secularization initiatives were precipitated by the 1937 amendment to the Turkish constitution. Turkishness came to be identified with the state that he was the founder and architect of. For further insights see, Ellen K. Trimberger "A Theory of Elite Revolutions," in *Studies in Comparative International Development* 7: 3 (Fall 1972): 191–207; Ellen K. Trimberger, *Revolution from Above: Military Bureaucrats and Development in Japan, Turkey and Peru* (New Brunswick, New Jersey: Transaction Books, 1978), 41–44. For further information see Robert Olson, ed., *The Kurdish Nationalist Movement in the 1990s* (Lexington: The University Press of Kentucky, 1996), 173–177; Nader Entessar, *Kurdish Ethnonationalism* (London: Lynne Rienner Publishers, 1992), 82.

114. David McDowall, *A Modern History of the Kurds* (London: T. B. Tauris, 1997), 194–95. See also, Nader Entessar, *Kurdish Ethnonationalism*, 83–83.

115. Kaveh Bayat, *Shooresh-e Kurdhigh-e Tur keyyeh va Taasir-e on Dar Ravabet-e Khary-e Iran* (The Revolt of Turkish Kurds and Its Impact on the Foreign Policy of Iran) (Tehran, Iran: Nashr-e Tarikh-e Iran, 1374), 19–22; Robert Olson, *The Emergence of Kurdish Nationalism, 1880–1925* (Austin: University of Texas Press, 1991), 155.

116. V. Hamdi, *Kurdistan va Kurd Dar Isnad-e Mahramanei Britania* (Kurdistan and Kurd in the British Confidential Documents), 189, F0371/1867 Magor Hareace, see also, F0371,1925; Martin Van Bruinessen, *Agha, Shaikh, and State* (London: Zed Books, 1992), 291–296.

117. McDowall, *A Modern History of the Kurds*, 194–96.

118. Van Bruinessen, *Agha Shaikh and State*, 291.

119. Entessar, *Kurdish Nationalism*, 84.

120. McDowall, *A Modern History of the Kurds*, 197–98.

121. Van Bruinessen, *Agha, State, and Shaikh*, 290–291; McDowall, *A Modern History of the Kurds*, 200.

122. Entessar, *Kurdish Nationalism*, 85. However, Bruinessen and McDowall argue against Nader Entessar's assertion that the Nuri's rebellion was nationalistic.

123. See McDowall, *A Modern History of the Kurds*, 202–204.

124. Ibid., 205. See also Gerard Chaliand, ed., *People Without a Country* (London: Zed Books, 1980), 65.

125. Entessar, Kurdish Nationalism, 84–85. See also Chaliand, *The Kurdish Tragedy*, 37–38.

126. Quoted by Chaliand, ed., *People Without a Country*, 65; Entessar, *Kurdish Ethnonationalism,* 86; Chaliand, *Kurdish Tragedy*, 38.

127. Chaliand, ed., People Without a Country, 65.

128. Kendal Nazdar, "Kurdistan in Turkey," in Chaliand, ed., *People Without a Country*, 65–66.

129. McDowall, *A Modern History of the Kurds*, 207.

130. Chaliand, *The Kurdish Tragedy*, 39. For more elaboration on this claim, see Kendal, "Kurdistan in Turkey." in Chaliand, ed., *People Without A Country*, 67.

131. See F0371/34977 from Sir E. Spears Beirot 10 May 1943. Apparently this document, which is reflective of racism in its very ugly form, might have been released to Komala Khoyben by the British Embassy in Lebanon, for the above mentioned footnote comes from the British confidential documents. See Hamdi, *Kurdistan va Kurd*, 195–6.

132. See Kendal, "Kurdistan in Turkey," in Chaliand, ed., *People Without A Country,* 68.

133. Kendal, "Kurdistan in Turkey," in Chaliand, ed., *People Without A Country,* 68; see also, Entessar, Kurdish Ethnonationalism, 86–87; Edgar O'Ballance, *The Kurdish Struggle, 1920–1994* (New York: St. Martin's Press, 1996). 16.

134. See Hamdi, *Kurdistan va Kurd*, 195–196.

135. Ibid., 196.

136. See Nezan Kendal, "Kurdistan in Turkey" in Chaliand, ed., *People Without A Country,* 72–74. See also Chaliand, *The Kurdish Tragedy*, 44; and Entessar, *Kurdish Ethnonationaism*, 87.

137. McDowall, *A Modern History of the Kurds*, 395–400.

138. Ibid., 403.

139. Kendal, "Kurdistan in Turkey," in Chaliand, ed., *People Without A Country*, 74; Entessar, *Kurdish Ethnonationalism*, 88.

140. McDowall, *A Modern History of the Kurds*, 404.

141. Quoted by McDowall, *A Modern History of the Kurds*, 404.

142. Ibid., 405.

143. Entessar, *Kurdish Ethnonationalism*, 89; see also, Chaliand, *The Kurdish Tragedy*, 45.

144. McDowall, *A Modern History of the Kurds*, 406.

145. Entessar, *Kurdish Ethnonationalism*, 89–90; Kendal, "Kurdistan in Turkey," in Chaliand, ed., *People Without a Country*, 97.

146. See Chaliand, *The Kurdish Tragedy*, 45.

147. Ahmet Samim, "The Tragedy of the Turkish Left," *New Left Review* 126 (March–April 1981): 60–85.

148. Kendal, "Kurdistan in Turkey," in Chaliand, ed., *People Without a Country*, 97.

149. See Chaliand, *The Kurdish Tragedy*, 45; see also Entessar, *Kurdish Ethnonationalism*, 89–90.

150. Kendal, "Kurdistan in Turkey," in Chaliand, ed., *People Without a Country*, 98.

151. Michael M. Gunter, *The Kurds in Turkey: A Political Dilemma* (Boulder: Westview Press, 1990), 16; Entessar, *Kurdish Ethnonationalism*, 90.

152. McDowall, *A Modern History of the Kurds*, 418–419; Chaliand, *The Kurdish Tragedy*, 47; Entessar, *Kurdish Ethnonationalism*, 94; Gunter, *The Kurds in Turkey*, 57; *Roosnamei Sobh-e Imrose* (Today's Morning Newspaper) in Yalcin Kucuk, *Dastan-e Dubareh Zistan: Khaterat va Andishahie Abdullah Ocalan* (Tehran, Iran: Hamida Publisher, 1378), 288–289. See also Munir Morad, "The Situation of Kurds in Iraq and Turkey: Current Trends and Prospects," in Philip G. Kreyenbroek and Stefan Sperl, eds., *The Kurds: A Contemporary Overview* (London: Routledge Press, 1992), 121.

153. Van Bruinessen, "Between Guerrilla Wars and Political Murder: The Worker's Party of Kurdistan," *Middle East Report* 16, no. 4 (July–August 1986): 41; "The Kurds Between Iran and Iraq," *Middle East Report* 16, no. 4 (July–August 1988): 24–27.

154. Ibid., 42; see also Bruinessen's article, "The Kurds Between Iran and Iraq," *The Middle East Report* 16, no. 4 (July–August 1986): 14–27.

155. Gunter, *The Kurds in Turkey: A Political Dilemma,* 59; Entessar, *Kurdish Ethnonationaism*, 95. For more information, see Ocalan Abdullah, *Islam va Meehan Doosty, Jame-ah-iKurdistan va Tarh-e Trror-e Man* (Islam and Patriotism, Kurdish Sovereinty, and the Plan of My Terror), translated from Turkish by Mohammad Raof-Marady (Tehran, Iran: One Nashr-One Publishers, 1379), 80–83.

156. Quoted by Gunter, *The Kurds in Turkey*, 59–60; and Entessar, *Kurdish Nationalism*, 95–96; Ocalan, *Islam va Meehan Doosty,* 74.

157. See McDowall, *A Modern History of the Kurds*, 420, Gunter, *The Kurds in Turkey,* 71–72.

158. Mao Tse-Tung, *Selected Works of Mao Tse-Tung*, vol. 1, 4th ed. (Peking: China: Peoples Publishing House, 1977), 207–208.

159. See McDowall, *A Modern History of the Kurds*, 420.

160. Ibid., 420–421.

161. Ibid., 421. See also Entessar, *Kurdish Ethnonationalism*, 98–99.

162. Cited by O'Ballance, *The Kurdish Struggle*, 146.

163. Ibid., 154.

164. McDowall, *A Modern History of the Kurds,* 421–423.

165. Ibid., 423.

166. Ibid., 422.

167. Ibid., 422–423.

168. *Human Rights Watch/Helsinki, New York* (March 1993): 12. See also Chaliand, *The Kurdish Tragedy*, 49.

169. Cited by McDowall, *A Modern History of the Kurds*, 423.

170. "The Kurds of Turkey Killings, Disappearances and Torture," *Human Rights Watch/Helsinki, New York*, March 1993, 11–13.

171. *Turkey—Facts and Figures, Which Turkey for What Europe*, 23, see also http://burn.uscd.edu/archives/kurd-1/1995/0139.html, p. 4 of 5.

172. Ibid., 23–24.

173. Ibid., 24.

174. "Under the Title of the Scorched Earth Policy in Kurdistan and State Terror in Turkish Kurdistan, *International Herald Tribune* 9 June 1994, 44. This newspaper has documented the villages destroyed by the Turkish Army. Hundreds of villages, which were destroyed, were mentioned by name. The report goes on to say the Kurdish towns of Sirnak, Kulp Lice and Cukurca have been altered into ghost towns. Half the population of others have fled as a result of state sponsored terror and assassination." In the last two years they have assassinated 1638 Kurdish intellectuals, political personalities, trade unionists and teachers, including the Kurdish poet Musa Anter, 74 years of age, member of the Parliament Mardin Mahmet Sincer and 72 other caders of his democracy party and 34 journalists and news agents. Many thousands of Kurdish political activists are in prison, solely because of their opinions . . ."

175. See Milliyet, 25 July 1995. See also, *Human Rights Report*: 1994, "A Summary" (July 1995): 7.

176. Medhi Zana, *Prison No. 5: Eleven Years in Turkish Jails,* published in French, Editions Arlea, Paris: 1995.

177. *Turkey—Facts and Figures, Human Rights Report*, "White Turkey for White People," 1994: 23.

178. *Kurdish Life*, no. 35 (summer 2000): 1. See also Chris Kutchera, "Mad Dreams of Independence: The Kurds of Turkey and the PKK," *Middle East Report* 189 (July–August 1994): 12–15.

179. Ibid. See also Aliza Marcus, "City in the War Zone," *Middle East Report* no. 189 (July–August 1994): 16–19.

180. See, for example, Abudullah Ocalan, *Dastane Doubareh Ziestan: Khaterat va Andi Shaheil Abdullah Ocalan, Sobhi Imroz* (The Story of Rebirth: Ocalan's Memoirs and Political Thoughts) 31, January 1999. Indexes from the Iranian media to the aforementioned source.

181. *Kurdish Life*, no. 35 (summer 2000): 2. See also Isam al-Khafaji, "Almost Unnoticed Interventions and Rivalries in Iraqi Kurdistan," *Middle East Report*. Accessed on 24 January 2001, http://www.merip.org/miro/miro012401.htlm.

182. Ibid.

183. *Kurdish Life*, no. 34 (spring 2000): 5.

184. Frank Cunningham, *Democratic Theory and Socialism* (Cambridge: Cambridge University Press, 1988), 58–59.

185. Andrew Levine, *Arguing for Socialism: Theoretical Considerations* (Boston: Roudledge and Kegon and Paul, 1984), 132.

186. Ertugrul Kurkcu, "The Crisis of the Turkish State," in *Middle East Report* (April–June 1996): 3–9; Sami Zubaida, "Turkish Islam and National Identity" in *Middle East Report* (April–June 1996): 10–15; *Kurdish Life*, no. 29 (winter 1999): 9.

187. *Kurdish Life*, no. 35 (summer 2000): 1; *Kurdish Life*, no. 36 (fall 2000): 1–6.

188. "Abduction of Abdullah Ocalan," *Kurdish Life*, no. 29 (winter 1999): 1–10. See also *Kurdish Life*, no. 35 (summer 2000): 1.

189. *Kurdish Life*, no. 29 (winter 1999): 9.

190. Ibid., 1

191. "Turkey hardens stances over Ocalan extradition." 16 Nov. 1998. http://can .com/world/europe/9811/16/Italy.ocalan/index

192. Aijaz Ahmad, "Imperialism and Progress," in *Theories of Development: Mode of Production or Dependence?* eds. Ronald H. Chilcote and Dale L. Johnson (London: Sage Publications, 1983), 44.

193. *Kurdish Life*, no. 31 (summer 1999): 1–3.

194. Ibid.

195. Ted Robert Gurr, *Why Men Rebel* (Princeton, New Jersey: Princeton University Press, 1970), 68–69.

196. Ibid., 12–13.

197. McDowall, *A Modern History of the Kurds*, 444.

198. Ibid.

199. Kurdish Life, no. 23 (winter 2000): 13.

200. Professor Doug Ergil authored the results of a survey conducted in 1995. The survey indicates that two-thirds of Kurds polled are in favor of self-administration within the Republic (only 11 percent favored secession.) Cited by McDowall's updated version, *A Modern History of the Kurds*, 446; see *Kurdish Life*, no. 33 (winter 2000): 15.

Chapter Six

Autonomy and Kurdish Political Problems

The concept of autonomy is seen as a solution to the political problems of minorities seeking socio-political and economic justice within multi-ethnic societies. David Held defines the concept of autonomy in the following way:

> Persons should enjoy equal rights (and, accordingly, equal obligations) in the framework that generates and limits the opportunities available to them. That is, they should be free and equal in the determination of the conditions of their lives, so long as they do not employ this framework to negate the rights of others.[1]

The right to participate in the process of political collective decision-making should not be limited by distinctions of creed, political persuasions, color, sex, or minority status. However, autonomy does not guarantee that decisions reflect the "will of all" (the general will). It is instead based "on the deliberation of all."[2]

It is crucial to distinguish between state sovereignty and popular sovereignty. Advocates of state sovereignty vest ultimate power in the state to determine the normative code of behavior and define for citizens their rights. Supporters of popular sovereignty assign to the state the role of class mediation, and its crucial function is to implement "will of all". In fact, both of these approaches involve tyranny and jeopardize individual autonomy and liberty. Hence, both must be viewed with prudence and skepticism and a system of checks and balances must be integral to each. The supremacy of one or the other can pose a threat to democratic ideals.[3] Government (or power) and freedom do not mix, one is the anti-thesis of another. Yet, both are critical values for human interaction: a government that is effectively in control and a government that is effectively controlled. An increase in one will come only at the cost of the other. Government control would be legitimate only if people, in turn, controlled government.[4] Thus for democratic autonomy to be realized, it has to be enshrined in a legitimate framework that enables and limits the sovereignty of the state and its citizens. The survival of civil society can only be insured within a constitutional system, with a bill of rights, free and competitive elections, and a constitutionally limited federation of democratic states.[5] Autonomy without democracy cannot be realized. In order to substantiate the validity of this claim, it is crucial to define what democracy really is.

Seymour Martin Lipset states, "Democracy is not only or even primarily a means through which different groups can attain their ends or seek the good of society; it is the good society itself in operation."[6] This definition is problematic. Defining democracy as a means to a particular end negates the value of the political and social components of democracy. Philip Green's argument further illustrates this problem. Genuine democracy involves political equality, which is absent in liberal capitalism. A true democracy is where "everybody should count for one and nobody for more than one."[7] A democracy is based on a component of social equality: a form of material equality guaranteed by equal access to the means of production with no oppressive division of labor.

Although Norway, Denmark, Sweden, Germany and a number of other European countries are social democracies, they do not meet Green's theoretical expectations. Green refers to a democratic deficit in these social democracies; a failure to promote social protection mechanisms and eradicate unemployment. In some of the European countries, inequality, marginalization and exclusionsim remain to be solved. In fact, the social democratic desire for egalitarianism and a class free society is doomed to fail. The notion of "egalitarianism at all costs" troubles Michael Walzer. He states:

> Simple equality of that sort is the bad utopianism of the old left . . . political conflict and the competition for leadership always make for power inequalities and entrepreneurial activity always makes for economic inequalities . . . none of this can be prevented without endless tyrannical interventions in ordinary life. It was an historical mistake of large proportions, for which we [on the left] have paid heavily . . ."[8]

In spite of many other shortcomings such as waste, insensitivity to consumer goods, overloaded bureaucratic states, and stagnated economic growth, social democracy is a radical improvement over the prevailing liberal democracies.[9] Liberal democracies have failed to deliver any degree of material equalities, which should be corrected by the liberal state's interventionism. But, as Andrew Levine correctly observes, under capitalism, the function of the state precisely is to maintain the existing unequal social relations of production.[10] As long as income and wealth are unequally distributed, the inequality of power will remain a dominant factor in liberal democracies, stifling democratic freedom and liberty.

In terms of income distribution, Anthony Giddens claims that the United States is the most unequal of all industrial and liberal democratic countries. "The proportion of income taken by the top 1 percent has increased substantially over the past two or three decades, while those at the bottom have seen their average incomes stagnate or decline." Compared to Sweden and Norway, poverty in the US in the early 1990s was five times as great. "Poverty levels were 20 percent for the US, as compared to 4 percent for the other two countries."[11]

Under a neoliberal approach, capital is concentrated in fewer and fewer hands. Clyde Barrow cites similar statistics. In the United States, ". . . the top 1 percent of American families own 61 percent of all outstanding corporate stock and 41 percent of total personal income goes to the top one-fifth of families."[12] Since the 1920s this pattern of capital concentration has persisted and grew wider during the 1980s. E. Digby Baltzell has referred to the class division in the US as a "business aristocracy." Inheritance transmits accumulated wealth that creates islands of exclusive wealth.[13] The inequality of wealth undermines political equality, rights, and opportunities for minorities. Pluralistic political participation and the abolition of the influence of wealth in politics would allow autonomy for minority and majority groups.

Donald L. Barlett and James B. Steele address the inequalities in the US, a country with wealth and power,

> "The top 1 percent of households controls almost one-third (30.4 percent) of the nation's total wealth not income." The next nine percent hold another third (36.8 percent) of the nation's wealth." Consequently, "the top 10 percent of households own two-thirds (67.2 percent) of the nation's wealth. The remaining 90 percent account for 32.8 percent of the wealth."[14]

Thomas Palley's research reveals that in the US, the income of the top 5 percent of households rose by 20.5 percent between 1970 and 1993, middle class income declined 8.5 percent, and the lowest fifth's income declined 12 percent within the same period. Palley, as opposed to Barrow, maintains that in 1992 the top 1 percent of wealthy American households owned 49.5 percent of all stocks and the top 10 percent owned 86.3 percent of all stocks.[15] These statistics show the great unequal distribution of wealth and income in American society. Political freedom and liberty require a degree of material equality since many of life's choices are defined by the availability of capital. When choices are limited due to material inequalities, liberty is denied. Freedom from material want is a natural right and is crucial for self-fulfillment. In a liberal democratic society, such as the US, the equality of opportunity does not secure an equality of conditions that is critical for the realization of democratic rights. Arbitrary distributions of wealth and status maintain a class system that deprives minorities an equal access to public goods.

Opposed to this unequal distribution of social justice, social democrats believe that when society is sharply divided into haves and have nots, liberalism's individualistic autonomous values are compromised. In reality, goods and services in a liberal democratic representational system are not distributed in accordance to their social meanings, which negates the very meaning of democratic autonomy. Walzer's analysis further supports the validity of this thesis.

"The disregard of these principals [of autonomous distribution] is tyranny. . . . In political life—but more widely, too—the dominance of goods makes for the domination of people . . ."[16]

In this sense, the autonomy of individuals, both politically and socially, is lost. Material inequality promotes the domination of a class system that blocks the political access points. Private wealth is used to control political decision-making and shape public opinion in favor of the dominant class interest. When the masses support dominant interest as their own interests, this is referred to as false consciousness.

Similar imbalances exist in North-South relations where the liberal democratic model has promoted self-interest. As Brian Barry argues:

"We should regard as self refuting any theory of justice claiming that there is nothing unjust about a world in which poor countries are making net transfers to rich ones, and in which the USA uses up to 40 percent of total resources, while a quarter of the world's population goes without the most basic necessities."[17]

Social forces in class-dominated societies suffer from inequalities, unemployment, under-employment, and injustices perpetuated by exploitation, corruption, and the unequal distribution of goods and services. Under the prevailing class-divided conservative world system, it is difficult to realize human ideals and autonomous rights. The democratic realization of rights for working men and women and minorities remains to be seen.

The Kurdish demand for autonomy in autocratic governments is not a fundamental solution. In defense of ethnic minorities and nationalities in the former USSR, Rosa Luxemburg wrote that autonomy is an empty concept if the centralized autocracy is not democratized. She made a distinction between the modern concept of autonomy and medieval particularism. Autonomy attends to the local needs of the people and advocates political participation.

Medieval particularism uses political power as paternalistic accommodation. Under capitalism, autonomy is not a practical solution to nationality problems. "So long as the capitalist states exists and imperialistic world politics determine and regulate the inner and the outer life of a nation, there can be no national self-determination, either in war or in peace."[18]

The capitalist world system conflicts with democratic ideals. It is a system of inequality rooted in the process of capital accumulation. The dominant world system perpetuates social injustices and human sufferings. Karl Kautsky feels that the problems of language and nationality can be solved only in a truly democratic system based on a universal franchise and equal direct participation in elections. Feudalistic privilege in the state must be abolished. When these conditions are met, democratic autonomy will be a solution to the political problems of Kurds and other minorities.

Both Luxemburg and Kautsky supported social democracy as a political solution to minority and nationality problems in the former Soviet Union, although the credibility and applicability of their thesis to the modern day Kurdish problems has been questioned. But the prevailing socio-economic and political problems in Russia today, which are attributed to the so-called electoral democracy, support the validity of Luxemburg's and Kautsky's propositions. Although many scholars claim that the democratic internationalization of the existing international order is critical, it is not enough. Democracy needs to be defined in terms of both political and social components and must be reinforced by the globalization of human rights, effective enforcement of these rights, and corruption containment.[19]

However, the irony is that democracy of this kind, with the exception of a few social democracies in Europe in need of restructuring and structural reformations, remains to be seen at the core of the world system, let alone in the Middle East or Kurdistan. Under these circumstances, the Kurdish demand for autonomy under the existing political structures functioning nationally and internationally is problematic.

In Iran, for instance, the Kurds need to be reminded of the constitutional movement of 1905–1909 that led to the creation of a progressive social democratic document. The movement was a struggle between those who stood for the status quo and those who sought liberation from oppression, corruption, and domination. The upheaval of Tabriz, along with the demands from other progressive social forces, especially the social democratic orientation of Haydar Khan Amu Ughli, culminated in the creation of democratic institutions. The document that was drawn up to support this new democracy was referred to as Supplementary Fundamental Laws and contained two main sections. The first section included a bill of rights, guaranteeing equality before law, protection of life, property, and honor, safeguards from arbitrary arrest, and freedom of the press.[20]

The second section provided for checks and balances, although the legislative branch appeared to have supremacy over the executive branch. More importantly, this new constitution declared that sovereignty would be derived from the people, not from God: "The sovereignty is a trust confirmed (as a divine gift) by the people to the person of the king."[21] This progressive constitution, born out of revolution like the Articles of Confederation, a product of the American Revolution, continued to live for twelve years from 1909–1921. Had this trend of constitutionalism succeeded, no ethnic group in Iran, including the Kurds, would have needed any justification for autonomy.

But sadly, the revolution of 1905–1909 overthrew the Qajar dynasty's "despotism" and replaced it with a progressive constitutional system. In 1921, a coup d'etat supported by the British resulted in the shelving of the newly created democratic parliamentary structure and the establishment of the Pahlavi dictatorship. The Reza Shah's autocracy abruptly ended the new democratic experimentation.[22]

However, constitutional and liberation struggles continued on two fronts with British imperialism in the south and Russian Tsarism in the north. This was reflected in the Anglo-Russian Agreement of 1907 that divided the country into possessive zones of influence and the dictatorship of Reza Khan. The Jangal (the jungle) movement, led by Mizra Kuchek Khan, fought the Russian forces of occupation. The movement was supported by Tagizadeh and Iranian students studying in Germany, who published a periodical called *Kaveh*. Kaveh was the name of a legendary blacksmith who had revolted against an unjust king. With the occurrence of the October Revolution of 1917 in Russia, the movement received a boost from this revolution. In Gilan, the Jangalies entered into an alliance with Khalu Gurban and Ehsanullah Khan's forces. The former organized the gum workers and Kurds from Kermanshah, and the latter, educated in Paris, brought democratic forces from Tehran. According to Abrahamian, by the end of 1917, the Janglies were a fundamental force in the North.[23] The October Revolution also helped the movement to offset the British occupation forces in the South, securing socialistic ideals, robbing the rich and feeding the poor.

But this movement, too, was short lived; Raza Khan's forces did slay its leader, Mirza Kuchek Khan. To prove that the Jangal movement was defeated, Mirza Kuchek Khan's head was put on display in Tehran, the capital of Iran.[24] Yet, this was the beginning of a new class struggle in Iran which culminated in the formation of socialist and communist parties that enhanced the struggle for liberation from an externally imposed dictatorial system. Whereas the progressive forces were committed to the cause of liberation, the imperial powers attempted to pit one faction against another by supporting the central government's control of the social forces, rather than repelling the dominating foreign powers. The class of "fifty three" formed the foundation of the revolutionary struggle aimed at the liberation of the oppressed. The leader of the fifty-three was a thirty-six year old professor of physics from Tehran University, Tagi Arani, who graduated from Berlin University, Germany, and was known for his promotion of political debate and critical thinking. But these intellectual debates came to an abrupt end in 1937 when the fifty-three were arrested by the police and Arani died (probably murdered) in prison.[25] The state increasingly utilized violence to control the masses. Had the allied forces not occupied Iran in August 1941, the Reza Khan's rule would have possibly been overthrown by a social revolution since there was little popular support for his regime.

With the forced abdication of Reza Shah in 1941, a degree of political openness developed that promoted further politicization, radicalization, and factionalization. It was in the absence of the incapacitated central government that the Firgeh-i Demokrat-e Azerbaijan, the democratic party of Azerbaijan led by Ja'Far Pishavari and the Kurdish Republic of Mahabad under Gazi Mohammad were formed in 1944–45. The Red Army supported both movements and when the Soviets, under pressure from the United States withdrew from Iran, both republics collapsed.

As a result of the elimination of the centralized dictatorial power and the weaknesses of the new shah, Mohammad Reza, the son of the abdicated shah, Mosaddeg, sought to restore the constitution of 1905–1909, a carbon copy of existing social democratic constitutions. Again, democracy was on the rise, especially when Dr. Mosaddeg, the Prime Minister, nationalized the Anglo-Iranian oil company. The US and Britian consented to Mosaddeg's position, but when he called for the nationalization of the oil industry, he was forced out of the country. However, in a CIA sponsored coup d'etat in 1953, the Shah was re-imposed on the Iranians.

The political climate changed drastically and a period of what Iranians call, KhaFagan, meaning a period of strangulation, began again. For nearly twenty-five years, despotism ruled the lives of Iranians. Summary execution, disappearances, chain killings, and tortures were the destiny of dissenting forces. By 1978–79, a popular mass-based revolution overthrew this despotic regime. Although the revolution restored national honor and provided for electoral participation, the implementation of the 1905–1909 constitution and the democratic ideals remain to be seen. One wonders if the Kurdish claim to democratic autonomy has any meaning. When an overwhelming majority of the country has been restricted for almost over a century, how can the Kurds live an autonomous and free life within this unfreedom?

In Iraq, under the centralized dictatorship of Saddam Hussein, political rights were restricted, as in Iran. Political dissenters were terrorized, and Saddam imposed a lengthy and very expensive eight-year war on Iran, invaded Kuwait and then marched into northern Iraq to destroy Talabani's forces. Saddam's atrocities toward the Kurds is well documented. During the Iranian/ Iraqi war, he gassed down five thousand Kurds at Halabja, a small Kurdish town located near the Iranian border, southeast of Sulaymaniya. This took place when Iranian armed forces, supported by Kurdish Peshmergas (guerrilla fighters), occupied Halabja. Iraq considered them enemy combatants or their accomplices and retaliated with chemical weaponry supplied by the West.

Following the Halabja tragedy, the Iraqi government continued its systematic violation of not only Kurdish rights, but retaliated against those who had protested Saddam's human right's violations. However, most of the gas victims of Halabja were civilians, women and children.[26] According to Martin Van Bruinessen, chemical attacks led to refugee crises and the government of Iraq embarked on the mass deportation of Kurds. They were shuffled from their homes in the north to the south where they were resettled in new governmental towns and subjected to forced Arabization and assimilation. By 1991, four thousand out of seven thousand Kurdish villages had been subjected to destruction. Halabja, and other strategic areas, had been demolished[27].

Human Rights Watch reported that between 1987 and 1988 an estimated 20,000 Kurdish civilians were killed with poison gasses. No one is sure how many Kurds were gassed down, but the Kurdish countryside was depopulated. The government had the entire population of Gala Diza, a minimum of 50,000 people, deported. What is more, as a result of the Iraqi gas attacks more than 100,000 Kurds had been forced into exile.[28] Although these atrocities captured worldwide media attention, it did not result in punitive action for Saddam. The US and other Western countries refused to criticize the mass killings.[29] According to Noam Chomsky, US and British responses to what he calls "the ultimate horror" supported Saddam's action, because his actions were "with our [US and British] support."[30]

Both The *Human Rights Watch* and *Amnesty International* provided an authentic summary of the abuse of human rights in Iraq, but lacked a macro analysis. The microanalysis was limited to a mainstream status quo interpretation. The devastating issues of colonization, Balkanization of the Middle East, the negative impact of neocolonialization, and the divide and conquer policy of the core of the world system was neglected. *Human Rights Watch* and *Amnesty International* failed to link the genocide practices of the Iraqi government to the atrocities of the neoconservative world system.

The concept of human rights has been used as a political tool by the core of the world system in defining its own material interests. This applies to the core countries themselves. Conflict between the rights of selfish interests and human rights are generally settled in favor of material self-interest. The core promotes division between the various factions in the peripheral regions in a deliberate effort to create friction.[31]

Human Right Watch and *Amnesty International* also failed to point out that Iraqi Kurds had more rights, especially political and cultural rights, than the Kurds in Iran and Turkey. They have their own parliament, language, universities, and security forces, to name a few. More important, the degree of Kurdish autonomous existence in Iraq proves our assumption that autonomy without democracy has no value. According to Noam Chomsky, Britain's divide and rule policy has always been present in the political realm. The Nazi forces exercised this tactic by using Jews to control Jews. Today it is happening with the Kurds. "The West is trying to mobilize Iraqi Kurds to destroy Turkish Kurds, who are by far the largest group and historically the most oppressed."[32]

The contradictory policies associated with capital accumulation and surplus extraction are ignored. If Saddam was such an abuser of human rights, why did the world core support him during his eight years of bloody war against Iran? Why did the West give Saddam a green light to invade Iran and did not condemn the use of gas in Kurdistan, but when the conquest was carried out against Kuwait, he was punished? An analysis that excludes the contradictions of the prevailing world system is faulty logic; it is only participation in state-approved ideological intellectualism.[33]

Chomsky claims that the West uses the Iraqi Kurds as sabotage for the prevailing Iraqi system. The goal is to create Western-style stability by installing a government in Iraq that would comply with Western desires. Why does the West support the Iraqi Kurds, but refers to the Kurdish political movement in Turkey as a terrorist organization?[34] The Iraqi Kurds and Turkish Kurds have the same culture, the same identity, and the same desire for an autonomous Kurdistan. Why doesn't the West take action against Turkey's atrocities against the Kurds? Why doesn't the West recognize the rights of Turkish Kurds? These questions can only be answered by using a holistic approach.

State sponsored political violence must be brought under democratic control by the rule of law which, according to Jurgen Habermas, ". . . is the recognition of the freedom belonging equally to all human beings with the power of will."[35] A legal political order is critical to transfer to "individuals the power of will objectively incorporated in law: Right is a power or rule of will conferred by the legal order."[36] Unfortunately, the world system's elites generally side with illegitimate state elites in the peripheries.[37] The elites at the core of the system use convenient concepts such as human rights, the rule of law, and democratic ideals as a means for the realization of its hegemonic world domination, which only promote contradictions that result in political violence, revolutions, and conflicts demonstrated by the experience of the Kurds in Turkey.

The Kurds in Turkey have less cultural and political rights than in Iran and Iraq. In Turkey, the Kurds are deprived of their identity by a denial of their social and cultural rights. They are referred to as the "mountain Turks," and are not allowed to exercise their unique culture or utilize their mother tongue. To say that the Kurds are not Kurds, but "mountain Turks," denies their identity and poses a threat to the healthy functioning of the Turkish whole. *Human Rights Watch/Helsinki*, claims that although the law outlawing the speaking of Kurdish on the street was repealed,[38] it is still illegal to speak the Kurdish in courts, official places, and public gatherings. The destruction of Kurdish villages and towns in the southeast remains in effect. Collective punishment is inflicted on villagers who refuse to join the so-called village guard system to fight against the PKK. People are also punished for providing food or shelter to the Kurdish guerrillas, the PKK. In the event of a PKK attack on military forces, a Kurdish village is to be vacated, and then the village is destroyed by governmental security forces.[39] Some scholars call this behavior "state sponsored terrorism."[40] The Turkish military solution to a political problem is no solution at all. It culminates in exclusivity, radicalization, and more politicization that threaten the continuity of the Turkish state. It further destroys any hope for political and national integration.

Consequently, the concept of democratic political autonomy is problematic. It is often defined by the Kurds as an exercise of self-determination within the framework of the prevailing systems. Although Kurdish inhabitants are established in the northern part of Iraq and in the east and southeast of Turkey, this is not the case in Iran where the Kurds claim possession to territories that have been owned by others for decades. Apart from definitional problems associated with a desire for territorial acquisition and possession of land, Kurdish political autonomy will be politically costly to all three countries. It will mobilize and encourage other politically important minorities to demand the similar autonomous rights, which may result in political backlash, disintegration, and dismemberment in those countries. In a sense, these ethnically formed nation states may cease to exist. This is the political dilemma that continues to overshadow and frustrate the issue of minority rights.

Kurdish rights to self-determination will be realized when the artificially drawn boundaries are redefined in the colonized Balkans and divided Middle East. Short of such a radical restructuring, the idea of the Kurdish homeland, Kurdish state, or a democratic political autonomy may be only a political dream. A redefinition of the boundaries in the region would be a radical structural transformation of the prevailing conservative and status quo order. It is unlikely that this change would be acceptable to current political cultures and structures since there is a conflict between Kurdish autonomy, the continuity of a stable world system, and the balance that favors the dominating internal and external political structures.

The fragmented traditionalistic political culture, tribal affiliations, informal group politics, and the conservative mode of thinking undermines the realization of the Kurds' desire for autonomy. The most debilitating contradiction between the Kurdish traditionalistic leadership and the desire to liberate Kurdish society from externally created internal domination is Kurdish dependence on imperial forces for liberation; a reliance on the oppressors. This logic has prevented the development of Kurdish class solidarity and political consciousness. The Kurdish quest for political autonomy and self-determination, especially in Iraq, has been consistently reactionary. This mode of behavior and political factionalism has played a key role in defeating the idea of political autonomy for the Kurds.

The Kurds have been used as a policy tool by neocolonial and regional powers for realizing their political and military ends. This negative state of affairs, coupled with factionalism, undermines the efforts of left wing Kurdish forces, such as the Komala or the Kurdish Worker's Party (though the latter has been accused of terrorism by the *Helsinki Human Rights Watch*). Jala Talabani, the founder of the Patriotic Union of Kurdistan (PUK), and the leading critic of the Kurdish Democratic Party led by Masud Barzani, was forced to accept the regional government's military support, a setback for Kurdish unity.

The Kurdish left represents itself as an advocate for the working people and poor peasants, and claims that the Iraqi KDP is a feudal organization, and that the KDP Iran is the class ally of the tribal elites and the urban bourgeoisie class. This view is not acceptable to the Iraqi KDP, since their support originates from the tribal forces. The tribal forces have supported the landed classes both in Iraq and Iran, and most of its cadres come from the urban upper middle classes. However, the vast majority of all Kurdish political organization membership can be sought either in tribalism or in the landed class. Critics of the Komala and the Kurdish left point out that many of the leftist leaders also are from a feudal background.[41] The Kurdish left has maintained that the traditionalistic KDP cannot affect a successful political liberation struggle. Mr Talabani, in alliance with the Kurdish left, was able to form the PUK in June 1975. This party played a critical role in promoting political consciousness of the Kurdish people, but unfortunately the KDP's rejection of PUK's political stand has resulted in further factionalization and conflict between the two.

Kurds killing Kurds is a political pattern. It blocks the formation of national unity and class solidarity, which are critically vital for the Kurdish realization of autonomy. Aspirations for autonomy are destroyed with divisive political strategies, the development of political consciousness is blocked, and the Kurds remain, as Marx described, a class in itself, but not yet for itself.

Observers of ethnic conflict regard federalism as a solution to the problems of ethnically divided societies. Federalism allows the integration of diverse groups into a single system, permits diversity, distributes power widely, and fosters the autonomy of minority groups. Different policies, laws, and institutions reflect the diverse constituency. Access points for political participation and accommodation increase opportunities for self-government. People are linked to government and taught lessons in democracy. Social mobility for the different ethnic members is also possible. The federation of Nigeria with forty million people (at the time of independence in 1960), and 250 distinct languages, has been cited as a model for accommodation and integrative political development.

According to Cynthia H. Enloe, domestic mobility and immigration can effectively alter the intensity of the ethnic conflict. Population movement can be accelerated when one part of a country develops faster than the rest. Expanding labor markets and better living conditions provide major incentives for population movements. This incentive-based push and pull movement leads to the dilution of the ethnic homogeneity of the groups and results in a voluntary cultural assimilation.[42] Enloe cites the African Americans in the United States as an example of a population movement from the deep South (77 percent in 1940, 53 percent in 1968, and before 1970, a little more than half of the African Americans lived in the South) to the North and the Midwest where better economic opportunities and welfare benefits were available.[43]

Although this strategy makes sense, it is not a lasting solution. Federalism has failed to solve the issues of discrimination, racism, and political integration as the inner-city riots in Los Angeles, California attest. Federalism is also very costly. It requires an excessive number of government units, the duplication of efforts, and economic inequalities. Federalism has failed in Nigeria, Zaire, Ugada, and in the British West Indies.[44] However, federalism, though not a single vital prescription due to each country's unique cultural diversity, can potentially aid in conflict reduction politics. Yet, in Tito's Yugoslavia and former Soviet Union, as long as the dictatorship prevailed, stability continued, and federalism worked.

The concept of stability in dictatorships is an explosive factor when a structural split or friction occurs. An extended period of stability in these highly centralized societies convinced many ethnic study scholars that a centralized federation system could be a solution to multi-ethnic and multi-cultural societies, although this has proven empirically erroneous. Years of control, political socialization, and indoctrination failed to alter or assimilate religious, cultural, and nationality identities. This should illustrate to the ruling classes of Iran, Iraq, and Turkey that systematic repression and control of the people cannot survive for long.

The Swiss model is regarded as another successful approach to ethnic conflict resolution. The miracle of stability in this country is rooted in decentralization, low level political mobilization, homogeneity, and male participation. Swiss federalism has been effective in diminishing progressive ethnic conflict.[45] The democratic tradition and effective homogeneous cantons system characterizing Switzerland's approach, appear promising for countries plagued with serious conflict at the center, territorially separate groups, and significant sub-ethnic divisions.[46]

> Since the control of the center has been the main cause of friction and tensions between the different regions, thereby threatening national solidarity and integrity, the distribution of functions between the regions and the center should be reviewed and so arranged that only such subjects and functions as will engender the minimum of suspicion and friction among different groups are allowed in the hands of the federal government.[47]

Although the Swiss approach has continual validity, it is unlikely that the ruling classes in Iran, Iraq, and Turkey will adopt the model; they cannot allot the degree of power to their minorities as Switzerland has done with its ethnic groups. In Iran, Turkey, and Iraq, an externally imposed decentralization may culminate in a revolutionary social and political and structural transformation. What is more, national ruling classes and the world system are not in search of a democratic model.

The Kurdish left, Komala, and the PKK realize that Kurdish rights cannot be achieved under the prevailing political systems, and autonomy would have no meaning in an undemocratic state. Therefore, the leftist faction maintains that socialism is the only solution to Kurdish political problems. This leftist solution provides for the abolition of privileges and surplus extracted from the masses of oppressed working men and women. Unfortunately, its practicality is questionable; a pure Marxian notion of socialism has never been implemented and excludes the social-democratic forms of accommodation, integration, and reform. Pure socialism in a land-locked Kurdistan surrounded by anachronistic and autocratic systems of thought will be no more than a small island within the ocean of conservative, traditional, tribal, and semi-capitalist political cultures and structures.

A radical democratic solution is problematic in Iran, Iraq, and Turkey due to the fear of dismemberment and political disintegration. In these ethnic and class-divided societies, the security and continuity of the systems depend on a degree of centralized but legitimate political sovereignty. In addition, in severely divided societies democracy is not a viable option. John Stuart Mill maintained that democracy would be "next to impossible in a country made up of different nationalities."[48] Other scholars have also advanced the thesis that ethnic harmony is paramount in a stable government, not democracy. Societies experiencing ethnic conflict would be better off without democratic institutions and ideals. Exclusion of the ethnic minorities in elections would trigger separatist and violent political movements.[49] To avoid this scenario, the attainment of ethnic harmony should take precedence over democratization in ethnic and class-dominated societies.

Since a fundamental solution to ethnic conflict is riddled with theoretical and practical problems, conflict resolution theorists endorse a consociational democracy as a way to manage ethnic conflict. This is an alliance of all ethnically divided groups, and all ethnic groups have mutual veto power. Resources and the distribution of opportunities are allocated based on ethnic proportionality, and autonomy exists for each group. These measures mitigate the negative outcome of majority decisions in ethnically divided societies.

Eric A. Nordlinger mentions six conflict-containing steps. These measures overlap and also conflict with Lijphart's thesis. The goal is to contain, manage, regulate, and alleviate ethnic conflict. Coalition building would facilitate proportionality; mutual veto, the restriction of governmental intervention in political controversy (depoliticization), compromise, and concessions. Milton J. Esman suggests a balanced pluralism that consists of proportionality, territorial autonomy, federalism, and legal cultural autonomy.[50]

Although the measures of Lijphard, Nordlinger, and Esman are critical in conflict containment, they do not provide a long run solution to Kurdish political problems. It is true that Switzerland, Austria, Belgium, and the Netherlands maintain democracies and stability with heterogeneous populations using the consociational democracy model, but this approach has no functional utility when applied to the Kurds. It is a mistake to apply generalizations from the segmented pluralism of these European countries to the Kurdish conflict. The hostility between the Kurds and the nation states of Iran, Iraq, and Turkey presents a special case. The conflict has resulted in repeated armed struggle, and the clash between armed governmental forces and the Kurdish Peshmargas (guerrillas) continues. The Kurdish conflicts are more political and intense than what has occurred in the European countries practicing segmented pluralism.

Kurdish problems require a Kurdish solution based on the regional realities of the countries involved and on the reality of the prevailing world system. The prevailing political order attempts to preserve the status quo at any cost, while the Kurds are determined to achieve their politico-economic and cultural rights. In these ethnic and class-divided societies of the Middle East, the Kurds are victims of the prevailing status quo politics sustained by an anachronistic divisive world system whose continuity relies on divide and rule policies. In all three countries (Iran, Iraq, and Turkey), hegemonic control prevails. This applies more to Iran and Iraq than to Turkey, where Kurds are more repressed politically and culturally.

The Kurdish political world is deeply divided. The divisive rural social structure of Kurdistan is extremely conservative. This divisiveness blocks the creation of class solidarity and political consciousness. The Kurdish movement has failed to win the hearts and minds of the masses. In all these countries, other minorities are as oppressed as the Kurds. The failure to enter into a class alliance with non-Kurds, especially in Iran and Iraq, has led these discontented forces to believe that the Kurdish quest for autonomy involves separatism or secessionism.

A solution to the Kurdish problem is autonomy for Kurdistan. This was advocated by the late KDPI leader, Ghassemlou, as democracy for Iran, autonomy for Kurdistan. This is one of the most viable solutions to the problems of all minorities. This solution, in the form of political autonomy, occurs within the context of the nation-states. It does not mean independence, secession, or separatism, and its implementation first demands a definition of internationally recognized autonomous territories. Without a well-defined jurisdiction of the autonomous areas, the validity for an autonomous argument will be undermined. According to the supporters of this scheme, in an autonomous Kurdish region, the Kurds would control their own political, economic, and social affairs through regional and local administrations. The central government would be involved in planning and formulating defense strategies with the armed forces, directing foreign affairs, and overseeing the monetary system. The administration of internal affairs should be vested in the hands of the Kurds and their locally elected leaders. The Kurds may also have social and cultural autonomy, and their languages may be used officially in the administration of their internal affairs. Internal security issues would be handled by the locally recruited forces.[51]

According to Herbert Marcuse, neither the rational use of resources nor workers ownership in the means of production can abolish the structurally created problems. A bureaucratic welfare state can be a state of force and repression that could continue into the second phase of socialism when each is supposed to receive according to his need.[52] Hence, socialism, advocated by the Kurdish left, cannot be a viable solution to Kurdish problems either. In Marcuse's words, the chain of subordination and exploitation must break at its strongest link,[53] and not at its weakest one.[54] This is why a universalization of human rights and social democratic transformation of the globalized world order is so critical.[55] Without such a solution, no one in the peripheries of the prevailing international world order will be free, let alone the Kurdish minorities.

NOTES

1. David Held, *Political Theory Today* (Stanford, California: Stanford University Press, 1991), 228.

2. Ibid., 229.

3. Ibid, 227–232.

4. E.K. Bramsted and K.J. Melhuish, (ed.) *Western Liberalism A History in Documents From Locke to Croce* (London and New York: Longman,1978), 274–277.

5. Held, *Political Theory,* 232.

6. Seymour Martin Lipset, *Political Man: The Social Basis of Politics* (Garden City, New York: Doubleday Anchor, 1963, 403. Quoted by Frank Cunningham, *Democratic Theory and Socialism* (Cambridge: Cambridge University Press, 1988), 58.

7. Philip Green, *Retrieving Democracy: In Search of Civic Equality* (Totowa, N.J.: Rowman and Allenheld, 1985), 58–59. Quoted and discussed by Cunningham *Democratic Theory and Socialism*, 314, n. 40. Cunningham maintains that Green's analysis of democracy and protection of minority rights is contradictory. However, Green feels that the "protection of minority rights is an empirically necessary condition for making advances in democracy," pp 58–59.

8. Quoted by Anthony Giddens, "The Question of Inequality" in Anthony Giddens, ed. *The Global Third Way Debate* (Malden, Massachusetts: Polity, 2001), 178.

9. Bernard Susser, *Political Ideology In The Modern World* (Boston, Massachusetts: Allyn and Bacon, 1995), 115.

10. Andrew Levine, *Arguing for Socialism Theoretical Consideration* (Boston, Massachusetts: Routledge and Kegan Paul, 1984), 132.

11. Giddens, *The Global Third Way Debate*, 180–181.

12. Clyde W. Barrow, *Critical Theories of the State* (Madison, Wisconsin: University of Wisconsin Press, 1993), 22.

13. E. Digby Baltzell, *Philadelphia Gentlemen: The Making of a National Upper Class* (New Brunswick: Transaction Publishers, 1989). This also discussed by Barrow, *Critical Theories*, 22–23.

14. Donald L. Barlett and James B. Steele, *America: Who Stole the Dream* (Kansas, Kansas City: University Press Syndicate Company. 1996), 8. See also, Thomas I. Palley *Plenty of Nothing the Downsizing of the American Dream and the Case for Structural Keynesianism* (New Jersey: Princeton University Press, 1998), 57–59.

15. Ibid., 57–58.

16. Richard J Arneson, "Against Complex Equality," in *Pluralism, Justice, and Equality*, David Miller and Michael Walzer, eds. (Oxford: Oxford University Press, 1995), 236.

17. Brian Barry, "A Spherical Justice and Global Injustice," in Miller and Walzer, eds. *Pluralism, Justice, and Equality*, 79.

18. Rosa Luxemburg, *The Nationality Question: Selected Writings by Rosa Luxemburg, ed.* Horace B. Davis (New York: Monthly Review Press, 1976), 218, 219, 290; Raya Dunayevskaya and Rosa Luxemburg, *Women's Liberation and Marx's Philosophy of Revolution*, 2nd ed. (Chicago: University of Illinois Press, 1991), 55.

19. Nancy Bridsall, "Life is Unfair: Inequality In the World" in Robert Griffiths, ed. *Developing World*, 9th ed. (Connecticut: Dashkin/McGraw-Hill, 2000), 25. See also, Leslie Sklair, *Globalization, Capitalism and its Alternatives* (Oxford: Oxford University Press, 2002), 322–324.

20. Ervand Abrahamian, *Iran Between Two Revolutions* (Princeton, New Jersey: Princeton University Press, 1982), 88–89.

21. Ibid., cited by Ervand Abrahamian, 90.

22. Ibid., 103.

23. Ibid., 111–113.

24. Ibid., 119.

25. James A. Bill, *The Iranian Intelligentsia: Class and Change*, Ph.D. Diss., Princeton University, 1968, 178–184; see also, Abrahamian, *Iran Between Two Revolutions*, 156.

26. *Amnesty International Report* (Amnesty International USA New York, NY.):125–128. See also Iraq's crime of Genocide. "The Anfal Campaign Against the Kurds" *Human Rights Watch/Middle East* (Yale University Press, New Haven and London, 1995), XV, 1–2; Bill, *The Iranian Intelligentsia*, 180.

27. Martin Van Bruinessin, *Agha, Shaikh and State:,The Social and Political Structure of Kurdistan* (London & New Jersey: Zed Books Ltd., 1992), 42–45. See also, Sami Zubaida, "Introduction" in Philip G. Kreyenbroek and Stefan Sperl, eds. *The Kurds A Contemporary Overview* (New York: Routledge Press, 1992) 1–9. A detailed description of these events is documented by Isam al-Khafaji, "The Destruction of Iraqi Kurdistan," *Middle East Report* No. 201, Vol. 26. 4, October–December 1996, pp. 35–38.

28. *Human Rights Watch,* 1 (Winter 1991): 9.

29. See Nader Entessar, *Kurdish Ethnonationalism* (London: Lynn Rienner Publishers, 1992), 138–139.

30. Noam Chomsky, *Propaganda and The Public Mind* (Cambridge, Massachusetts: South End Press, 2001), 25–29.

31. A. Manafy, "The State and Human Rights: Critical Perspectives," *The Iranian Journal of International Affairs*, 1, vol. 8 (spring 1996): 120–139.

32. Noam Chomsky, *The Prosperous Few and the Restless Many* (Berkeley, California: Odonian Press, 1993), 58.

33. Manafy, "The State and Human Rights: Critical Perspectives," 133–135

34. Chomsky, *The Prosperous Few,* 58–59.

35. Jurgen Habermas, "Private and Public Autonomy, Human Rights and Popular Sovereignty," in Obrad Savic, ed. *The Politics of Human Rights* (London and New York: Verso, 1999), 51.

36. Ibid.

37. Barrow, *Critical Theories of the State*, 105.

38. *Human Rights Watch/Helsinki,* "The Kurds of Turkey, Killings, Disappearances and Torture," New York, Washington, Los Angeles and London, 1993, pp. 1–2.

39. *Human Rights Watch/Helsinki,* "The Kurds of Turkey, Killings, Disappearances and Torture," New York, Washington, Los Angeles and London, 1993, pp. 1–2.

40. This concept of "state terrorism" has been widely used by Professor Noam Chomsky and other scholars from the left.

41. See Martin van Bruinessen, "The Kurds Between Iran and Iraq" in *Middle East Report* (July–August 1986): 17–18.

42. Cynthia H. Enloe, *Ethnic Conflict and Political Development* (Boston, Massachusetts: Little, Brown & Company, 1973), 89–96: Donald L. Horowitz, *Ethnic Groups in Conflict* (Berkeley: University of California Press, 1985), 602–613.

43. Enloe, *Ethnic Conflict*, 94–95.

44. Horowitz, *Ethnic Groups*, 621–622.

45. Crawford Young, *The Politics of Cultural Pluralism* (Madison, Wisconsin: University of Wisconsin Press, 1976), 234.

46. According to Enloe, women were not allowed to vote in Switzerland until 1971. Based on her argument, Switzerland's integrative model has been able to sustain democracy and ethnic toleration by a lower level political mobilization and political participation. Yet she adds that the Swiss federalism may enter into a new era of uncertainty. Enloe, *Ethnic Conflict*, 98–100.

47. Cited by: Horowitz, *Ethnic Groups*, 615.

48. Ibid., cited by Horowitz. 681.

49. Ibid., 615

50. Ibid., 569–571.

51. Abdul-Rahman Ghassemlou, "The Clergy have confiscated the Revolution" in *Middle East Report* July–August 1981, 17–23.

52. Herbert Marcuse, *An Essay on Liberation* (Boston, Massachusetts: Beacon Press, 1969), 4.

53. Ibid., 3–6.

54. Ibid., 82.

55. During the height of the Iranian and Nicaraguan conflicts when I advocated the idea that these revolutions were taking place at the weakest link, a concept originally formulated by Lenin, Professor Harry Cleaver told me in his Political Economy class, that for a genuine liberation to occur the world capitalist system must be transformed, otherwise liberation movements will not be successful. I think he was right. See also Leslie Sklair, *Globalization Capitalism and Its Alternatives*, 3rd ed. (New York: Oxford University Press, 2002), 322–327.

Chapter Seven

Conclusion: What Is To Be Done?

The Kurdish political struggle is not in accord with the theories of national liberation movements. The Kurdish movements have lacked national solidarity and have been dominated by tribal and parochial values. The Kurdish leadership has lacked sophistication in political and educational knowledge. The Kurdish leaders and masses (with few exceptions) have suffered from lack of action-driven educational expertise, which is critical for the definition of political issues. In addition, tribalism has constituted the core of the Kurdish forces. In Derk Kinnane's words, "The major objective of the leadership is to weaken the central government for the purpose of self-realization."[1] Due to self-interest, Kurdish tribes were not on Gazi Mohammad's side in 1946, but had a pathological attachment to the Iranian Army. In national liberation struggles, national solidarity plays a critical role. Unfortunately, Kurdish leadership has always chosen particularism, refusing to ally with other aggrieved national minority forces. The Kurdish leadership, even under pressure from the former Soviet Union, refused to unite itself with the movement to Azerbaijan. Thus, both the Mahabad and Azerbaijan Republics in Iran came into being via support of the Red Army, and both collapsed when the Soviets, under pressure from the United States and Britain, withdrew from Iran. The problem is that the idea of nationalism in a modern sense has always been an alien concept in Kurdistan. The Kurdish people follow their tribal and religious leaders, and the existence of their tribal loyalty has deprived the Kurds of creative and pragmatic initiatives.[2] Furthermore, for the purposes of their own economically oil motivated interests, the colonial and neocolonial powers have imposed on the Kurdish tribes the culture of divide and rule policy in order to further enfeeble a unified Kurdish front. As the cheap production of oil continues, and as the petro-dollar capability of oil producing countries continues to create a competitive market for the western world's commodities, especially military goods, the imperial hegemony in the Middle East will remain prevalent. The Kurds, like the valuable oil resource, will be of a great importance for the imperial domination of the region. Consequently, in Turkey, where there is no oil, the Kurds have been placed on the terrorist list of the United States State Department, but the Kurds in Iraq are seen as freedom fighters. Yet, the Kurds in Iraq are far better off than the Kurds in Iran and Turkey. In comparison to the Kurds in Turkey, the Kurds in Iran have more political, economic, and cultural rights.

Mortaza Zarbakht mistakenly compares Barzani's march to Russia to that of Mao's national liberation and historical 1934 political march to Yan'an in the north.[3] One hundred and twenty thousand Chinese traveled more than 6,000 miles (10,000 km) in a hostile environment. This trek took over a year and approximately 20,000 men survived. Contrary to Barzani's revolt, which always depended on colonizing powers, the Chinese movement was nationalistic, self-reliant, and isolated from external forces.[4] Mao's objective was the liberation of China from colonial domination. Paradoxically, Barzani relied exclusively on the colonizing forces for the liberation of Kurds from the so-called internally colonizing powers. General Barzani repeatedly turned to Kurdish enemies for assistance. This illogical strategy permitted the external forces to use the Kurdish struggle as an instrument for the realization of their own ends.

As a result of external interventionism and internal divisiveness, the Kurdish liberation movements are doomed to failure. They have failed to forge national unity and have suffered from deep divisions and treachery within their leadership ranks. The leadership's lack of political insight and inability to learn from past mistakes is another critical factor hindering Kurdish liberation. Time and again, the Kurdish leadership has cooperated with external forces, which have been responsible for the failure of the Kurdish cause. This inconsistent behavior has resulted in the punishment of their own people. The Kurdish leadership has been provincial and parochial and possesses little political knowledge of the dynamics of the world system. They have failed to realize that the fate of the nations is decided behind closed doors at the core of the world system and "beyond the confines of the Middle East."[5]

Kurdish leadership has also failed to understand the implications of the Palestinian tragedy. The Arab world with its tremendous oil wealth has failed to give up its dependency on external forces and has also failed to promote a cause that the Arab elite's consider their own cause; the realization of the Palestinian dream of an independent state on the land freed from occupation. It was only during the Gulf War (Desert Storm) in 1991, that the United States called upon the Kurds to rise up against Saddam Hussein's government. They responded to this appeal, only to be abandoned and slaughtered. The Kurds have learned nothing from the experience of repetitive deceptions. It was just recently that Mom Talabani, on his visit to Turkey, asserted:

> We are looking to Baghdad, we are focusing on Baghdad, it is the capital. It is the main part of this country. We are not just looking through Kurdish glasses. We are looking through Iraqi glasses.[6]

Mom Talabani was prepared to strike Baghdad as soon as he was told to do so, with no assessment of a cost/benefit analysis or a political risk calculation. Although the United States is concerned about the brutal conflict among Iraqi's ethnic and religious groups and intend to limit the Kurds' role to the northern part of Iraq, Mom Talabani is ready to extend armed conflict to the heart of Baghdad.[7] Such a strategy contradicts the logic of national liberation movements. Rather, it is compatible with the theory of instrumentalism. The Kurds are being used as an instrument for the realization of political and economic ideals of the external as well as regional forces, rather than liberation of the Kurdish people. The Kurdish armed forces are there for rent. This assertion can be proven empirically. During the Iran-Iraqi war, Mom Barzani's forces sided with Iranian government, and Mr. Barzani lent invaluable assistance to Iranian forces, which were fighting Saddam Hussein's army of aggression. At Halabja, approximately 5,000 Kurdish civilians were gassed down.[8] This savagery was justified by the Iraqi regime under the pretext that the Kurds were aiding and confronting the enemy. While Mom Barzani forces were fighting for Iran and against Saddam Hussein, Mom Talabani forces were on the side of Iraq. During the eight years of Iran-Iraqi conflict, Saddam Hussein aided the Iranian Kurds, who in the process were defeated by Mom Barzani's forces. This contradictory behavior has occurred repeatedly during Kurdish armed political conflicts and is not totally attributed to parochial tribal values or the lack of education of the movement's leaders. Highly educated and enlightened members of the Kurdish democratic party have behaved like those leaders of the illiterate tribal forces. In 1966, the intellectuals called "Jash of 66" sided with the Iraqi Army. Talabani is a highly educated lawyer, but yet he, along with Ibrahim Ahmad, Ali Askari, Helmi Sharif, and Omar Dabbabeh were Iraqi sympathizers. Based on Chris Kutshera's argument, their justification was the liberation of the Kurdish movement from Barzani's backward tribal organization. Financed by the Iraqi government, they recruited 2,000 Kurds. This group continued fighting Barzani forces until 1970.[9]

Kurdish leaders do not deny these allegations of contradictory behavior. They argue that this behavior is necessary for the survival of the Kurdish people. Of course, with limited resources, it is extremely difficult to fight liberation struggles against highly equipped, organized, and the well-trained modern armies. However, the concept of self-preservation is problematic, for it reflects self-serving hypocrisy. It is not a "mass line," but a feudal line devised by the Kurdish people's enemies to inhibit the Kurdish liberation struggle and use the Kurdish movement as a vanguard for the realization of status quo political and economic interests.[10] The beneficiaries of inter-Kurdish rivalry conflict are the international and national elites. It is not a credible claim that contradictions in Kurdish leadership decisions are prompted by the desire for Kurdish survival. Wars waged against one's own people are not consistent with the theory of mass line. Yet, empirical data show that the regional and external alliances were devised to maintain the hegemonic domination of one Kurdish leadership over another. When Kurds kill other Kurds, the survival argument loses its credibility.

Kurdish political organizations are mainly dominated by traditional forces such as Shaikhs, Agas, religious leaders, or their family related clientele loyalists. No matter how radical their agenda maybe, they are conservative and want to preserve their current system. Although the traditional forces have criticized the power structure of feudal lords and their class privileges, they have never attempted to abolish the class interests of these dominant forces in Kurdistan.[11] It can be argued that the Kurdistan Workers' Party of Turkey (PKK) has adopted a radical agenda in comparison to the KDP of Mom Barzani and the PUK of Mom Talabani. Although Syria provided a training haven for the PKK forces, the party did not rely on imperial powers for the liberation of the Kurds. Thus, its agenda was political and, as a result, was placed on the United States' terrorist list.

Washington has never even openly criticized the state-sponsored terrorism inflicted on the Turkish Kurds by the Turkish Army. Yet, the Kurds of Turkey are more economically, politically, and culturally disadvantaged than the Kurds in Iraq and Iran. The CIA's report lends credence to our claim:

"The [Turkish] eastern provinces have received only 10 percent of state industrial investment and only 2 percent of all commercial investment."[12]

The report points out that there are few hospitals and educational facilities in eastern Turkey, unemployment is higher than the national average, illiteracy among the Kurds is almost 80 percent, and more than half of the villages do not have drinking piped water, roads, or electricity.[13]

Deprivation in southeast Turkey is the critical variable that triggered the PKK's armed struggle to liberate the Kurds from the discriminatory apartheid situation. According to Aziz Nesin, one of the leading Turkish critical writers, "If these people cannot admit that they are Kurds, there is no way to put democracy into practice in this country."[14] The PKK feels that the ruling classes of Iran, Iraq, and Turkey are the colonizing powers of Kurdish lands, although the Kurds in Iran and Iraq are far better off than the Kurds in Turkey where, their status socio-politically and economically is worse than colonized people. Although Western colonization robbed and colonized nations, they did not take away the people's cultural tradition. The British did teach English to Indians and Pakistanis, but never forced them to assimilate or abandon their mother tongue. Kurds in Iran and Iraq speak several languages and are not denied their national identity.

The PKK claims that the Shaikhs, Agha's, and Jashes (Kurds who are the agents of regional governments) are the agents of colonization forces. The Kurdish national liberation struggle must also be directed against the Kurdish ruling class, but the party has deviated from this ideology. Leadership and the Kurdish people allied themselves with so-called patriotic Aghas against the collaborating ones (those forces that side with the colonizers). The Kurdish liberation movement is more like tribal warfare.[15] Rivalry among the Kurdish leadership factions is a deep-seated tradition. Kurds killing Kurds over rivalry and factionalism continues non-stop, "as is Kurds killing Kurds out of reverence for strangers."[16] Both Mom Jala and Mom Barzani, as part of their agreements made with regional and external governments, participated in the destruction of the PKK Kurds.

Kurdish leaders tend to blame their own self-inflicted failure on others. The Kurds assert that during much of the last decade, destructive confrontation with the PKK Kurds was the job of Barzani's KDP forces, and now, the KDP criticizes Mom Jalal's PUK for doing so. It appears that the PUK was motivated by a desire to compete with Barzani over the special favors delegated by Ankara on economic and trade issues.[17]

While Kurds are killing Kurds in a competitive pursuit of favor from Ankara, the Turkish general has this to say: "We say our homeland, state, language and flag are one, and there can be no freedom to increase them to two."[18] Apparently, the Kurdish leadership either consciously or unconsciously uses the Kurdish people as an instrument geared toward the realization of the exploitive neocolonial/imperial forces.

The key component of domination and exploitation is conflict. Without conflict and the policy of divide and rule, there can be no militarization of the region. Oil, lucrative markets, and arms sales constitute the backbone of the so-called regime change. The Kurdish leaders should know these goals depend upon subservient puppet regimes. Michael Klare's article "Oiling the Wheels of War" supports our claim. Iraq has proven reserves of 112 billion barrels of oil and posses a great area of "unexploited hydrocarbon potential." According to Klare, the Iraqi fields of petroleum far exceed the untapped fields in Alaska, Africa, and the Caspian. Whoever controls these fields in

Iraq will control the pulse of the world energy markets.[19] Hence, the Iraqi Kurds accrue an importance not shared by the Kurds in Iran and Turkey.

Jonathan Randal describes Kurdish leadership as clumsy, traditional, provincial, and politically unaware of the core of the world system,

> . . . where the fate of nations is decided beyond the confines of the Middle-East and the often paranoid mindset there. At times Kurdish leadership was broadly traditional, as in Iraq, at others newly minted from the repressed underclass, as in contemporary Turkey.[20]

Provincial Kurdish leadership promotes false consciousness, which contradicts the ideology of national liberation struggles. False consciousness is not just associated with the Kurdish leadership. A Kurdish writer has been cited by Randal as saying, "The mutual interest between Americans and Kurds constitutes a 'marriage made in heaven' because we [the Kurds] have the oil and want democracy, and you in America have democracy and want the oil."[21] This pattern of false consciousness and political naiveté prevents the Kurds from realizing the ultimate motives behind the actions of the United States. The United States wants Iraqi oil, otherwise the United States would have sided with the Turkish Kurds. What other explanation can logically justify why the Turkish Kurds are seen by the United States as terrorists and Iraqi Kurds considered "good" Kurds? In spite of Iraq's brutalities, the Baghdad government has tolerated the Kurdish political and cultural freedoms to a greater extent than Turkey. In Iraq more than 80 percent of Kurdish books are published in Kurdish, the Sorani language. No other country in the Middle East, including Iran, allows this. Randal claims that "in Turkey, until President Turgut Ozal changed the law in 1991, the only Kurdish language publication for nearly seventy years was printed in Europe and smuggled back into the country."[22] Does this indicate an exclusionary policy or democracy? Why does the United States withhold democracy from the Turkish Kurds, but offers it to the Iraqi Kurds? The Iraqi Kurds are granted more parliamentary-based autonomy than the Turkish and Iranian Kurds.

The fallacy of the Kurdish leadership lies in the fact that it expects the core of the world system to facilitate Kurdish liberation, the system that deliberately thwarts Kurdish liberation movements. Amir Hanssanpour, a Kurdish intellectual, feels that the Kurdish movement has been persistently contradictory in comparison to other national liberation movements. The discrepancy arises with traditional leadership that tends to perpetuate the status quo and the demands of the relatively modern society it attempts to liberate.[23] Obviously, the Kurdish liberation struggle is contradictory. It fails to meet the expectations of the theory and practice of national liberation movements. The

Kurdish liberation struggle has relied on the external forces to liberate the Kurds in Iran, Iraq, and Turkey from the so-called internal colonialism. Given the imperatives of the regional politics, the Kurds have also used these regional powers to defeat their fellow rival Kurds. The regional governments do not hesitate to use the various Kurdish factions as a means to achieving their own political ends.

Kurdish political ideology is not consistent. At times, the Kurdish leadership seeks solutions and strives for the acquisition of more democratic rights within their own respective country. At other times, this goal disappears from their political agenda. For instance, Ghassemlou in Iran pursued the famous slogan: "Democracy for Iran-Autonomy for Kurdistan," but, in practice, he violated his own tenet by involving his Peshmargas (guerrilla fighters) in an armed conflict with the Turkish speaking Turks of Nagadeh in western Azerbaijan. The memory of this bloody confrontation has never been forgotten. Ghassemlou repeated the tragedy that Ismael Agha Simko of the Shikak tribe inflicted on Armenians and Assyrians in Rezaeih (now Urmia), the capital of western Azerbaijan. This example of regressive behavior does not suggest a struggle for democracy and inclusionism. If Kurdish leadership genuinely seeks democracy, the Turkish government adheres more to democratic principles than either Iran or Iraq. Why wasn't the Kurdish leadership inclined to join the social democratic party of Turkey? Social democracy is the only viable means for seeking and realizing social justice. This mode of behavior with Iranian, Iraqi, and Turkish authorities reflects separatism, not democratic autonomy.

Jonathan Randal characterizes the Kurds as "stubborn survivors and steady losers, likeable for their warmth, humor, courage, charm, and distinguished by a streak of unpredictable violence."[24] They are warriors. The Kurds are unique people who cling to their tradition, culture, custom, uniform, and language. The Kurds offer a critical contribution to the notion of multiculturalism, diversity, and pluralism. The continuity and longevity of the Kurdish way of life outdates the Europeans.[25] The international community has a moral responsibility to protect the rights of all minorities since democracy without diversity, dissenting views, and cultural pluralism cannot flourish.

The Kurds have been victimized by their own leadership. They have paid heavily for internally divisive tribal values. The internal divisiveness is aggravated by regional and external forces, which are primarily concerned with their own selfish interests. The British government has repeatedly misused the Kurdish people. To secure access to the valuable oil resources in the Middle East, Britain has used regional governments to inflict harm on their adversaries or balance the region's conflicting demands.

What can be done to protect the political, social, and cultural traditions and rights of this vulnerable Kurdish minority? As mentioned in Chapter VI, some scholars have seen autonomy as a solution to the political problems of minorities. This solution can be rejected on the ground that autonomy in a dictatorship has no political value; autonomy is a solution only if the country is democratic. Only a genuine democracy in the tradition of the Scandinavian countries, Germany, and France can secure rights for the Kurdish people.

The United States offers another solution for post-Saddam Iraq: federalism. In Iraq, the majority of the population is Muslim, 60 percent of the populace are Shi-i Muslims. The remaining population is Sunni Arab Muslims, and Kurds, who are mostly Sunni, predominantly speak Kurdish, while the remaining speak Arabic. How will the language issue in terms of official governmental communication be solved? In terms of territorial concentration of the population, Kurds can be allowed to either live in their own area or be socially mobile, free to work and live in any part of the country they choose. The problem of representation will be solved by the rotation in presidency. A possible scenario would be that every four years one ethnic group leader would be chosen as president, administering the country for all populations.

Parliamentary politics would be decided by proportional representation, each group would receive parliamentary seats in proportion to the number of votes each party wins in an election. This model allows formerly excluded or partially included forces to participate in the political decision making processes, enabling them to articulate their own interests. It also allows most parliamentary decisions to be submitted to popular will, in an institutional model of direct democracy.[26] This model maintains, stabilizes, and secures national sovereignty while allowing competing and conflicting groups to voice their legitimate demands on a system created by consensus. A federalist arrangement is a creative solution, not only for the Kurdish people, but also for the other forces in the Middle East. The creation of administrative units would accommodate the Sunni Kurds, Mom Barzanis, Shi'i Muslims, and the Sunni Arabs with veto power. But granting veto power will discriminate against the majority faction. There fore, it would not be acceptable. Nonetheless, federation based on a constitution, a legal system, justice, civil rights, state political parties, and a parliament in accordance with proportional representation may be a better solution. The states' autonomy would include financial and organizational autonomy, and financial support would be available via horizontal and vertical equalization payments, as in Switzerland. It would be critical to grant the states enough power to shape federal policies and in turn, be shaped by the federal government.

However, the implementation of this model in Iraq would be problematic if the details were determined in Washington without consent from the masses. For almost half a century, the United States government has selected the head of governments in the third world countries, installing numerous puppet regimes. This shortsighted policy works temporarily toward the realization of imperial ideas and interests. These appointed agents have no legitimization and their position is precarious, as demonstrated in Iran, Nicaragua, Philippines, Chile, and Guatemala, to mention just a few. In Iraq, the United States is motivated to possess the oil and gas resources of the region. If at any time during the continuum of the federation in Iraq, the United States' interest is questioned; the federation will cease to exist.

The Kurdish political parties (the KDP, PUK and PKK) are rivals. Currently in northern Iraq, there are two rival leaderships, the KDP and the PUK. Mom Jalal and Mom Masud have always conflicted over leadership issues. What about the Kurds in Turkey? Given the democratic nature of the Turkish government, the Turkish Kurds may join left to center parties, either liberal or social democratic parties, and fight for the realization of their collective rights. However, the unique nature of the Kurdish language and cultural tradition presents a problem. For political integration and democratic unity to succeed, the Turkish government must relinquish its policy of Turkification and assimilation of the Kurdish people. Whether the Turkish government would accept cultural plurality remains to be seen. Nonetheless, with Turkey joining the European Union, the Kurdish political problems may be solved in Turkey.

In Iran, the Kurdish culture is deeply rooted in the Persian civilization. Federation imposed from the outside would be a precarious arrangement due to the lack of legitimization. The most feasible solution would be the democratization of the prevailing orders in Iran, Iraq and Turkey. Political problems, Kurdish and otherwise, can only be solved within the context of a democratic order. The pursuit of equality forms the heart of a progressive mode of thinking. Without a just and democratic society, there can be no human value, and without justice, peace or stability can not be realized.[27]

The Kurds, along with other discontented and victimized minorities, are tired of servitude, foreign interventionism (colonial/neocolonial), economic and political deprivation, and more importantly, political repression. Minorities were hopeful that with the demise of the former Soviet Union, their just demands would no longer be seen as communistic. Within a democratic framework, minorities could surely attain their socio-political ideals. Washington, with its interventionist policy of unilateralism, instead of providing moral leadership, seeks domination by pitting one group against another. Recent revelations by Noam Chomsky indicate that the United States, Turkey, and Israel are attempting to agitate nationalistic forces in northern Iran to move toward a linkage of the Iranian Azerbaijan with Azerbaijan of the former Soviet Union which had been possessed forcefully by Tsarist Russia.[28] This may culminate in the disintegration and dismemberment of the country. Therefore, the solutions to Kurdish, other minorities, or even dominant majority problems cannot be sought under capitalistic structures of the prevailing world system, which negate justice, democracy, and peace, offering only control and domination.[29] .

Paul A. Passavant and Jodi Dean argue that "both the imperial world and capitalism are oppressive forms of power that are parasitic upon our labor power, but the very conditions that define empire will enable the possibility of its overthrow and the self organization of democracy."[30] Hence, containment of conflict in the periphery of the world system, through vertical and mechanical devices, is a short run solution to the problems of unfreedom. In the long run, in order to stem the tide of international violence and restore rights and responsibilities, the creation of a social democratic order at the global level is the only solution to the problems of humanity that suffers from the fatal viruses of a sick and unfree world. However, on an optimistic note, the trend is toward liberalization and democratization, which can be seen as an ultimate solution not only to the Kurdish problems, but also for all of the oppressed people in the world.

This analysis is further supported by Gramsci's theory of passive revolution, which is applied whenever the hegemony of the ruling class is threatened or its superstructure is unable to expand the force of production.[31] To maintain world domination, the elites at the core of the world system have attempted to control political consciousness, conceal their ideology, and maintain a highly secretive administrative network. But in the periphery of the world system, the states have failed to control political consciousness, failed to conceal their ideology, and have been unable to maintain administrative secrecy.[32] Under this set of circumstances, where force is no longer a viable method of control in the periphery, the bourgeoisie attempts a passive revolution, labeled as democratization.[33] Although electoral democracy and democratic federation can be seen as critical reforms, they may only contain conflict. Professor Leslie Sklair claims:

> I cannot accept the optimistic hope that capitalism can become much more humane, globally than it already is, or that Stalinist communism can ever produce a decent society, in my view the next step in the quest for human progress has to be in the transformation of capitalist globalization into socialist globalization through the globalization of human right.[34]

Otherwise, the prevailing peripheral states, as well as the world system itself, will suffer from a serious legitimization crisis that in turn will enhance the severity of political conflicts and social movements.[35]

NOTES

1. Derk Kinnane, *The Kurds and Kurdistan* (Tehran, Iran: Negah Publishers, 1372), 206.

2. Ibid., 206–207.

3. Zarbakht Mortaza, *Az Kurdistan-e Iraq Ta onsoye Roud Aras Rah paymaie Tarikh-e Mulla Mostafa Barzani* (Tehran, Iran: Azadeh Publisher, 1337), 3–5.

4. Michael G. Roskin, *Hard Road to Democracy: Four Developing Nations* (New Jersey: Prentice Hall, 2001), 21.

5. Jonathan C. Randal, *After Such Knowledge, What Forgiveness: My Encounter with Kurdistan* (New York: Farrar, Straus and Giroux, 1997), 12–13.

6. Dexter Filkins, "Iraqi Kurds Set Sights on Baghdad," *New York Times*, 17 November 2002, Section 1.

7. Ibid., 17.

8. David McDowall, *A Modern History of the Kurds* (London: I.B. Tauris, 1977), 358.

9. Chris Kutschera, *Le Mouvement National Kurde* (Paris: Flammarion, 1979). Translated into Farsi by Junbish Milli-e Kurd by Ibrahim Unisi (Tehran: Negah Publisher, 1373), 322–24.

10. *Kurdish Life*, no. 36 (Fall 2000): 1.

11. For a detailed analysis of Kurdish political organizations, see Martin Van Bruinsessen, *Agha, Shaikh, and State: the Social and Political Structures of Kurdistan* (London and New Jersey: Zed Books Ltd., 1992), 316.

12. National Foreign Assessment Center (U.S. Central Intelligence Agency), "The Kurdish Problem in Perspective," cited by Michael M. Gunter, *The Kurds In Turkey A Political Dilemma* (Boulder, Colorado: Westview, Press, 1990), 125.

13. Gunter, The Kurds in Turkey, 125.

14. Cited by Gunter, *The Kurds in Turkey,* 126.

15. Martin Van Bruinessen, "Between Guerrilla War and Political Murder: The Worker's Party of Kurdistan," *Middle East Report,* no. 153, 40–46.

16. *Kurdish Life*, no. 36, Fall 2000, 1.

17. Ibid.

18. Ibid., 2.

19. Michael T. Klare, "Oiling the Wheels of War." *The Nation* Oct. 7, 2002. 6–7.

20. Randal: *After Such Knowledge*, 8.

21. Ibid., 13.

22. Ibid., 45.

23. Amir Hassanpour, "The Kurdish Experience," *Middle East Report* (July–August 1994): 2–7 and 23.

24. Randal: *After Such Knowledge*, 32.

25. Ibid., 20.

26. For further discussion of federalism, see Wolfgang Luthardt, "Direct Democracy in Western Europe: The Case of Switzerland," *TELOS: A Journal of Critical Thought* 90 (Winter 1991): 92.

27. Anthony Giddens, ed. *The Global Third Way Debate* (Cambridge: Polity Press, 2001). 8–9.

28. Noam Chomsky, "Imperial Ambition," *Monthly Review* (May 2003):15. See also, Noam Chomsky *Hegemony or Survival: America's Quest for Global Dominance* (New York: Henry Holt & Company, 2003), Chapters 2 and 5.

29. From now on Kurds cannot, or must not, expect liberation from foreign, external or regional forces. They cannot rely on foreign aid or support. This dependency has led to the defeat of the Kurdish movement. They must not limit the fight to one state only. That would mean failure. The Kurds must incorporate other aggrieved forces and follow the formula of other national liberation struggles. See Kutschera, *Le Movement National Kurd*, 442.

30. Paul A. Passavant and Jodi Dean, eds. *Empire's New Clothes* (New York and London: Tautledge Publishing, 2004), Chapter 3; see also, Michael Hardt and Antonio Negri, *Empire* (Cambridge: Harvard University Press, 2000), Chapters 1, 3, 4.

31. Anne Showstack Sasson, "Passive Revolution and Politics of Reform," in *The Approaches to Gramsci* (London: Writers & Readers Publishing Cooperative, 1982), 133.

32. Ibid.

33. Claus Offe, "The Theory of the Capitalist State and the Problem of Policy Formation," in Leon Lindberg, ed,. *Stress and Contradiction in Modern Capitalism* (Lexington, Mass.: D. C. Heath, 1975), 127.

34. Leslie Sklair, *Globalization, Capitalism and its Alternatives*, 3rd ed. (Oxford, New York: Oxford University Press, 2002), 324.

35. For a better understanding of the transition from the prevailing mode of unfreedom, see Chalmers Johnson's provocative book, *The Sorrows of Empire, Militarism, Secrecy, and the End of Republic* (New York: Metropolitan Books, 2004), Chapter 1, 8, and 10.

References

Abrahamian, Ervand. *Iran Between Two Revolutions*. Princeton. New Jersey: Princeton University Press, 1982.

Ahmad, Aijaz. "Imperialism and Progress." In *Theories of Development: Mode of Production or Dependence*. Edited by Ronald H. Chilcote and Dale L. Johnson. London: Sage Publications, 1984.

Ahmad, Eqbal. "Revolutionary Warfare and Counter-Insurgency." In *National Liberation in The Third World*. Edited by Norman Miller and Roderick Aya. New York: The Free Press, 1971.

Al-Khafaji, Isam. "Almost Unnoticed Interventions and Rivalries in Iraqi Kurdistan." *Middle East Report*. Accessed on 24 Janurary 2001, pp 1–5. http://www.merip.org/mero/meroo12401.html

Amin, Samir. "The Future of Socialism." In *The Future of Socialism Perspectives From the Left*. Edited by William K. Tabb. New York: Monthly Review Press, 1980.

———. "The Real Stakes in the Gulf War." *Monthly Review* (July–August 1991): 14–24.

Amnesty International Report. Amnesty International USA, New York, NY, 1990.

Baltzell, E. Digby. *Philadelphia Gentleman: The Making of a National Upperclass*. New Brunswick: Transaction Publishers, 1989.

Barrow, Clyde W. *Critical Theories of the State*. Wisconsin: University of Wisconsin Press 1993.

Barry, Brian. "A Spherical Justice and Global Injustice." In *Pluralism, Justice and Equality*. Edited by David Miller and Michael Walzer. Oxford University Press: Oxford, 1995.

Bartlett, Donald L. and James B. Steele. *America: Who Stole Thy Dream*. Kansas City: University Press, 1996.

Bartlett, Richard J. and R. Miller. *Global Reach: The Power of the Multinational Corporations*. New York: Simon and Shuster, 1979.

Bayat, Kaveh. *Shooresh-e Kurdhigh-e Turkkeih va Ta asir-e on Dar Ravabei-e Kharej-e Iran* (The Revolt of Turkish Kurds and its Impact on the Foreign Policy of Iran). Tehran, Iran: Nashr-e Tarikh-e Iran, 1374.

Barzoei, Mojtaba, *Ovza-e syasie kurdistan* (Political Conditions of Kurdistan). Tehran, Iran: Nashr-e Feker-e, 1378.

Berberoglu, Berch. *The Internationlization of Capital Imperialism and Capitalist Development on a World Scale*. New York: Praeger, 1987.

―――― . *Turkey in Crisis*. London: Zed Press, 1982.

Besikci, Ismael, *Masalei-e Kordestan Dar Turkkieh va Iragh* (The Kurdish Problem in Turkey and Iraq). Translated from Turkey into Persian by Mohammad Raooph. Tehran, Iran: Hamida Publisher, 1378.

Bill, James A. The *Iranian Intellectuals: Class and Change*. Ph.D. Diss., Princeton University, 1968.

Bill, James A. and Robert Springborg. *Politics in the Middle East*. 4th ed. Harper Collins: College Publishers, 1994.

Bill, James A. and William John Aiden. *Roman Catholics and Shi, i Muslim: Prayer, Passion, and Politics*. Chapel Hill: The University of North Carolina Press, 2002.

Bill, James A. *The Eagle and the Lion*. Connecticut: Tragedy Haven, 1998.

Bramsted, E. K. and K. J. Melhuish, eds. *Western Liberalism: A History in Documents from Locke to Croce*. London: Longman, 1978.

Bridsall, Nancy. "Life is Unfair: Inequality in the World." In *Developing World*, 9th ed. Edited by Robert Griffiths. Connecticut: McGraw-Hill, 2000.

Bruinessen, Martin Van. *Agha, Shaikh and State*. London: Zed Books Ltd., 1992.

―――― . "The Kurds Between Iran and Iraq." *Middle East Report* (July–August 1986): 1–18.

Carnoy, Martin. *The State and Political Theory*. New Jersey: Princeton University Press, 1984.

Chaliand, Gerard, ed. *People Without a Country The Kurds and Kurdistan*. Zed Press: London 1980.

―――― . *The Kurdish Tragedy*. London: Zed Book Ltd., 1994.

Christenson, Reo, et al. *Ideologies and Modern Politics*. 2d ed. New York: Harper & Row Publishers, 1975.

Chomsky, Noam. "Imperial Ambition." *Monthly Review* (May 2003): 15.

―――― . *The Prosperous Few and the Restless Many*. Berkeley, California: Odonian Press, 1993.

Chomsky, Noam. *Hegemony or Survival Americans Quest for Global Dominance*. New York: Metropolitan Books, 2003.

Clive, Thomas. *The Rise of the Authoritarian State in Peripheral Societies*. New York: Monthly Review Press, 1984.

Cunningham, Frank. *Democratic Theory and Socialism*. Cambridge: Cambridge University Press, 1988.

Drydale, Alasdair and G. H. Blake. *The Middle East and North Africa: A Political Geography*. New York: Oxford University Press, 1985.

Enloe, Synthia. *Ethnic Conflict and Political Development*. Wisconsin: The University of Wisconsin Press, 1976.

Entessar, Nader. *Kurdish Ethnonationalism*. London: Lynne Rienman Publishers, 1992.

Faroughi, Omar, *Negah-i Beh Tarikh va Farnhang-i Kurdistan* (A Look at the History and Culture of Kurdistan). Tehran, Iran: Sharg Publishers, 1362

Filkins, Dexter. "Iraqi Kurds Set Sights on Baghdad." *New York Times* 17 November 2002, p. 7.

Friedman, Thomas. "A View from Tehran." *New York Times* September 1996, p. 21.

Giddens, Anthony. "The Question of Inequality." In *The Global Third Way Debate*. Edited by Anthony Giddens. Malden, Massachusetts: Polity, 2001.

Ghassemlou, A.R. "Kurdistan in Iran." In *People Without a Country*. Edited by Gerard Chaliand. London: Zed Press, 1980.

Green, Philip. *Retrieving Democracy: In Search of Civic Equality*. Totowa, New Jersey: Rowman and Allenheld, 1985.

Goldstein, Joshua. *International Relations*. 5th ed. New York: Longman, 2003.

Gunter, Michael M. *The Kurds in Turkey: A Political Dilemma*. Boulder, Colarado: Westview Press, 1990.

Gurr, Robert Ted. *Why Men Rebel*. Princeton, New Jersey: Princeton University Press, 1970.

Habermas, Jurgen. "Private and Public Autonomy, Human Rights and Popular Sovereignty." In *The Politics of Human Rights*. Edited by Obrad Savic. London, New York: Verso, 1999.

Hamdi, V. *Kurdistan va Kurd Dar Asnad-e Mahramanei Britania* (Kurdistan and Kurd in the British Confidential Documents). Hamadan, Iran: Noor-e Elm Publishers, 1378.

Hassanpour, Amin. "The Kurdish Experience." *Middle East Report* (July–August 1994).

Hardt, Michael and Antonio Negri. *Empire*. Cambridge, Massachusetts: Harvard University Press, 2000.

Hedges, Chris. "Baghdad's Move Puts The Future of Kurdish Haven in Doubt." *New York Times* 4 September 1996, A-6.

Held, David, ed. *Political Theory Today*. Stanford, California: Stanford University Press, 1991.

Holub, Ronate. *Antonio Gramsci: Beyond Marxism and Postmodernism*. New York: Routledge, 1992.

Horowitz, Donald, L. *Ethnic Groups in Conflict*. Berkeley: University of California Press, 1958.

Ichiyo, Muto. "For An Alliance of Hope." In *Global Visions Beyond The New World Order*. Edited by Jeremy Brecher, J. Brown Hills and Jill Coulter. Boston, Massachusetts: South Ends Press, 1993.

Izady, Mehrdad. *The Kurd: A Concise Handbook*. Washington & London: Crane Russak Taylor and Francis International Publishers, 1992.

Jawad, Sa'ad. *Iraq & the Kurdish Question, 1958–1970*. London: Ithaca Press, 1981.

Jehl, Douglas. "Some Iraqis Are Still Dying Inside the Kurdish Regime." *New York Times* 8 September 1996, 14.

———. "50,000 Fleeing:Iraq's Kurds City Abandoned Without a Fight." *Denver Post* 10 September 1996, A-3.

Johnson, Chalmers. *The Sorrows of Empire Militarism, Secrecy and the End of Republic.* New York: Metropolitan Books, 2004.

Kendal, Nezan. "The Kurds Under Ottoman Empire." In *People without a Country, the Kurds and Kurdistn.* Edited by Gerard Chaliand. London: Zed Press, 1980.

Kinnane, Derk. *The Kurds and Kurdistan.* Oxford: Oxford University Press, 1984.

Kinzer, Stephen. "Key Kurd Says Deal with Iraq is Stop Gap." *New York Times* 5 September 1996, A-11

Klare, Michael T. "Oiling the Wheels of War." *The Nation* 7 October 2002, 6–7.

Koohi-Kamali, Fereshteh. "The Development of Nationalism in Iranian Kurdistan." In *The Kurds: A Contemporary Overview.* Edited by Philip G. Kreyenbroek and Stefan Sperl. London: Routledge, 1992.

Kreyenbroek and Stefan Sperl. *The Kurds: A Contemporary Overview.* London: Routledge, 1992.

Kreyenbroek, Philip G. "On The Kurdish Language." In *The Kurds: A Contemporary Overview.* Edited by Philip Kreyenbroek. London: Routledge, 1992.

Kurkcu, Ertugrul. "The Crisis of the Turkish State." *Middle East Report* (April–June 1996): 3–9.

Kutschera, Chris. *Le Movement National Kurde.* Paris: Flammarion, 1979.

Levine, Andrew. *Arguing for Socialism: Theoretical Consideration.* Boston: Routledge, Kegon and Paul, 1984.

Luthardt, Wolfgang. "Direct Democracy in Western Europe: The Case of Switzerland." *Telos: A Journal of Critical Thought Quarterly* 36 (Winter 1991).

Luxemburg, Rosa. *The Accumulation of Capital.* New York: Monthly Review Press, 1964.

———. *The Nationality Question: Selected Writing.* Edited by Horace B. Davis. New York: Monthly Review Press, 1976.

Luxemburg, Rosa and Raya Dunayevskaya. *Women's Liberation and Marx's Philosophy of Revolution.* 2d ed. Chicago: University of Illinois Press, 1991.

Magdoff, Harry. "Militarism and Imperialism." In *Readings in U.S. Imperialism.* Edited by K. T. Fann and D. C. Hodges. Boston, Massachusets: Porter Sargent Publisher, 1971.

Manafy, A. "The State and Human Rights: Critical Perspectives." *Iranian Journal of International Affairs* 1 (Spring 1996): 120–139

Mao-Tse Tung. *Selected Works of Mao Tse Tung*, Vol. 1. Peking: Foreign Language Press, 1977.

Marcus, Aliza. "City in the War Zone." *Middle East Report* 189 (July–August 1994): 16–19.

Mardukh, Shaikh Mohammad. *Tarkh-i Mardukh, Tarikh-i Kurd va Kurdistan* (Mardukh's History: The History of the Kurd and Kurdistan). (No name for publisher and the place of publication), 1979.

Mayer, Arno J. "Beyond The Drumbeat: Iraq, Preventive War, Old Europe." *Monthly Review* 54 (March 2003): 17–21.

McDowall, David. A Modern History of the Kurds. I. B. Tauris, London, New York, 1997.

Minorskii, Vladmir Fedorovich. *Kurd*. Translated by Habiballah Tabani. (Tehran, Iran: Gustardeh Publishers, 1379).

Morad, Munir. "The Situation of Kurds in Iraq and Turkey: Current Trends and Prospects." In *The Kurds: A Contemporary Overview*. Edited by Philip G. Kreyenbroek and Stefan Sperl. London: Routledge Press, 1992.

Myers L. Steven. "A Failed Race Against Time: U.S. Tried to Head Off Iraq." *New York Times* 5 September 1996, A-11.

Nelson, Brian R. *Western Political Thought From Socrates to The Age of Ideology*. 2d ed. New Jersey: Prentice Hall, Inc. 1996.

Nikitine, V. *Kurds va Kurdistan*. Translated by M. Gazi. Tehran, Iran: Nilofan Publication, 1366.

O'Ballance, Edgar. *The Kurdish Struggle, 1920–94*. New York: St. Martin Press, 1996.

Ocalan, Abdullah. *Dastarn-e Doubareh Ziestan: Khaterat va Andishahi-e Abdullah Ocalan* (The Story of Rebirth: Ocalan's Memoirs and Thought). Tehran, Iran: Hamida Publishers, 1378.

Ocalan, A. *Islam va Meehan Doosty Jamea-i, Kurdistan va Tarh-e Terror-e Man* (Islam and Patriotism, Kurdish Sovereignty and the Plan of My Terror). Tehran, Iran: Nashr-e Ona Publishers, 1379.

Offe, Claus. "The Theory of the Capitalist State and the Problem of Policy Formation." In *Stress and Contradiction in Modern Capitalism*. Edited by Leon Lindberg. Lexington, Massachusetts: Heath Publishers, 1975.

Olson, Robert, ed. *The Kurdish Nationalist Movement in the 1990*. Lexington: The University Press of Kentucky, 1996.

Osman, Mahmud. "Modern Capitalism." *The Kurdish Journal* 4:1 (March 1967): 3–7.

Passavant, Paul A and Judi Dean, eds. *Empire's New Clothes*. New York and London: Tautledge, 2004.

Pelletiere, Stephen C. *The Kurds: An Unstable Element in the Gulf*. London: Westview Press, 1984.

Peng, Martin Khon Kor. "Reforming North Economy, South Development and World Economic Order." In *Global Visions Beyond the New World Order*. Edited by Jeremy Brecher, John Brown Childs, and Jill Coutler. Boston, Massachusetts: South End Press, 1993.

"The Pike Report." Reproduced in *The Village Voice*, 23 Feb. 1976.

Poulantzas, Nicos. *Political Power and Social Classes*. London: New Left Books, 1974.

Quaye, Christopher. *Liberation Struggles in International Law*. Philadelphia: Temple University Press, 1991.

Randal, Jonathan, C. *After Such Knowledge, What Forgiveness: My Encounter with Kurdistan*. New York: Farrar, Straus and Giroux, 1997.

Randal, Jonathan and John Mintz. "Kurdish Feuds and Surrogate Powers." *Washington Post* 1 September 1996, A34.

Roosevelt, Archie Jr. "The Kurdish Republic of Mahabad." In *People Without A Country The Kurds and Kurdistan*. Edited by Gerard Chaliand. London: Zed Press, 1980.

Roskin, Michael G. *Hard Road to Democracy: Four Developing Nations*. New Jersey: Prentice Hall, 2001.

Sabine, George. *A History of Political Theory*, 4th ed. London: Holt, Rinehart and Winston, 1973.

Samim, Ahmet. "The Tragedy of the Turkish Left." *New Left Review* 126 (March–April 1981): 60–85.

Sanadaji, Mirza Shukr Allah. *Tuhfah-i Nasiri Dar Tarikh va Joghrafiay-i Kurdistan* (Nasiri's Gift in The History and Geography of Kurdistan). Tehran, Iran: Amirkabeer Publications, 1987.

Sasson, Showstack. "Passive Revolution and Politics of Reform: The Approaches to Gramsci." London: Writers and Readers Publishing Cooperatives, 1982.

Sipah-i Pasaran-i Inqilab-i Islam, Kurdistan. Tehran, Iran: The Revolutionary Guard of Islam, Daftar-i syasie sipah-i Pasdaran-i Ingilab-i Islami, 1980.

Sklair, Leslie. *Globalization, Capitalism and its Alternatives*, 3d ed. Oxford University Press, New York, 2002.

Skocpol, Theda. *States and Social Revolutions: A Comparative Analysis of French, Russia and China*. London: Cambridge University Press, 1979.

So, Alvin Y. *Social Change and Development, Modernization, Dependency, and World System Theories*. London: Sage Publications, 1990.

Susser, Bernard. *Political Theory in the Modern World*. Boston, Massachusetts: Allyn & Bacon, 1995.

Tavahoudi, Kalim. *Harakat-i Tarikhi-i Kurd Beh Khurasan* (The Historical Move of the Kurds to Khurasan), 2 vols. (No publisher and place of publication).

"The Kurds of Turkey, Killings, Disappearances and Torture." *Human Rights Watch/Helsinki*. New York, Washington, Los Angeles, and London, 1993.

"The Anfal Campaign Against The Kurds/ Human Rights Iraq's Crimes of Genocide." *Human Rights Watch/Middle East*. New Haven and London: Yale University Press, 1995: XV, 1–2.

Trimberger, Ellen K. "A Theory of Elite Revolutions." *Studies in Comparative International Development* 7:3 (Fall 1972): 191–207.

———. *Revolution from Above: Military Bureaucrats and Development in Japan, Turkey and Peru*. New Brunswick, New Jersey: Translation Books, 1978.

Tucker, Robert. W. "The Radical Critique Assessed." In *American Foreign Policy*. Edited by John Ikenberry. Boston, Massachusetts: Scott Foresman and Company, 1989.

Vanly, Ismet Sheriff. "Kurdistan in Iraq." In *People Without a Country*. Edited by Gerard Chaliand. London: Zed Press, 1980.

Wallerstein, Immanuel. *The Modern World System: Capitalist Agriculture and the Origins of the European World Economy in the 16th Century*. New York, London: Academic Press, 1974.

———. *The Capitalist World Economy*. New York: Cambridge University Press, 1979.

Weisskopf, Thomas. "Capitalism, Socialism and The Source of Imperialism." In *American Foreign Policy*. Edited by John Ikenberry. Boston, Massachusetts: Scott Foresman and Company,1989.

Young, Crawford. *The Politics of Cultural Pluralism*. Wisconsin: The University of Wisconsin Press 1976.

Zana, Mehdi. *Prison No.5: Eleven Years in Turkish Jails*. Paris, France: Arlea Editions, 1995.

Zarbakht, Mortaza. *Az Kurdistan-e Iraq Ta Onsoy-e Roud-e Aras, Rah Paymai-e Tarikh-e Mulla Mostafa Barzani* (From Kurdistan of Iraq to the Other side of Aras River, The Historical March of Barzani to USSR). Tehran, Iran: Azadeh Publisher, 1337.

Index

About the Author

Dr. A. Manafy is a Professor of Political Science at New Mexico Highlands University and author of numerous articles. He is currently working on a book entitled: The Meaning of Jihad in Islam and the U.S. Foreign Policy.